'A Pleasant Change from Politics'

Music and the British Labour Movement between the Wars

Duncan Hall

New Clarion Press

First published 2001

New Clarion Press
5 Church Row, Gretton
Cheltenham GL54 5HG
England

New Clarion Press is a workers' co-operative.

ISBN paperback   1 873797 29 X
          hardback   1 873797 30 3

Typeset in 10/12 Times New Roman by Jean Wilson Typesetting, Coventry
Printed in Great Britain by MFP Design and Print

Contents

Acknowledgements

There are many people to acknowledge and thank for their assistance in the production of this book. First and foremost I must thank Professor Tony Mason and Professor Carolyn Steedman who supervised my doctoral research, from which this book is drawn. Their tireless and constructive criticism and advice has been of immeasurable value; access to their expertise and knowledge in a wide variety of areas of social and cultural history was a considerable privilege, their enthusiasm for the project a source of strength during the more difficult times. Special mention should also be made of Chris Bessant and all at New Clarion Press for their labours in making this book. I would also like to thank the Graduate School at Warwick University for providing the funding that made the project possible, and both the Centre for Social History (sadly no more) and the Department of History under whose auspices the research was carried out. Ros Lucas, the Graduate Secretary in the History Department, was a tower of strength throughout.

Various people at record offices, libraries and archives have been extremely helpful. Particularly, I should mention all at the Modern Records Centre (Warwick), especially Richard Temple for pointing out some specific records, the staff at Ruskin College Library, the Imperial War Museum sound archive, the National Museum of Labour History (Manchester), the Library of Working Class History (Salford), Birmingham Central Library, Bradford Central Library, West Yorkshire Archives (both the Bradford and Keighley divisions), the Bodleian Library and Warwick University Library (particularly John Bennett).

Individuals who have helped my progress over the last three years, through assistance, encouragement and advice, or through suggesting or providing source material, include Gareth Williams, Roger Fagge, Stephen Yeo, Mary-Beth Hamilton, James Hinton, Gwyn Lewis, Colin Jones, Matthew Thomson, Rana Mitter, Michelle Dowling, Natalie Suart, Alan Burton, Jonathan White, Ruth Livesey, Tonya Blowers, Claire McManus, Paul Long, Neil Ormerod, David Ayrton, Neil Carter, Seth Denbo, Chris Brader, Angela Jones, Matt Adams, Toby Haggith, Cedric Binns, Helen Sheehan, Michael Holt, Claire Nebesnuick, Michael

Hunter, Nick Hall and many other friends and colleagues. Special mention must be made of my parents, Brian and Virginia Hall, whose support and encouragement could not have been stronger.

Duncan Hall

Abbreviations

AEU	Amalgamated Engineering Union
BICS	Birmingham Industrial Co-operative Society
BLMDU	Birmingham Labour Musical and Dramatic Union
BUF	British Union of Fascists
CVU	Clarion Vocal Union
DLP	Divisional Labour Party
EFDSS	English Folk Dance and Song Society
ILP	Independent Labour Party
IWM	Imperial War Museum
LLCU	London Labour Choral Union
MCC	Marylebone Cricket Club
NEC	National Executive Committee
NLCU	National Labour Choral Union
NMLH	National Museum of Labour History
NUM	National Union of Mineworkers
NUR	National Union of Railwaymen
NUWM	National Unemployed Workers Movement
SCW-SA	Spanish Civil War – Sound Archive
TUC	Trades Union Congress
WMA	Workers' Music Association
WTM	Workers' Theatre Movement
WYA	West Yorkshire Archives

Introduction

> Music has always been an integral part of the Labour Movement, but never has such interest been aroused as at the present moment.
>
> *Sydney A. Court, conductor of the Deptford Labour Choir, 1924*

Labour movement activism in the 1920s and 1930s was enlivened by music. At meetings, social gatherings, demonstrations and campaigns, music of various genres was employed for the cause. For most it was a pleasant way to the pass the time: a break, a diversion or an entertainment. For some it was so important that it could occasionally eclipse the movement's other business altogether. In this book I shall explore this music and what it meant to labour performers, audiences and commentators during the inter-war period.

The musical culture of Britain between the wars was one that was experiencing rapid commercialization and was being revolutionized by new technology in production, distribution and consumption. Inevitably, interest in this musical revolution – and particularly its implications for the most popular musical forms of the day – eclipses historical and scholarly investigation into the amateur and voluntary musical culture that continued to co-exist with the dance craze and the jazz explosion. Indeed, histories of the 'grass roots' of music – the many performers who were never 'stars', and the various audiences – have been few and far between. Until some recent social histories, such as Dave Russell's *A Social History of Popular Music in England, 1840–1914*, the history of music has tended to centre on the 'great composers'. Furthermore, despite important catalysts for musical change between the wars – gramophone, wireless, electronic recording – the history of the period's popular music has tended to be told as part of broader studies such as histories of broadcasting, or as an introduction to histories of popular music over a much longer period. A recent Oxford Ph.D. thesis, 'Popular music and the popular music industry in Britain, 1918–1939' by James J. Nott, is one exception.

The British labour movement between the wars underwent important realignments and formalization in the early part of the period, as well as electoral growth, but then endured troubled times owing to social unrest,

1

political divisions and – despite two short-lived minority Labour govern-
ments – the persistent political dominance of the Conservative Party. The
labour movement can be narrowly or broadly defined; in this book I shall
use a broad definition. Here the labour movement is taken to mean the
Labour Party, the trade unions and the co-operative movement (the 'official' movement) as well as the Communist Party and various small fringe
socialist groups and parties (the 'unofficial' movement). The 'official'
and 'unofficial' descriptions are borrowed from Stephen Jones, amongst
others, and are not always entirely satisfactory; some groups bridged the
two, like the London Labour Choral Union, and others moved from one to
the other during the period, such as the Independent Labour Party (ILP). It
is generally felt that between the wars the goals of the official movement
became more practical: winning Keighley or Smethwick was prioritized
over building the New Jerusalem.

One may be forgiven for looking at these two 'worlds' – the nation's
musical culture and the British labour movement – and feeling that there
should be little connection or interaction between the two. It is not surprising that historians of the labour movement have tended to concentrate
on politics and industrial relations – after all, that is the purpose of a
labour movement – but it was clearly felt between the wars that the movement had a pressing aesthetic duty as well. It is the purpose of this book to
consider that duty and how it manifested itself with regard to ideas about
music and commitment to music making.

The labour movement's interest in music has not been entirely ignored
by historians. Chris Waters, in particular, has made a close study of
labour music making in the period 1880–1914, but despite its important
place within the labour movement between the wars, the labour music of
that period has been neglected. That it did attain a place of importance is
clear, whether that be evidenced by the legions of choirs, bands and orchestras in every town or by the many contemporary books, pamphlets
and articles produced on the subject. However, despite the feeling at the
time that the movement's musicality was increasing and developing,
more interest has been expressed in the musical pursuits of socialists at
the end of the nineteenth century than between the wars.

Perhaps another reason for the lack of academic interest in labour
music is that we cannot explicitly see much in the way of the products of
that inter-war cultural production in the present. The primary socialist
composers of the period are surprisingly neglected in contemporary repertoires; popular labour songs were rarely recorded. There are socialist
choirs who have had unbroken service since this period, such as the Clarion Singers in Birmingham who were formed in 1939, but they have not
retained their places of prominence in the movement. Some political

songs written in this period will still be heard in folk clubs, but often by dwindling and non-political audiences. The long debates about the suitability of 'The Red Flag' and the search for a successor were not replicated in the discussions surrounding 'Things Can Only Get Better' in 1997. And yet it is the contention of this book that the musical culture of the British labour movement between the wars had an important impact upon the popular culture of these islands, and beyond, in the twentieth century, even if that impact is rarely obvious.

Historians such as Chris Waters, Stephen Yeo, Stephen Jones and Ian Watson have paid some attention to the British labour movement's musical activity. Waters and Yeo concerned themselves with the late Victorian period as part of broader questions: socialist attitudes to popular culture and the religiosity of the late Victorian labour movement respectively. Stephen Jones studied the inter-war period in *Workers at Play* and *The Labour Movement and Film, 1918–1939*, but music played only a small part in both books. However, as well as providing useful background to ideas about working-class and popular culture between the wars, *Workers at Play* includes an interesting chapter on labour movement approaches to working-class culture.

Ian Watson's work in this area includes a book, *Song and Democratic Culture in Britain* (1980) and a particularly useful article, 'Alan Bush and left music in the thirties' (1978).[1] Both pieces explore the idea of what Watson calls a 'Second Culture' (an 'alternative' or 'democratic' culture) with particular reference to socialist music and 'protest song', which I explore in some detail in Chapter 4. Watson's book does not limit its focus to a particular time period and, as its focus is 'song' not 'music', analysis is weighted towards lyrics rather than tunes. The article is of more specific usefulness for this book: it includes a brief but insightful summary of music in the service of socialism in the 1930s and then an interview with the communist composer, Alan Bush. I look at the contribution made by Alan Bush to the 'labour musical movement' in Chapter 5. Both the article and the interview seek to promote the aforementioned 'Second Culture' argument and identify a 'Thirties Movement' of 'left music' to match that in the literary world. Despite that preoccupation, I draw on both when considering Alan Bush in Chapter 5, the London Labour Choral Union in Chapter 3 and the use of music during strike action in Chapter 4.

Richard Hanlon and Mike Waite have also paid some attention to Bush and his contemporaries in an article 'Notes from the left: communism and British classical music', included in Andy Croft (ed.), *A Weapon in the Struggle: The Cultural History of the Communist Party in Britain* (1998). Although this is a useful article, as with other articles about Bush the emphasis is on his prolific composing career after the Second World War rather than on his pre-1939 works.

Another way in which all the secondary literature was useful was in formulating ways to write about music. Very few pieces of historical writing say much about the sound of music. Even Roy Palmer's *The Sound of History* (1988), for all that it is an extraordinary annotated anthology, is really a literary analysis and does not dwell much on the *sound* of history at all. Perhaps it is an impossible undertaking to say very much about the sound and effects of music without betraying oneself to the metaphysical vagaries that lie outside the positivistic boundaries of musicology, or to the obfuscation of the over-technical. After all, although I am interested in what labour activists heard at meetings and concerts between the wars, is it perhaps one of those historical black holes like 'what did food taste like?' Even a piece by a serious composer, where the tempo, dynamics and every rest and playing instruction are included in the manuscript, is not *really* frozen in time to be brought back to life as a historical artefact at every performance. There is room for interpretation around the most complete notation by conductor, musician and, perhaps most importantly, the listener.

However, this inevitable limitation should not prevent us from saying what we can about what was heard. We can say quite a lot about a piece of music from looking over a manuscript – or, indeed, simply from knowing a tune – and from descriptions, criticisms and personal accounts of listening to music. For the actual method of describing music, I must cite a number of 'literary' influences, not least the popular musicology of the inter-war labour music writer H. G. Sear, and musical biography such as Michael Hurd's *Rutland Boughton and the Glastonbury Festivals* (1993) and Ian Kemp's *Tippett: The Composer and His Music* (1984). Articles from the *Musical Times* and the *Listener* also helped me to develop a method of comprehensible 'music writing'.

Music played an important role in various aspects of labour movement life, but it was generally considered as something outside or alongside the movement's primary political and industrial activity. As such, it would never attain detailed description, exploration or explanation in the minutes of branch meetings, for example. What might usually be the richest primary source for researching labour movement history is not especially fruitful, then, when researching musical aspects of the movement. The best one might expect to find in the minutes of a branch meeting are the details of the organization of social events, the cost of hiring bands and financial concerns regarding the particular group's rooms, club or venue. Such information is occasionally useful, but hardly inspiring.

The richest source for researching the musical culture of the labour movement between the wars, and for assessing its importance, is the labour press: the movement's means of communicating with itself. Newspapers like the *Town Crier* in Birmingham and the *Pioneer* in Bradford were full of musical advertisements, reports, criticism, articles and even songs. Just as with the late Victorian period (when, according to Yeo, music was 'the main cultural thrust of the movement'), through the pages of the labour press, music is given extraordinary weight and significance. While this might be more an illustration of the musicality of amateur journalists and editors than of the movement as a whole, such a conclusion does not account for the vast number of 'musical items' given at labour meetings across the country. Furthermore, it suggests that the producers of labour papers felt that music – and writing about music – was what their readers wanted from a newspaper, or possibly what they needed. But labour newspaper readerships were not vast; like many of the choirs and orchestras whose progress they narrated, labour papers fought off perpetual crises in their struggle for existence. Similar language was employed in both struggles: it was the duty of good socialists to take the *Daily Herald* and their local labour paper, just as it was their duty to support the local choir or band. The musical culture of the labour movement, suggested in the pages of the labour press and detailed here, was a small culture, lovingly defended and championed by that culture's mouthpieces. At various points in time, musical socialists found themselves larger audiences, but often they played, sang to, and criticized each other.

Because music touched so many aspects of what it was to be a socialist between the wars, it is not surprising that it runs through memoir and autobiography. This is true not only of socialist musicians, such as Ewan MacColl writing *Journeyman*, but also of general activists, such as in Wal Hannington's recollections of unemployment demonstrations in the 1920s and 1930s, and in oral history collections. This forms another useful source. The subjectivity of autobiography and memoir, as well as that of political journalism, is what makes it particularly useful here, rather than being a minefield for the historian. Appreciation of music *is* subjective; I was actively seeking out attitude, opinion and prejudice, not looking to avoid them. That is not to say that I turned a blind eye to the problems of using autobiography and memoir (and newspapers and journalism) as historical sources, rather that those problems proved to be their most useful feature.

Certain individual socialists were keen to write at great length about music whether in the pages of the labour press or in their own books and pamphlets. Rutland Boughton, Arthur Bourchier, H. G. Sear and 'Casey' Hampson all contributed to a vast literature on the meaning of music to socialists and what made music 'good' or 'bad'. Biographical information about these individual musical socialists is rare – except with the popular composer, Boughton – but helped to piece together the story of this musical culture.

The last useful source was the music itself, mostly in the form of song. The production of labour songbooks continued apace through the inter-war years. They often included the favourite anthems of the pre-war period, such as Carpenter's 'England, Arise!' and various William Morris lyrics. Songs from that earlier period began to attain a special place of prominence that they had not enjoyed prior to the First World War: particularly 'The Red Flag' and 'The Internationale'. New songs were regularly to be added to the repertoire, but these last two fought off all contenders and retained their special place at meetings and events, alongside 'Jerusalem', 'Auld Lang Syne' and, in Yorkshire, 'Ikla' Moor Baht 'At'.

A review of the literature, particularly Chris Waters' material, revealed the existence of a strong musical tradition in the labour movement by 1918. By the beginning of the inter-war period, there was a history of musical associations and musical theories and ideas. Chapter 1 explores this late Victorian legacy and considers the broad areas of socialist and labour interest in music. The next three chapters consider the labour movement's use of music in various aspects of its activity. Chapter 2's focus is the everyday use of music in meetings and social events. Chapter 3 concentrates on specifically musical associations: choirs, bands and orchestras. Although there is some consideration of the national picture in these two chapters, they make close studies of the cities of Birmingham and Bradford, and their neighbouring districts. Chapter 4 looks at the use of music in protests and strikes, and at other times of struggle. Numerous questions are raised in the first four chapters about musical genres, and a number of tensions are uncovered within labour ideas about music. These form the focus of the last two chapters. Chapter 5 focuses on Western art music, while Chapter 6 concentrates on the popular music of the day and the Folk Revival.

Was music just 'a pleasant change from politics'? Was it simply a diversion, an entertainment and a reward for hard political work? Or did it have a more important role to play in the work and life of the labour movement in this period? These are the central questions that shape this book, although others emerge and join them during its course.

1

Socialism and Music

This chapter is intended to perform two key functions. Firstly, the background of what came to be called the 'Labour musical movement' is explored in an attempt to sketch an idea of the musicality of the British labour movement at the start of the inter-war period. Secondly, I shall seek to identify important theoretical themes and problems that will inform the book as a whole and introduce some of the key questions.

A socialist musical legacy

The year 1918 saw the labour movement emerge from the First World War, altered in a number of ways. The main organizational change was the unveiling of the new model Labour Party with its new constitution drafted by Sidney and Beatrice Webb. The Russian Revolution set in chain a reorganization and realignment of socialist politics outside the Labour Party as well, leading to the establishment of the Communist Party of Great Britain in 1920. It is often argued that the movement turned away from its 'heroic', 'religious', pioneering phase and began specifically to consider socialist programmes for municipal or national government, in the case of the Labour Party, and organizing for the revolution on the part of the communists. There is considerable debate as to the precise impact of the First World War on Labour politics and whether or not these processes were already under way.[1] While it is sometimes argued (by Ross McKibbin, for example)[2] that the Labour Party in 1918 was unchanged in its fundamental character – 'propagandist and evangelical' – others (like Tom Nairn)[3] have suggested that the war made the modern Labour Party. Certainly there were changes in the Labour Party, exemplified by its new constitution and policy documents, but there were important areas of continuity too, as we shall see.

As this book will demonstrate, earlier 'extra-curricular' activities of socialists changed but did not vanish, and the comrades still made time for singing and playing, as well as for other 'cultural' pursuits. In order to place this account of music in the labour movement between the wars in its context and to identify the source of some of the popular labour theories about music and the arts, it is essential to consider music in the late Victorian and Edwardian labour movement.

Transforming the individual

In his article 'A New Life: the religion of socialism', Stephen Yeo insisted that music was 'the main cultural thrust' of socialism in the period 1883 to 1896.[4] Chris Waters has identified two traditions of 'music in the service of socialism' at work in the late nineteenth century: the first a tradition of middle-class social reform, considered 'philanthropic'; the second, 'utopian'.[5] Both traditions believed that music could transform the individual personality or character and were influenced by a work by the Reverend Hugh Haweis, *Music and Morals* (1871).[6] Sometimes the ends for which the individual might be transformed by music were lost sight of behind the 'refining, elevating and delightful art'. Indeed, a close study of Haweis' text (particularly Books One and Four,[7] which dealt with these issues) shows that while he believed that music was capable of creating a moral transformation and refinement for the individual, he was not at all clear about the ends to which this should be put.

Morally good activity, for Haweis, was 'to respect and promote the healthful activity of society in general', as 'what is really morally healthful for the individual will be found as a general rule healthful to society at large'.[8] This aspiration is vague and arguably conservative, but it was sometimes the case that musical socialists, inspired by these traditions, would be interested in the moral reform of the individual *for its own sake*. Both the utopian wish that the reformed personalities would be revolutionary ones, and the essentially conservative philanthropic desire for new individuals to grow more attached to state and nation – or the related vagaries of Haweis himself – were often ignored and, for some, pure individual 'elevation' became the primary purpose of bringing music to the 'masses'. Strangely, although Haweis thought that 'the social effects of music would be a very interesting subject of discussion', he felt that they lay 'a little outside the purpose of our present article'[9] and made little attempt to address them.

British socialist writers or thinkers like Robert Blatchford and Edward Carpenter completed the picture in this area. For them 'social transformation began with a change in the heart of the human individual'.[10] Whether this really differed very much from a Marxist notion of a change in 'consciousness', other than in the choice of language used, is open to question.

The primary difference would appear to be with regard to the primacy of class. Class was never an all-important aspect of Carpenter's socialism, which was 'essentially religious',[11] although Blatchford did rehearse arguments about material class relations. *Merrie England* (first published, 1894), Blatchford's series of letters to John Smith, a fictional working man from Oldham, could be seen as an exercise in developing class consciousness, even though the quasi-religious imagery of the working class as a reluctant Messiah places it very much in a non-Marxist tradition.

> Dear Mr Smith, I am sorry to hear that you look upon Socialism as a base and foolish thing, and upon Socialists as base and foolish men.
> Nevertheless, since in you lies the hope of the world, I shall try to change your opinion.[12]

Although evidence of the Haweis tradition can arguably be seen in socialist writings about music, the question of *how* music transformed the individual was not explored. Although Haweis claimed to be scientific, his study really required a leap of faith. His theory, put as simply as possible, was that music was the only art that adequately expressed (and promoted) emotions because they shared a number of scientific properties: elation and depression, velocity, intensity, variety and form.[13] He argued that these properties of emotions transferred themselves to music via the scale, tempo, dynamics, harmonies and counter-melodies and form of music respectively. This was the part of his study that he considered scientific and 'proved' that music was the art most capable of 'exciting the deepest emotions' for good or ill.[14] Emotions are imbued into a piece of music at various points: the composer clearly does most of this, but then 'the executive musician' has opportunities to 'interpret' the composition, and finally the listener imbues emotion into his or her own interpretation of a piece of music. People on different intellectual or moral 'planes' may interpret the same piece very differently: 'mean and gnawing spite in a low plane becomes an emotion of bitter and just vengeance in a high one'.[15]

Haweis makes the link between emotions and morality with a remarkable absence of analysis, considering the 'scientific' exertions and diagrams he uses in making the connection between music and emotions. The best examples of music having an effect on morals, for Haweis, were patriotic songs and communal hymn singing. The 'invariably earnest and dignified' music of patriotic tunes and national anthems had the power 'of pitching high the plane of the emotions, and driving them home with the most efficacious and incomparable energy'.[16] Converts to Nonconformist churches 'found in hymn tunes and chants a great medium of expressing the rush of a new religious life upon their spirits'.[17]

This final point is important in understanding the central place of music during what has variously been called the 'heroic' phase of British socialism or the period of the 'New Life' or 'religion of socialism', when music appeared to be the main cultural thrust of British socialism. It must also be borne in mind that Haweis was quite far from being a socialist himself. His concerns for music were not shared with concerns for social or political matters. Haweis would appear to have been a confident nationalist with pride in British institutions.

> When we have a national school of music, and not before, we shall have high popular standards, and the music of the people will then be as real an instrument of civilisation in its way, and as happily under the control of public opinion as the Press, the Parliament, or any other of our great national institutions.[18]

By 'music of the people' he did not mean music that was popular, or music that had in some way been composed in any broad sense by 'the people', but instead simply meant music that was British, or English. Furthermore, Haweis scorned working-class musical tastes in a manner perhaps not as far removed from some socialist comment as one might suppose: 'Music is not to our lower orders a deep-rooted need, a means of expressing the pent-up and often oppressive emotions of the heart, but merely a noisy appendage to low pastimes.'[19]

If Haweis was as influential as Chris Waters and Dave Russell suggest, then some of his views on what constituted good or bad music – as well as just *morally* good or bad music – might have influenced labour movement thinkers. Therefore some of his other views might have to be borne in mind when we come later to consider taste and musical discrimination. It is important to note that Haweis, and others like him, were an influence not just on the embryonic British labour movement, but on the musical life of the country more generally. They constituted part of what, for want of a better term, we may consider a 'movement' behind what Dave Russell calls 'music for the people'. This was not an organized, politically or socially homogeneous movement, but rather a wide range of attempts to bring music to the working class by a variety of mainly middle-class 'activists' for a variety of ends. Those ends largely centred around the idea that music could act as 'an object of social utility and balm for society's many evils'.[20] The 'activists' might have been middle-class philanthropists, radical politicians, socially aware amateur musicians, entrepreneurs or municipalities; the 'ends' could vary from temperance (providing alternatives to concert rooms in public houses and music halls) to alleviating class antagonisms (either in a general sense or in the sense of industrial relations in a single place of work).

Making socialists

The importance of music to the labour movement was not only considered in terms of morality and the transformation of the individual. On a less metaphysical level, socialists recognized that music played an important part in the lives of the workers and believed that it was an interest which could perhaps be harnessed on behalf of the 'cause'. Whether it was the music hall, hymns and church music or a parlour instrument (piano or harmonium) at home, many workers listened to – or even performed – music. Music education had become a central feature of state elementary schools since 1871,[21] and by the early part of the twentieth century instrumental lessons at school were becoming commonplace.[22] Piano ownership became more widespread at the turn of the century as competition from Germany brought down the cost, and as the First World War approached, 'full employment and rising wages enabled a far larger proportion of the working class than hitherto to purchase a long coveted status symbol'.[23]

Some socialists from the pioneering period before the First World War introduced or promoted a number of other musical forms or activities that were directed at the workers in the desire to 'make socialists' and build their movement. The problem was that, as we shall see, working-class people generally just did not like or appreciate what the socialists considered to be 'good' music. Socialists would often despair of working-class tastes, particularly the 'music hall fare' that they considered to be particularly banal.[24] The same debates re-emerged between the wars regarding jazz music (see Chapter 6). However, there were a number of strands of labour and socialist interest in music from before the First World War, which can be followed through to the inter-war years. These raise a number of important questions.

The first of these strands is the interest in folksong and the related interest in other 'pre-industrial' musical forms. Folksong collection, and the appreciation of the music collected, was an interest shared by people of various political persuasions. It was, however, embraced particularly warmly by socialists: here was a music that laid claim to authenticity and was considered free from the bonds and stain of commercialism.[25] A 'national treasure' of popular song also sat well with the *Merrie England, Britain for the British*, popular nationalist strain of Clarion socialism.

Of course, there was an internationalist tradition in the movement as well, which was visible, among other occasions, in some socialists' opposition to the First World War, or support for the Bolshevik government in its defence against the White Russians and Western intervention. Folkloric influences can give music its national or regional character, and the choice of overseas folk tunes for certain performances could help evoke internationalist sentiments. In a review of the 'Hands off Russia' Conference of 1918, the Glasgow *Worker* noted that 'when the Russian violinist played the Russian Funeral March and the delegates stood with uncovered heads in a tribute to the memory of our murdered, German comrades, the grandest feature of our movement – its internationalist character – was clearly revealed'.[26] Clearly, the sad melody of the Russian funeral march (whichever specific piece this was) would have helped create the atmosphere for the part of the conference described above, and the particular melodic and harmonic features of this music that associate it with Russia and eastern Europe would have assisted in the internationalist flavour of the tribute more successfully than a traditional English funeral march.

The idea of music being an international language that can communicate to workers everywhere was a repeated one – 'The Internationale' springs to mind, and the idea re-emerges during the Spanish Civil War – but it stands in interesting conflict with the preoccupation of many with the *Englishness* of music. Clearly this was a central preoccupation of the Folk Revival, but it was also a major concern of composers and critics from the labour movement, such as Rutland Boughton.

The debates that have emerged about folk music's claims to authenticity, as well as the interest in industrial folksong pioneered by the Workers' Music Association (founded in 1936), will be considered in Chapter 6. The important point here is simply that a number of socialists found some music more fitting for socialism than others and that this discrimination was based on factors other than the technical quality of the music or purely aesthetic considerations. Indeed, Montague Blatchford, the founder of the Clarion Vocal Unions and brother of Robert, believed that workers did not want 'high art', which they would not understand, and that they should have, instead, 'art of their own'. Blatchford, with peculiar reasoning, felt that Tudor madrigals best fitted this description. The questions arising for this book from this strand of late Victorian/pre-war, socialist interest in music are firstly, how far did socialists continue to search for an 'art of their own' for the British working class? Furthermore, did they consider industrial folksong or types of popular music in that search, or did they continue to prioritize agricultural folksong and Tudor madrigals? These questions are addressed in Chapter 6.

These considerations about what music socialists should enjoy or perform were rehearsed and expanded upon in the music columns of the labour press. Chris Waters identified a desire on the part of music writers in the socialist press of his period to improve popular tastes, bringing together the 'better elements' of several musical traditions, which included folksong and Tudor madrigals. Georgia Pearce, music columnist for the

Clarion before the First World War, would frequently mystify her readers with technical musical terminology and commentary, and correspondents to the paper would express their wish to hear the music she spoke of because they imagined that they would like it.[27] While music columnists would continue to concentrate upon 'art' music in the papers between the wars, as we shall see in Chapter 5, opportunities for working-class readers actually to hear such music increased considerably. The music programme provided by the BBC on the wireless, the increased ownership of gramophones and the improvement in sound quality and extent of recorded music available meant that much more of this music was within easy reach of most working-class families. Whether these dramatic changes in the world of music represented a democratic revolution for 'art' music, and whether it was consequently welcomed by socialists, must be considered in greater detail. As we shall see, between the wars the labour press took advantage of the increased opportunities for their readers to hear music. Furthermore, they did attempt to 'popularize' their music columns by including items on dance or variety music, and began to offer record reviews like those included in the popular press.

Another strand of labour interest in music to consider is the singing, composition and appreciation of socialist songs and anthems. According to Waters, 'while almost forgotten today, socialist songbooks published prior to 1914 played a prominent role in the movement's associational life'.[28] Before 1914 songs such as Edward Carpenter's 'England, Arise!' were among the most popular (along with musical settings of William Morris's poetry), whereas later favourites such as 'The Red Flag' were not so popular. None of the songbooks that Waters analysed contained that song, although it had been sung for some time, composed as it was in 1889. Debates surrounding the socialist anthems at this time included the suitability of some of the well-known tunes chosen and whether the songs came from within or from outside the labour movement and the working class. Well-known tunes were adopted for many songs so that the ability to read music was not a prerequisite skill for those wishing to communally sing them at meetings. By the 1880s, elementary schools were encouraged financially by the government to teach vocal music by note rather than by ear. While the teaching of standard notation was being taught at only a minority of schools, the tonic sol-fa method of musical notation was taught at most schools by the 1890s. The capacity for singers to learn unfamiliar tunes would have been much higher by the inter-war period than at the time when many of the major socialist anthems were written.

Some songs in Carpenter's *Chants of Labour* (first edition, 1888; sixth edition, 1922) were set to tunes such as 'Rule Britannia!'[29] and 'God Save the Queen'.[30] The famous case of 'The Red Flag' being set to 'Tannenbaum' rather than the lyricist Jim Connell's preferred 'White Cockade' was also part of this debate. If one believes a theory that a tune contains within it emotions and a moral message (and that any words serve only as a secondary communicator, which was certainly the view of the Reverend Haweis) then the dangers of using 'capitalist' or 'imperialist' emotions to convey socialist words are paramount. Even if the appropriation of a tune could be considered ironic or subversive (such as 'To Liberty' to the tune of 'God Save the Queen', where the 'Queen' is the feminine personification of Liberty herself), the danger remains. While the sheer volume of socialist songbooks, often featuring many of the same songs, was not repeated after the First World War, new songbooks were produced, old ones were reissued (such as *Chants of Labour*) or updated (such as the Socialist Sunday School hymn books) and these songs continued to be an important feature of meetings, particularly large demonstrations and rallies.

Some musical organizations of the labour movement that existed before the war continued their work into the inter-war period, most notably the Clarion Vocal Unions (CVUs). Before the First World War the CVUs constituted the largest socialist choral body in Britain.[31] This was not much of a claim as it was the only national body (if the northern-centred movement could be described as 'national') mentioned in the existing literature, but it was quite a significant organization, founded by Montague Blatchford in Halifax. The CVUs performed primarily Victorian choral music at May Day celebrations, socials, bazaars and other fund-raising activities. They had annual competitions from 1898 and the competitive element became central, arguably leading to a diminution of the socialist aspect of their work and a demand for more technical musical training. While the competitions might have attracted a larger and more enthusiastic audience for the choirs – audience reaction has been compared with that of sports crowds – some who joined organizations like the CVUs for fellowship were put off by the prospect of the greater musical training required for success in competitions. Some of the choirs, such as the Keighley one, competed in choral festivals outside the movement as well.[32] While some socialists were uncomfortable with the competitive element, Blatchford defended it by insisting that the aim of the socialist was 'not to pull down but to lift up' and that competition was the way to get the best performances out of people.[33]

The competitiveness of these choral festivals – and the unease about it that was engendered – existed on a larger scale outside the labour movement. While the sport-like partisanship of the choirs' supporters has been commented on, there is no suggestion that it came close to the audience reaction to choral festivals in South Wales at the same time, where tens of thousands sometimes broke out into fighting and violence.[34] 'Proponents of music as a civilising and refining force' despaired of 'disgraceful scenes' of 'mob law' in the Welsh musical press.[35] Labour choral exploits never reached that level of popularity or enthusiasm, although trade unions and political organizations had a growing role in the eisteddfods between the wars. This was almost inevitable as, in 1930 for instance, a third of the singers at the Three Valleys Festival were out-of-work miners and their families.[36] The Welsh discourse probably influenced the debates around the CVUs' competitions, and similar debates raged in the Brass Bands movement.

The CVUs' competitive tradition was perhaps rather more on the model of the competitive music festival movement begun in the 1880s by Mary Wakefield. She was a Ruskinian, radical suffragette who might have felt at home in the Clarion movement, and her Westmorland Festival in 1885 sparked off at least sixteen festivals based on her model by 1900. The festival was itself inspired by the eisteddfod, but looked to avoid 'prize-hunting and self-glorification'.[37] It is no coincidence that the roots of elements of the amateur music movement were closely connected with the roots of elements of the labour movement, and that these shared beginnings – whether they were radicalism, Ruskinian anti-industrialism or Nonconformist religion – led to shared passions and prejudices.

After Montague Blatchford's death, Rutland Boughton took his place at the helm of the CVUs. His role of organizing a similar but larger organization for the Labour Party in the 1920s is considered in Chapter 3. Waters argues that the CVUs did 'make socialists' by bringing people into contact with socialists and their associations, even though the Unions themselves were not as explicitly political as some people wanted.[38] They existed alongside and, to a certain extent, as part of a wider choral movement that was particularly strong in the north of England, especially West Yorkshire, which was also the cradle of the CVUs. The story of the CVUs raises questions about the purpose of such musical adventures in the labour movement: were they for 'making socialists' or for performing the best music to the best of the players' abilities? How could the former purpose be maintained when, in the interests of competent public performance, the latter goal became increasingly important?

By placing the musical culture of the British labour movement between the wars in this historical context, it is clear that the movement already had a musical tradition in 1918. Any inter-war musical projects and ventures were not pioneering experiments but instead would have been seen by labour activists as part of this history. Socialists in 1918 were quite used to a discourse about music, and had seen the prominent role of music in the

Clarion, Labour Church and other movements – indeed, some historians would extend the 'heroic' phase of the British labour movement to 1924.[39] However, while the benefits of music as entertainment and as a fund-raising activity were well understood, along with the idea that music had a solidarity-building role, socialists before the First World War were not as clear about the potential or desirability of a project to 'build' or 'create' a socialist culture. It had been hinted at with the interest in folksong and notions of an 'art of their own', as well as in the opposition to commercial culture, but the idea was not well articulated and British socialist thought on this matter was full of contradictions. As time went on, comparisons with the labour movement in Germany, and approaches to the arts in Soviet Russia, led to these considerations becoming more widespread.

Music and socialist thought

Attempting to piece together a variety of ideas from different, broadly Marxist intellectuals, comparing and contrasting them with inter-war opinions and prejudices, in order to identify a broad socialist or Marxist musical theory, is a task fraught with difficulties. One problem is the changing meanings of key terms as well as that of applying ideas articulated in Russia, Germany and Italy (and in Russian, German and Italian) to inter-war Britain. An illustration of the problem is the changing and ambiguous nature of the word 'culture' and the question of what Antonio Gramsci, for example, meant by it. Raymond Williams, in *Keywords* (first published, 1976), described 'culture' as 'one of the two or three most complicated words in the English language'.[40] This is due to the word's complex development in several languages and several academic disciplines. While recognizing Gramsci as perhaps the most influential Marxist theorist of culture, and therefore an important thinker to consult here, it is certainly worth questioning to what extent he included 'the arts' within his definition of culture. When the Turin Socialist Party decided to form a 'Cultural Association', it was welcomed by some of the party's leading figures because of the opportunities for 'diversion', 'relaxation' and 'education' that it offered. It was hoped that it might steady the 'wavering' convictions of those who 'have drifted away from our political organisations, lured by the appeal of mere amusements'. The proposal and the language sounded similar to some of the projects suggested in the British labour movement, but Gramsci welcomed it with rather different language, comparing the Association with the Fabian Society in Britain and not seeming to consider any cultural pursuit other than political education.[41] Such ambiguity inevitably makes this task all the harder. In this section I will seek to identify some broad tensions within socialist thought that we can explore throughout this book, as they apply to the inter-war labour movement.

'The best music available' versus 'art of their own'

If we begin with the concept of 'good music', we may first consider some of the ideas of Theodor Adorno, the Marxist musicologist, sociologist and philosopher, who made detailed studies of 'art' music, as well as hostile criticisms of some music, most famously in his essay 'On jazz'. For Adorno, there was not just 'good' and 'bad' music, but there were 'good' and 'bad' ways of *listening* to music. A 'good' mode of listening is to do so 'with a concentrated and whole-hearted engagement with the work as an independent totality'.[42] While this led to him deploring commercial 'popular' music with its repetitive themes and rhythms, it also meant that he was opposed to a popularization or democratization of 'art' music, meaning that the project of many socialists who wished to bring 'the best music' to 'the masses' would have been at odds with Adorno's position. He felt that the increasing number of 'bad' listeners at concerts actually changed the nature of music *composed*, as well as that selected to be performed. When socialist music columnists, such as H. G. Sear who wrote for Birmingham's *Town Crier*, tried to persuade their readers that music by the great composers was as easy and pleasurable to listen to as so-called light music, he would have been encouraging a 'bad' mode of listening. As such, he was risking changing the art of music altogether.

Like Adorno, the socialist composer Rutland Boughton recognized that 'the new public of the radio, especially, has little understanding of the fact that to listen to music is itself an art'.[43] For him a good mode of listening required 'a surrender, rather than an effort, of the conscious part of the mind'.[44] The BBC shared some of these concerns and made efforts to ensure that broadcast music was not 'background' music through such means as leaving long silences between pieces.

Adorno's observation that the new audience for music, particularly via the gramophone and the wireless, might change the art itself need not *necessarily* mean that it would change for the worse. Walter Benjamin, for instance, observed that

> For the first time in world history, mechanical reproduction emancipates the work of art from its parasitical dependence on ritual. To an ever greater degree the work of art reproduced becomes the work of art designed for reproducibility . . . the total function of art is reversed. Instead of being based on ritual, it begins to be based on another practice – politics.[45]

This meant that once art was free of the ritual of 'the moment' (for our purposes, once music was free of the ritual of the concert), it changed the relationship between the artist and the consumer. Benjamin would appear to mean 'politics' in a very broad sense, but this does introduce a further question, and one that concerned many between the wars – can art, or should art, be political?

Certainly Adorno's position would appear to preclude any *use* of music beyond the aesthetic. Adorno deplored jazz for manipulating the senses, but if that was the purpose of the music, does its success not, in some way, make it 'good'? Is it possible for a 'bourgeois' European musicological tradition, to which Adorno belonged, to make judgements and generaliza-tions in a different musicological arena in its own terms? If we were to consider ethnomusicology or 'pop' musicologies, different types or modes of listening might be considered perfectly legitimate. Further-more, there is nothing to stop a popular piece of music – say, a piece of 'hot' jazz – being listened to as an interdependent whole, especially if we can consider it in terms of Boughton's 'surrender'. Also, *should* lyric-music, either song or opera, be listened to in that manner? If so, surely thought-provoking or engaging lyrics cause bad listening, as would interesting drama in an opera. As such, would not Adorno's 'good' mode of listening lead to a degradation in the standards of lyrics, librettos and drama, just as the masses' so-called bad mode of listening might lead to a degradation in music? Finally, is a 'good' mode of listening essen-tially one (despite Adorno's Marxist position) which has emerged from the right background, the right education – essentially meaning that music should remain the property of the ruling class, or a better-educated elite? There is little or no room within Adorno's position for alternative art or art as counter-culture, let alone explicitly political art or agit-prop. How-ever, Gramsci's thinking on hegemony opens up an alternative Marxian view.

There was little concept of the possibility of counter-culture in Britain between the wars, although it would be wrong to suggest that there was none at all. Gramsci's writing certainly did not influence British socialists and, while Lenin was more widely read, it is unlikely that his less sophis-ticated but not dissimilar views on society having two cultures had much influence. But there *were*, for all that, some embryonic notions of an 'art of their own' or, for our purposes, 'music of their own'. These included folksong (or folk arts), to be considered in more detail in Chapter 6, and 'simple' music – that is, minimalist music with purity and beauty that was not 'too high' for the workers to understand. The problem with consider-ing this as 'art of their own' is that these pre-industrial tunes and songs had very little relevance to the lives of the working class in twentieth-century Britain. Both Montague Blatchford and Rutland Boughton saw such music as 'people's music' – the lost culture of the working class that could be returned to them. If this was as far as ideas of 'art of their own' ever got, then they had much more in common with vague nostalgic utopianism than with any embryonic Gramscian analysis.

Ideas of alternative cultures were, in some ways, old and well rehearsed by the inter-war years. The 'new life' for socialists – particularly the activities of the Clarion movement – was essentially an attempt at an alternative culture away from commercialism. Similarly, the preoccupation of the likes of Edward Carpenter and Rutland Boughton with small-scale farming and self-sufficiency was part of the desire to form anti-industrial alternative sub-cultures. But these tasks are different from considering industrial working-class culture as a potential counter-culture and developing cultural activities with some sort of counter-hegemonic project in mind.

As for music, there are a number of reasons why an 'art of their own' did not extend far beyond agricultural folksong. A. L. Lloyd and Ewan MacColl had not yet brought to light their collections of industrial folksong, and even when they did, they were mostly of nineteenth-century origin and were only a significant part of the cultural life of certain small communities. Popular music (variety/music hall, jazz, dance, swing, etc.) was arguably not *of* the working class because of its commercial nature. Instead it was 'sold' to the workers by capitalists and, as such, if its socialist detractors had approached a Gramscian analysis, it was *part* of the bourgeois hegemony. The fact that folksong was thought to be the product of workers was important for its socialist champions.

There was a common theory that industrialism and capitalism destroyed the creative spirit of working people and their families. For Boughton, for example, 'conditions of life in which ordinary people had initiative caused them to make music as they worked, and music in celebration of work they had accomplished. Christian civilisation [Boughton's euphemism for capitalism], being developed without reference to the general welfare, made an end of such music.' He went on to say that 'the creative spirit which produced folk-music was checked by unfair conditions and then swamped by the echoes of the music halls'.[46] Boughton was placing the composition of folksong in an imagined 'golden age', as most people did in this period, and was not aware that people continued to write songs about work and other facets of life throughout industrialization. Furthermore, he would not appear to have been looking for art in times of struggle, even though he was championing the art of 'ordinary people'.

However, there is occasional evidence of British socialists between the

wars getting rather closer to a concept of counter-hegemony or counter-culture. The Workers' Theatre Movement, a dramatic organization
firmly in the bosom of the Communist Party, performed an almost exclusively agitational and propagandist role. Their monthly bulletin *Red
Stage* considered the role that the arts and entertainment played in class
domination and, as such, *did* approach a crude concept of hegemony,
probably grounded in some of the writings of Lenin.

> Every form of popular art and entertainment, public opinion and 'moral
> direction' is controlled by capitalist interests – or their agents, the Gov-
> ernment and the Church . . . Even 'sport' is a commercialised affair
> which reflects the dirty mismanagement of its capitalist promoters . . .
>   And should [the worker] dare to start thinking along different lines
> the Labour Party and the ILP will look after his interests to see that he
> doesn't get too far . . .
>   That is what we are up against. A capitalist state; capitalist control;
> capitalist propaganda making use of every form of thought to poison
> the thinker, or, better still, to keep him from thinking at all . . .
>   We are not competing with capitalist entertainment, we are exposing
> it.[47]

This was not the analysis of Gramsci, despite certain similarities. While
the writer acknowledged the conservative power of the arts and recreation, he was suggesting not that they should attempt to use art in the same
insidious way and 'compete' with 'capitalist entertainment', but that they
should use their agitational and propagandist style to 'expose' the hegemonic 'trick'. The question of artists 'competing with capitalist
entertainment' will be returned to in Chapter 3 when we consider choirs,
bands and orchestras in the movement, including the Workers' Theatre
Movement's singing troupes and bands – the formative elements of the
Workers' Music Association.

   In 1936, Left Theatre Ltd declared that its role was to counter the effects of 'capitalist theatre', referring to 'reactionary' songs such as
'Tipperary' and 'Keep the Home Fires Burning'.[48] This would suggest
that members of the Left Theatre, by 1936, had some embryonic concept
of a socialist counter-culture. It is interesting that the same year saw the
founding of the Workers' Music Association, which always considered
the dual functions of promoting music *of* the workers and providing
music *for* the workers, with varying success.[49]

   Those who held the position that the working class should be tutored
to appreciate 'good' music (or 'the best') were not always in conflict
with those who claimed to believe that the working class should have
'art of their own'. Indeed, the arguments sometimes even came from the
same people. While very few would have disagreed with Lenin that 'the

best of bourgeois art' should be included in a socialist culture,[50] few would have agreed with Trotsky that 'proletarian art' was necessarily 'pock-marked'.[51] If one can talk about an inter-war socialist musical culture in Britain, then it must really constitute a combination of these various components and seemingly contradictory ideas. As such, this socialist culture, in so far as it existed, was often at odds with the popular – or working-class – culture of the day, as we shall see in the next section.

Socialist musical culture versus popular musical culture

Did the attempts at moulding a socialist culture aim to engage with the popular, working-class culture of the day? If we were first to consider the 'traditional' or 'serious' aspects of an industrial working-class musical culture, the two great movements would be brass bands (from the north of England and the Midlands) and male voice choirs (particularly from South Wales). We might add the choral movement of Yorkshire and Lancashire as well. By 1918 there was some tradition of socialist engagement in these fields, especially the choral movement, and this continued and grew through the inter-war period, as we explore in Chapter 3. But these were localized traditions, long established and arguably in decline. Even music halls – the commercial villains of pre-First World War labour writing on music – were transforming into 'variety' clubs and being eclipsed by the craze that was to take working-class life in Britain by storm through the 1920s and 1930s: dancing.

Dance music was genuine big business, with songs and tunes played on the wireless selling vast quantities of sheet music so that all the dance bands in the dance halls up and down the country would be right up-to-date with the popular 'hits'. There was no unified or typical labour response to the phenomenon, but one can find some theoretical (and some just plain prejudiced) opposition to jazz and related music on the left, while at the same time finding dances and jazz bands becoming increasingly prominent aspects of labour movement activity. The common objections to dance music were not the complex musicological and sociological objections of Adorno, or certainly not expressed in the same terms. Musically, jazz was considered banal and repetitive. Politically, the commercial nature of the popular music industry was considered to be capitalism intruding into the aesthetic arena. For some, there would appear to have been further objections to the American – and possibly the African – origins of the music. The question of how socialists responded to commercialism and professionalism in art, and particularly the art of music, will be considered in the next section. The important question here is whether the labour movement, while engaged in popular politics, realized the possibilities of popular culture.

This problem was not confined to music. Socialists had various concerns about whether they should encourage seaside holidays, football, racing (and, more particularly, gambling), pub culture and all manner of frivolous pursuits. The reasoning behind socialist papers including a sports page and betting news, for instance, would appear to have been primarily the practical decision that it was the best way to keep in business. The *Bradford Pioneer* with its betting news flourished, while the more ascetic attitude of the *Bradford Labour Echo* contributed to its floundering.[52]

When it came specifically to music, a single newspaper could carry instructions in the art of musical discrimination from its music columnist and elsewhere enthuse about the variety shows coming to town, and try to sell tickets to a Labour Party dance. These internal contradictions could regularly be seen in Birmingham's *Town Crier*. There is nothing necessarily problematic about a paper that was aimed at a readership united by politics, not cultural tastes, appealing to a wide range of interests and musical opinion. But the language of the music columnists, such as H. G. Sear at the *Town Crier*, did not suggest the indulgence of one interest group amongst many. Sear was evangelizing to all:

> I will promise not to be technical. I will not tire you with the rules of music. I will seldom mention key or time. You shall not be bothered with augmented sevenths or enharmonic minors. If I cannot make you realise the personality of that man behind the music I shall have failed utterly and will withdraw. But I think I can.[53]

But even such an evangelist as Sear eventually found himself making nods in the direction of popular culture, whether under editorial pressure or not, we cannot say. By the late 1920s, his music columns included a survey of the week's new gramophone releases, including dance music, which he reviewed seriously and without the prejudice displayed by some. The movement's engagement with popular music will be explored in Chapter 6.

Amateurism versus professionalism/commercialism

'It . . . is abominable to think that the products of man's deepest emotions should be carried to market like a pound of butter.'[54] Rutland Boughton made many statements such as this, highlighting his distaste that artists should have to attempt to make their living from their art. Boughton believed that in a socialist future all artists would work and all workers would have the opportunity to become artists because of the expanded leisure time afforded to them. In the meantime, he seriously looked at the possibility of combining music with farming so that the authenticity and aesthetic independence of the music would not be endangered by the perils of having to pay for itself. This was one aspect of his plans for Glastonbury music festivals and music classes that never received wider support, and it remained an unfulfilled dream that his scholars should sow and harvest crops between learning their arpeggios. Eventually, Boughton got his farm and it was 'a sanctuary for any composer who does not object to being cut off completely from all the amenities of modern times'. Apparently there was 'not a neighbour's wireless set for miles'.[55]

While Boughton was something of a maverick, he did reflect a broader tendency within the labour movement in favour of amateurism in music as in other areas of recreation and leisure. There was also some inconsistency here. The same labour newspaper could carry a music column despairing of the compositions of those who wrote pieces in order to sell them and a trade union column encouraging readers to boycott a particular cinema that did not pay Musicians' Union rates for the players. The amateurist tendency on the left led to the Musicians' Union not always being treated as seriously as they would have liked, and some trade unionists felt that the semi-professional majority of the union's members should only have been paid for one job, which should be the 'proper' job. The anti-commercial strand of labour thought was part of a long tradition among utopian elements of the movement.

Music and 'the good time coming'

To consider music and utopia, with particular reference to the British labour movement, one can look at three particular sources. The first is socialist writing about music, the second is the lyrics to socialist anthems and songs, and the third is the actual music itself. The first two sources are the most readily usable. We can look for utopian themes and imagery in lyrics, and find a lot of them, and also look in socialist writing for utopian ideas about the role of music, both in bringing about the 'Co-operative Commonwealth' and in the place it would play in that future state. The most difficult task, and as such the most interesting, is to look for evidence of the utopian imagination in the actual music that socialists wrote, performed or championed.

Socialist writing about music

To begin with, let us consider the meeting of music and utopia within the writing of British socialists. One popular socialist theme after the First World War was the 'right to leisure'. Much writing surrounding this issue focused on the campaign for a forty-hour week. This was hardly a utopian aspiration; indeed, the modesty of the goal adds to the interest of the utopian language of much of the discourse. 'Leisure' was considered as a material thing – a prize that could be won. 'Life will become a romance full of glorious adventures for the workers once they have leisure.'[56] So read an article on 'The right to leisure' in the Glasgow *Worker* in 1919. It was believed by many, including the writer of that article, that leisure would be used in a constructive, rational and intellectual way to bring about a socialist future: 'leisure [is] the gateway to economic freedom', he wrote; 'workers who have leisure for thought and recreation will soon evolve a culture which will not tolerate exploitation or subjection'. The article was forward thinking in so far as it considered the possibility of workers evolving a culture for themselves, as well as being practical in arguing for the attainable goal of a forty-hour week. And yet it is written in the utopian form and uses the utopian imagination. There was surely an aspiration way beyond attaining the forty-hour week in the prediction that 'life will become a romance full of glorious adventures for the workers'.

The discourse on what workers would do with their leisure time in the future – whether after small trade union victories on hours of work or in the future co-operative state itself – contains many musical musings in the utopian voice. At the extreme end of these considerations come Rutland Boughton's ideas about how much manual work musicians should have to do in a future socialist state, along with the economic position of artists generally. He concludes: 'two hours a day in materially productive labour would not injure the soul of any artist; but, on the contrary, lead him to understand the thoughts and feelings of his fellow workers, and make him fitter to express them in terms of art'.[57] These considerations stemmed from debates before the First World War, ranging from those who, like William Morris or Edward Carpenter, felt that 'work itself must be so transformed as to become a pleasure',[58] to others, such as James Blackwell, writing in *Justice*, the organ of the Social Democratic Federation, who argued: 'We consider work, however necessary it may be, an evil to be avoided if possible, and we consider pleasure – *true rational pleasure that is* – the end and aim of existence.'[59]

An anonymous 'member of Yorkshire's socialist fraternity' remarked that 'the socialist choir could serve as "a first promise what enjoyment may be obtained from life, when under the socialism which these choirs are using their voices to promote, all men and women will have leisure to devote to intellectual pleasures"'.[60] The occasional rather prosaic perception that music made a 'pleasant change from politics' or helped to 'brighten' the movement is expressed differently here with utopian lyricism – the importance of pleasure and brightness in the labour movement is shown to have an importance beyond entertainment.

Utopianism in the British labour movement was not always entirely characterized by a discourse of the future. There were a number of British socialist thinkers for whom a rural idyll of the past was their utopia. For some – particularly Edward Carpenter, who was inspired by Thomas Carlyle[61] – a critique of capitalism was also a specifically anti-industrial position. It was, essentially, the 'green and pleasant land' as opposed to the 'dark satanic mills'. While various writers would have denied such conservative nostalgia, there was quite a 'Ruskinian' tradition, arguably including Morris and Blatchford, certainly Carpenter, and the considerable socialist interest in folksong and morris dancing was largely due to their 'unspoilt' nature. William Morris's utopia in *News from Nowhere* (first published in 1890) was pre-industrial in character, the clothes, buildings, modes of transport and environment being derived from an imagined past rather than an imagined future. Women's dress, for instance, was 'somewhat between that of the ancient classical costume and the simpler forms of the fourteenth century garments, though it was clearly not an imitation of either'.[62] It is no accident that cultural production from the 'golden age utopians' was firmly in the romantic tradition, for that utopianism was a socialist (or communist) romanticism, distinct from the individualism of some of the famous romantics, such as Byron, but with a long tradition in the Chartist and radical movements.[63] I shall return later to the importance of this tradition to inter-war labour music making.

Socialist lyrics and music

Both the 'good time coming' and the 'golden age' were referred to in socialist lyrics, but for the most part in those hymns and anthems, it was the state which was to come that was sung about. Edward Carpenter's very popular song 'England, Arise!' talked of the 'long, long night' being over and of 'the dawn' appearing.[64] The imagery of a 'new dawn' is found in many socialist lyrics. On the ethical, Labour Church side of the movement, utopia might be expressed as 'a heaven on earth'.[65] Such images of utopia are compared with dystopic images of the capitalist present:

> Comrades, brothers, do you see
> Want and mis'ry all around,

> Flaunting wealth and luxury,
> Side by side on earth abound?[66]

But, of course, 'the night is darkest before the morn'.[67] References to a utopian 'golden age' are more difficult to find. There was certainly a common theme in socialist lyrics that life under capitalism was 'unnatural':

> Oh help, my brothers, to bring the day
> When you and I shall both be free
> To live our lives in nature's way
> The call's to you and me.

The librettos of Rutland Boughton's music-dramas were often based on poetry that evoked pre-industrial society, relying heavily on Celtic mythology and Arthurian legend, as well his setting for the Thomas Hardy poem, 'The Queen of Cornwall'. His most famous music-drama, *The Immortal Hour*, was 'steeped in Celtic myth and legend'.[68]

A far more difficult task is to search for evidence of the utopian imagination at work in the actual music that socialists wrote, performed, enjoyed or championed. Evocation of a pre-industrial 'golden age' is noticeable in the folk tunes, rhythms and cadences used in much socialist composition and played its part in the choice of folksong and English renaissance pieces of music to fill the repertoires of socialist musical combinations. Just as Boughton often used Celtic and pre-industrial themes for the drama and librettos of his works, similarly the music was heavily imbued with 'folky' and Celtic ornamentation and the use of simple tunes and rustic rhythms. While Boughton's music and words and their relation to his world-view will be looked at in greater detail in Chapter 5, much of his output does demonstrate a Ruskinian-style utopian imagination at work. While many socialist anthems were sung to tradi-· tional tunes, it is most likely that a rather more practical consideration led to their choice: simply that the tunes ought to be well known in order to assist mass singing. That is not to say that specific tunes might not have been selected for other reasons – the general hymn-like qualities of the songs might just have arisen from the limitations of four-part choral arrangements and the limitations of communal singing. However, both types of music might be seen to be heralding the good news of a new Jerusalem and share some characteristics accordingly.

Keith Nield has attempted to explain why earlier labour historians had neglected the role of the likes of Edward Carpenter and why, for a time, Carpenter's work had an 'intense, but brief, popularity'. This was a consideration of Carpenter as a poet, but Nield's ideas can be applied to the musical life of the movement as well. Carpenter had been neglected, it is argued, because his work could be viewed as 'conservative nostalgia for a non-existent pre-capitalist idyll', 'inconsequential utopianism with no purchase on the real world' or 'diversionary dreaming in the path of the political struggle'. The reason for his brief popularity was that 'the *form* of his writing – its utopianism, its mysticism, even its "diffuseness" – may result from . . . the power, density, and historical specificity of the cultural hegemony which he and his contemporaries confronted'.[69] In other words, the specific historical context of late Victorian and Edwardian Britain's liberal/capitalist hegemonic consensus was such that certain methods of expressing alternative values were more appropriate and effective than others. Rather than confronting audiences and readerships with analyses of capitalist society and economics, and the details of socialist organization to defeat it, he simply showed how the status quo was not necessary or inevitable and hinted at the possibilities of an alternative. It was utopian, clearly, as it did not take into account political agency, but it was able to attract interest that 'scientific' Marxism could not. This is backed up by the famous quotation from the *Manchester Guardian* that 'for every convert made by *Das Capital* [*sic*], there were a hundred made by *Merrie England*'.[70]

Can this same analysis be applied to the *music* of socialists? Certainly, as we have considered, there was great interest in vague utopianism, pre-capitalist nostalgia and Celtic mysticism in the music of the movement. As such, the utopian anthems and Boughton's mystic music-dramas can be viewed alongside such writing as Carpenter's *Towards Democracy* as the cultural production of the movement. The popularity of the product is rather more difficult to assess. We are assured that Carpenter had a brief but ardent popularity, Blatchford sold over two million copies of *Merrie England*[71] and songbooks such as *Chants of Labour* ran to many editions, sold within the movement. In all these cases, one must assume that the readers shared the values of the poet, writer or musician. In the case of *Merrie England*, sold for threepence, many copies were bought by socialists and then distributed for propaganda work.

The popularity of Boughton's *Immortal Hour* cannot be viewed in the same way. It was quite possible to enjoy the music and the drama of *The Immortal Hour* and other works without sharing the values by which it was inspired. Imbued as it was with mysticism and pre-capitalist nostalgia, it was essentially a piece of escapist theatre enjoyed, much to Boughton's embarrassment, by aristocrats and society people in London, although it did have successful runs in more popular or democratic venues such as the repertory theatre in Birmingham. Reviewers in the labour press sometimes recognized the political impulses behind the work:

> There never was a time when we were more in need of dreams; dreams to beckon and dreams to command. Today, as always, we have to pass by way of dreams to the Land of Heart's Desire.
> The 'Immortal Hour' is a beautiful work . . . Greater even than beauty is the desire for beauty, and from such a feast we rise hungrier than we sat down . . .[72]

Boughton's popularity waned after he joined the Communist Party in 1926 and his political position became more public. Be that as it may, if it is true that the most effective counter-culture to the late Victorian and Edwardian hegemony could have been via the utopian form, all the vagaries and contradictions of the pre-1914 labour musical movement may have had their uses and successes after all. However, if 'socialists like Edward Carpenter and Robert Blatchford, who concerned themselves chiefly with a quest for "the new life", were to find themselves out of harmony with the growing parliamentary movement and its more limited aims',[73] did music have to carve out a new niche for itself in a more 'labourist' inter-war movement?

The question of an advent of 'labourism' is a vexed one. If labourism could be distinguished from socialism by being passive rather than active, reflexive rather than educative, empirical rather than ideological, pragmatic rather than principled, evolutionary rather than revolutionary, practical rather than intellectual, imbued with an 'ethic of responsibility' rather than one of 'ultimate ends' and distinguished from Fabianism because of its firm roots in the working class,[74] there was no overnight conversion from one 'ism' to the other in the British labour movement. Neither can many of the early British labour traditions be easily placed in one or other 'camp'. Where would the spirituality of ILP socialism sit? While trade unionism would normally be placed under the 'labourist' label, what about militant unionism and the role of revolutionary parties?

While not dismissing the 'labourist' thesis, it is a change from 'spirituality' to 'practicality' – away from pioneering, evangelical zeal – in both revolutionary and 'labourist' elements of the movement that has the most potential for upheaval in cultural production and consumption between the wars. One must also bear in mind that the use of the utopian form in labour art did not just have political significance; it was very much part of the romantic tradition, as I have suggested. The significance of the longevity of romanticism, via utopianism, extends far beyond the socialist/labourist debate in Labour Party history.

It is clear that music did not lose its important place in the movement in the 1920s. Sydney Court, a Labour Choir conductor from Deptford, asserted in 1924 that 'music has always been an integral part of the Labour Movement, but never has such an interest been aroused as at the present moment'.[75] It will be the focus of the next chapter to consider what role music played in the day-to-day associational life of the labour movement, notably regarding the important functions of entertainment, fund-raising and propaganda.

2

Pleasure, Pennies and Propaganda: Music in the Associational Life of the Labour Movement

The purpose of this chapter is to consider the role of music in the daily life of organizations and associations in the labour movement, with particular regard to the entertainment of activists, the raising of funds and the propagation of the socialist message. Associations are definitively local and therefore part of this chapter is necessarily in the form of local case studies. The cities and districts of Birmingham and Bradford were chosen partly because they provide regional, political and socioeconomic contrast. Particularly, Bradford was chosen as a Labour heartland city with an established and politically popular labour movement, and Birmingham, in contrast, had a small, pioneering but quickly strengthening labour movement, in local opposition. Both districts had a tradition of pre-war labour music making with Clarion Choirs and Labour Churches. Similarly, both cities had a vibrant musical life outside the labour movement.

Bradford was a city with a musical reputation. In 1900 Bradford had thirty choral societies, twenty brass bands, one amateur orchestra, six concertina bands, one bell-ringing team, two music halls and various 'popular concert' venues, all within 8 kilometres of the city centre.[1] While Birmingham might not have had a reputation for being as 'musically distinguished'[2] as Bradford in the past, its musicality progressed apace in the inter-war period. It acquired its first permanent orchestra in 1920 followed by a string orchestra in 1927 and the semi-professional Birmingham Choral and Orchestral Union in the same year, and it began holding a successful music festival in the late 1930s.[3]

The ILP was strong in both cities, particularly Bradford, and this was important as well. The ILP had an ambiguous role in the labour movement of the period and there was some debate as to its status and how long it could continue to operate as a 'party within a party' with individual membership and separate conferences. There was some attempt to carve out a specific role for the ILP that could be complementary to the work of the Labour Party without stepping on any toes. There was no doubt that those areas covered by this chapter – 'pleasure, pennies and propaganda' – were valid ILP activities. Propaganda and recreation were very much within the ILP's remit, and both tasks – particularly the former – required funds.

The chapter also sketches a national picture, paying some attention to music in trade union branches and national factions. Clearly the local detail cannot be replicated there, but, similarly, the local studies have their limitations: one cannot extrapolate national generalizations too confidently from local trends. By using both methods, I hope to present a picture of musical life in the associations of the British labour movement. The explicitly musical associations that existed in many local Labour Parties will be considered in Chapter 3, as they were generally choirs, bands or orchestras.

'The religion of socialism': a coda

As both Stephen Yeo and Chris Waters have suggested, British socialism had a zeal and fervour of religious proportions in the late Victorian period and, to a lesser extent, in the years just before the First World War. This fervency was particularly evident in the various socialist approaches to recreation: making the movement a 'total' experience (what Yeo referred to as a 'New Life') for devotees, with leisure time being spent amongst comrades in the Labour Church and Clarion movements. The various socialist organizations also attempted to provide this 'New Life' from cradle to grave through Socialist Sunday Schools, a variety of youth movements and then a wide variety of adult associations.

There is a standard thesis concerning this aspect of the early labour movement that runs something like this: as the Labour Representation Committee and later the Labour Party became more realistic electoral forces, and socialists ceased to be just a small sectarian minority that was variously persecuted and ridiculed in the popular press, so the zeal and fervour were concentrated upon winning elections rather than providing an all-round 'socialist' way of life.

Furthermore, in *Primitive Rebels* (1959) Eric Hobsbawm has characterized the Labour Churches as 'labour sects', placing them in a nineteenth-century working-class sectarian religious tradition. Fred Reid has considered whether this tradition could be seen as having extended into the inter-war years, demonstrated particularly by the Socialist Sunday Schools.[4] The surprising existence of inter-war Labour Churches in

Birmingham could add some weight to that suggestion. It must be borne in mind, however, that the Labour Churches were transformed considerably from a predominantly religious movement to a movement of secular ethics.

John Trevor himself, the founder of the Labour Church Union, lived until 1930, but his relationship with the labour movement had become strained much earlier. Trevor felt that the strong, and growing, relationship between the Labour Churches and the ILP was a threat to the spiritual side of the movement.[5] The other cause of his estrangement with the movement was that, despite the Labour Churches having been very anti-clerical from their inception, by 1899 he was beginning to consider the benefits of a clergy with little or no support. The more secular side of the Labour Church movement, represented by Fred Brocklehurst, gained the upper hand in the first decade of the twentieth century and Trevor lost interest when it became, in his view, 'a Sunday meeting of trade unionists and so lost its religious character.' Any Churches established after 1906 were more secular than the earlier ones.[6] The 1906 Labour Church Hymn Book contained a Statement of Principles:

i)   That the Labour Church exists to give expression to the religion of the Labour Movement.

ii) That the religion of the Labour Movement is not theological but respects each individual's personal convictions upon this question.

iii) That the religion of the Labour Movement seeks the realisation of universal well-being by the establishment of Socialism – a Commonwealth founded upon Justice and Love.

iv) The religion of the Labour Movement declares that improvement of social conditions and the development of personal character are both essential to emancipation from social and moral bondage, and to that end insist upon the duty of studying the economic and moral forces of society.[7]

The 'new' Labour Party and attendant movement that emerged in 1918 has generally been thought to be one without Labour Churches and with a smaller, marginalized and anachronistic Clarion movement. It is generally believed that 'between 1891 and 1910 about 120 Labour Churches can be identified . . . but only one or two survived the First World War'.[8] Although Socialist Sunday Schools grew after the war, the venom with which they were attacked by what the labour movement called the 'dope' press, which accused the schools of indoctrinating small children, could only have occasioned disquiet amongst electorally minded Labour Party members.

However, a close look at the labour movement in Birmingham after the First World War shows that there were some deviations from that thesis.

One of the most striking examples of the deviation is Birmingham's Labour Church movement. 'Birmingham's Labour Weekly', the *Town Crier*, began production in October 1919 and a prominent aspect of the associational life depicted in its advertisements and reports was the activity of the Labour Churches. From there being six Churches meeting (and advertising and reporting in the *Town Crier*) regularly in 1920, the numbers rose to a peak of seventeen in 1925, from which point there began a decline.[9] It is difficult to be absolutely confident of these numbers as not all Churches advertised every week – there would often be reports of a Labour Church meeting that had not been advertised and vice versa. Furthermore, although there was a Labour Church 'season' that lasted approximately from September to April, different Churches opened and closed at different times. Although the highest 'count' of Labour Church announcements was in 1925, there does not appear to have been a rapid decline after that date, and no concern was expressed in the pages of the *Town Crier* about Churches having to close.[10] Recreation was always an integral aspect of the Churches, but if anything it seems to become more central between the wars.

Music in the Labour Church movement

John Boughton describes a typical Labour Church meeting as opening 'with a song from the Labour Church hymn-book' followed by 'an address from a visiting speaker' and concluding with 'another Labour hymn or two'. Sometimes this would be followed by 'the performance of a musical item, a brief address or reading from the Chair and a collection'.[11] The extended metaphor with a Christian church was persisted with – this 'typical' meeting was often referred to as a 'service'.

In fact the musical item was a more regular feature than suggested by Boughton, and Labour Church advertisements would generally give the name of the speaker, the chair and the soloist. The Churches had pianists, who were normally drawn from among their members although occasionally the position would be advertised,[12] and a local or visiting singer would provide the entertainment. On occasion there would be instrumental solos (violins, cellos and cornets were popular) either instead of or as well as the vocal solo. Exactly how long the musical selections would last at one of these meetings would appear to vary. There are frequent references to the musical items: at Bristol Street Labour Church in 1921, 'Miss Doris Lawson sang two solos in fine style, and Mr W. A. Neill rendered several violin solos, which were very much appreciated.' At Rotton Park Labour Church in 1920 the 'Rotton Park Labour Church Choir' just 'gave a couple of musical items'. This aspect of Labour Church meetings continued throughout the 1920s and was such a standard part of the meeting that correspondents with the *Town Crier* did not always feel the need to comment on the music, often just making a passing reference. A correspondent from the Aston Labour Church gave the musical aspect of the Church its proper importance when announcing its opening for the 1921–2 'season': 'a first-class speaker, vocal and instrumental music and, in fact, everything which goes towards the making of a Labour Church'.[13]

The visiting speaker, sometimes referred to as a lecturer, would speak on a wide variety of subjects,[14] and it was not unusual for issues surrounding music to be considered. Although the most common talks were on topics related to spiritual or ethical aspects of socialism, lectures could be on music, literature, religion and a variety of issues with little or no connection or reference to the labour movement. On Sunday, 29 November 1925, for example, at the Balsall Heath Labour Church, 'Mr C. Mobberley gave an excellent lecture on the lives and works of the famous musical composers illustrated by selections from their compositions'. The enjoyment of this particular evening was 'added to' by 'Miss Jackson' and her singing.[15] A very similar lecture was sometimes provided at the Churches by the writer of the music column in the *Town Crier*, H. G. Sear, who was also the conductor of the Birmingham Labour Party Orchestra. The talk was entitled 'The Men Behind the Music' and was based upon his newspaper column.[16] As another example of the sort of recreational or cultural items of interest at Labour Church meetings, aside from music, Birmingham's embryonic People's Theatre Movement advertised in the *Town Crier* in July 1925 to offer to 'give Dramatic Readings at Labour Churches'.[17]

If the typical Labour Church meeting described above was a pattern, it was one from which there were regular deviations. The most typical alternative to the usual lecture – 'a pleasant change from politics'[18] – was a 'musical evening'. These were popular items in Labour Church calendars, often being used to open or close seasons. Church members and their friends would often provide the entertainment. For example, the Balsall Heath Labour Church held what was advertised as a 'Grand Concert' on 2 April 1922, tipped as 'a grand miscellaneous concert . . . which will include many tip-top artistes'.[19] Apparently the concert 'reached a high standard of excellence and the audience showed their great appreciation of the efforts of each artiste'.[20] It is perhaps worth mentioning at this point that the available 'criticism' of musical events in the Labour Churches comes in the form of reports submitted to the *Town Crier* by representatives of the Churches themselves. The absence of a separation of powers between criticism and advertisement helped to secure a general tone of enthusiasm and politeness when describing these amateur efforts.

This concert was referred to as 'miscellaneous' to explain that it was an evening of individual 'artistes' and not a choir, orchestra, band or concert party. Balsall Heath had had musical evenings on 26 February,[21] 12 March[22] and 26 March.[23] The week after the 'Grand Concert', the Amalgamated Engineering Union Male Voice Choir was making a return visit.[24] Although this is an unusual run of musical evenings, it demonstrates their popularity at the Churches. It was more usual for such evenings to be spread out across the season.

A number of Labour Churches formed their own choirs and 'orchestras'. The Rotton Park Labour Church had its own choir. After giving 'a couple of musical items' on 8 February 1920 at their own Labour Church, they offered their services more widely: 'it may be mentioned that this choir is ready to make arrangements to aid any of the other Labour Churches and the movement generally'.[25] Their pioneering work in this area was helped along by their conductor William MacBeath, who entered into some of the city-wide discussions and controversies regarding choirs, bands and orchestras.[26] The Selly Oak Labour Church followed Rotton Park's lead, exporting its choir and orchestra to other Churches in the city. The combination of choir and orchestra was sometimes referred to as the Selly Oak Musical Society and was much in evidence at Labour Church meetings[27] and other Labour concerts and social events. It is not clear whether the Selly Oak Choir later changed its name to the Selly Oak Choral Union[28] to tie in with the national Labour Choral Union movement,[29] or whether this was a separate group altogether. The latter choir primarily performed at Labour Churches and was popular, at least with the authors of Labour Church reports in the *Town Crier*. When it opened the 1925–6 season of the Stirchley Labour Church, the paper reported that 'the Selly Oak Choral Union, conducted by Mr T. Osborne, provided a magnificent programme of solos and part songs'. However, occasional reference was still made to the 'Selly Oak Labour Church Choir' after this.[30] In 1926 the Sparkhill and Tyseley Labour Church had its own 'orchestra' to provide selections at normal meetings rather than the usual soloists.[31]

Another type of musical evening that was occasionally held at Labour Churches was a gramophone night. This would be either a lecture illustrated by gramophone selections[32] or a whole night of music presented on a gramophone.[33] These events occasioned some excitement amongst the correspondents to the *Town Crier*, who would sometimes enthuse over what model the 'instrument' was and the modern design. This was still new technology and so the attendant excitement was quite understandable.

Community singing, while actually a long-standing aspect of labour movement activity at meetings and demonstrations, was popularized in Birmingham by a 'Festival of Community Singing' at the Hippodrome, sponsored by the *Daily Express*,[34] and became a national phenomenon around the same time. After this, many events that had presumably included community singing before began to advertise it and couch it in that term. Sometimes it would just replace the solo or musical item at the end of a normal meeting;[35] on other occasions it was the main feature.[36]

The singing of 'labour hymns' at Labour Churches was referred to more in *Town Crier* announcements and reports with the increased interest in community singing. John Boughton wrote that Birmingham Labour Church meetings opened with a song from 'the Labour Church hymn-book' and that 'England, Arise!', 'Lift up the People's Banner', 'Jerusalem' and 'The Red Flag' were particular favourites'.[37] The hymn book referred to was presumably John Trevor's collection from 1891 or the updated new editions (produced without Trevor) published in 1906 and 1907.[38] As well as popular old labour anthems and 'hymns', the Birmingham Labour Churches introduced a number of new songs and new 'musical settings' of old songs to the local labour movement, certainly from 1926, through the pages of the *Town Crier*. The Birmingham labour weekly expanded that year and 'Labour Church Hymns' became a new occasional feature.

A brief analysis of these songs – particularly their lyrical content – reveals quite a lot about the Church's utopianism, ethical socialism and ambiguous relationship with Christianity. The series began with a special one-off on 20 August 1926: a new arrangement of 'The Land Song', which was advertised in the following terms on 13 August: 'As we cannot repeat publication, we urge all who desire a copy of the "Land Song" to make sure of securing the *Town Crier* next week. Give your newsagent an order for an extra copy of next week's issue.'[39] Of course, the *Town Crier* was using the special item to try and increase its sales, and in the event the song was printed again on 27 August for those who had missed it. 'The famous "Land Song" [was] not as well known in the Labour movement as it should be', according to the *Town Crier*'s editor, W. J. Chamberlain. This was a 'new musical setting by a local Labour musician', which, Chamberlain declared, 'should be one of the musical items at all future Labour meetings', particularly 'in view of the Labour Party's "Land For The People" Campaign'.[40]

The following month 'Not "God's Will"' was included, set to a tune called 'Darwell'. The four-part choral setting was again included in the paper and again the arranger remained anonymous, as did the lyricist. The lyrics were not as 'religious' as the title suggests; they were rather a criticism of 'religious' defences of capitalism: ''TIS NOT GOD'S WILL! It is the grinding, crushing, curse of MAN-made Laws!' The final line of the song is less ambiguously secular: 'The LAND was God's great gift to MAN, TO ALL MANKIND'). The composer had written a band arrangement for his song: 'Band parts can be obtained. Apply *Town Crier*.'[41] In fact, the choral setting would have been appropriate for unaccompanied singing as well, being quite a traditional four-part hymn setting.

Another 'hymn' was printed the following week: 'BREAK THE CHAINS!' No reference was made to any choir or band parts being available;[42] instead the singer would have to be aware of the old tune to which it was set[43] and use existing choral arrangements. Again, the lyricist remained anonymous. The following week, another 'hymn' was printed: 'Heaven on Earth'. This song was again put to an old obtainable tune[44] and the lyrics called for a renewal of socialist 'vows', expressing a vague utopian yearning:

> Onward and upward, be our trend;
> Liberty sweet, with pity blend;
> Freedom and Peace, and honest Mirth,
> So shall we make a 'Heaven on Earth.'[45]

Another Labour Church hymn ('Plenty For Everyone – Too Much For None') was included the following month, on 5 November 1926. This was set to a new tune and the music was included in the paper. The *Town Crier* presented it as being popular and much in demand by printing it again on 12 November 'by request'. Another, on 26 November, was called 'Evening Hymn'. This one was set to the same tune as 'BREAK THE CHAINS!' and strangely the lyrics referred very little to socialism or religion in an explicit way. The final verse, though, appears to suggest that socialists will go to heaven:

> So may we live that we may dread
> The grave as little as our bed.
> Fearless whene'er the end's in view
> If to our conscience we've been true.[46]

The next Labour Church hymn included in the *Town Crier* was 'a Labour Christmas Hymn' set to the tune of the carol 'O Come All Ye Faithful'. The opening line was 'O Come! all good comrades . . .'

The very familiar tune might well have made this song, at least, a popular one at the Christmas Labour Church meetings. The question of quite how often these songs were actually sung is an important one with regard to their place in the associational life of the labour movement, whatever their merit or otherwise as pieces of music, poetry or complete songs. How well known the various 'Bristol Old English Tunes' were is difficult to estimate, but they would be unlikely to be known simply by the number. For Labour Choirs – let alone for community singing – the ability to read music could certainly not be taken for granted, even if most would have encountered tonic sol-fa notation at school. The 'hymns' with new tunes would have been even more difficult to learn without a competent musical director to tutor the 'congregation'.

The alleged popularity of 'The Land Song' and 'Plenty for Everyone – Too Much for None' would suggest that these were sung, and at least one of the printed hymns, 'Labour's "Soldier's Chorus"' was certainly performed. The latter was printed on 11 March 1927 without the name of the lyricist and – on this occasion – without any reference to the tune to which it was to be sung.[47] Sparkhill and Greet Labour Church (previously called Sparkhill and Tyseley Labour Church) took out a large advertisement in the *Town Crier* on 18 March 1927 to announce that 'Labour's "Soldier's Chorus" as inserted in last week's *Town Crier* specially adapted to Gounod's world famous "Faust" Music' would be sung on Sunday, 26 March at the Labour Church. Other songs were to be sung as well, by a soloist.[48] The advertisement did not say who would sing the new Labour Church hymn; one assumes, because of the nature and purpose of 'labour hymns', that the song would have been attempted by the audience. It is impossible to tell whether any of the hymns became the popular choice of the Church-goers, but they certainly did not dislodge 'The Red Flag', 'The Internationale' or 'Auld Lang Syne' from their positions of prominence at other labour meetings and outings.

Hymns continued to be printed at irregular intervals. John Boughton remarked that Sparkhill and Tyseley Labour Church 'even compiled its own hymn-book and hymns',[49] and although there was no suggestion in the *Town Crier* that its 'Labour Church Hymns' section was a serialization of the Church's efforts, it is one possible source. Of course, the *Town Crier*'s songs were also intended to be collected by Labour Church members right across the city in order for them to have their own hymn books.

There are certain similarities in style and choice of imagery (such as references to 'wealth' as a sentient being) which might suggest that these Labour Church hymns shared the same anonymous writer. Of course, this cannot be assumed and the similarities might be explained by the ethos of the Birmingham Labour Churches. The style of lyricism is not markedly different from the style displayed in the hymns and anthems of labour written around the turn of the century, which were well represented in Labour Church hymn books and Carpenter's *Chants of Labour*. However, I would conclude that the 'Labour Church Hymns' section of the *Town Crier* did not represent a renaissance in Victorian labour hymn writing in Birmingham, but rather was the work of a single writer.

Music and the survival of spiritual idealism

The interest in the Labour Churches amongst the wider movement, expressed via the *Town Crier*, continued and grew after the apparent peak in Labour Church activity in 1925. There was no immediate evidence of decline, and yet decline they did. Boughton asserted that 'by 1929 just four remained open and none survived the next few years'.[50] In fact, a few Churches continued to operate throughout the 1930s and some were reopened. However, they became considerably more isolated from the city-wide movement, failing to use regularly the advertising opportunities offered by the *Town Crier*, and the meetings appeared to lose some of their distinctive and recreational spirit. Church meetings from the 1930s involved the passing of resolutions and very political speeches with little or no mention of musical or recreational activity or thought.

John Boughton's comparison of this aspect of the Birmingham labour movement with activities in Sheffield is illuminating. The dominance of the Chamberlains and the Unionists in the politics of Birmingham, amongst many socioeconomic factors well documented in his thesis, resulted in Labour Party support remaining unusually low in Birmingham through the 1920s, while Sheffield saw the dominance of Labour as an electoral force. Sheffield labour newspapers and party records do not refer to any Labour Churches in Sheffield between the wars – there was a Sheffield Christian Socialist Church operating in 1919,[51] but it sounds like quite a different sort of organization: Birmingham Labour Churches were essentially secular. Boughton puts this difference between the labour movements in the two cities down primarily to the basic difference in their electoral strengths and suggests that the Birmingham Labour Churches declined as Labour Party supporters lost the 'veneer of spiritual idealism which had sustained the pioneers when their goal seemed distant'.[52] In other words, according to Boughton, Labour Churches were an element of the life of a sect – not His Majesty's Opposition, and certainly not the party of government.

This was certainly not perceived by Labour Church enthusiasts in Birmingham. In 1924, under the headline 'Extension of Labour Church Movement' in the *Town Crier*, an anonymous writer (probably a member of the Handsworth Labour Church) declared: 'One of the encouraging results of the awakening of interest in Labour is the extension of Labour Church activity in Birmingham. Handsworth supporters are anxious to have a Church in each ward . . .'[53] This statement of aims for Labour Church expansion was accompanied with the news of several new Churches being opened. It was felt that the local growth of support for the Labour Party was an opportunity for the Labour Churches to grow, and necessitated the party involving itself in more, not fewer, cultural and lei-sure activities. Activists in the Birmingham labour movement were not just sustaining an old socialist way of life beyond its natural course, they were attempting to extend the movement further into members' and supporters' free time in a variety of ways – some based on the past, some entirely new.

The Churches' primary roles would appear to have been recreational and educational, 'a combination of entertainment and self-improvement'[54] that had its roots in those notions of 'rational recreation' considered in Chapter 1 and by a number of historians, including Chris Waters.

Looking elsewhere in the country, there is certainly an argument to be made that there was more than a 'veneer of spiritual idealism' in the movement. Although Birmingham would appear to have been the only part of the country to have had a Labour Church renaissance under the old name, meetings of a similar nature under a variety of titles were not rare. At the same time, other sometimes short-lived and localized organiza-tions and movements displayed rather more spiritual idealism than the inter-war Labour Churches. Bradford had organizations like The Peo-ple's Church on Kirkgate, which held a long series of meetings aimed at labour activists entitled 'The Christ of Revolution'.[55]

Bradford and nearby West Yorkshire towns like Keighley were the early strongholds of the ILP and housed the earliest and largest Labour Churches. This strength of tradition in the spiritual and recreational sides of the movement might lead one to expect a more stable and well-established labour musical movement than that which we have docu-mented in Birmingham. The assertions in John Boughton's comparison between Birmingham and Sheffield, however, would make you expect Bradford more closely to resemble the latter city.

Neither Keighley nor Bradford Labour Churches survived the First World War, but the ILP did continue to hold Sunday evening meetings with lectures and music throughout the period.[56] Sometimes the Sunday evening meeting would include a 'musical service' and this continued right into the 1930s while Labour Churches were on the decline in Bir-mingham. Indeed, there is some evidence to suggest that meetings very similar in nature to the Labour Churches in Birmingham were organized by the ILP across much of its heartland. While the National Labour Church movement would not appear to have survived the war, local ILPs seem to have kept up the traditions, while choosing to keep the name only in Birmingham. An ILP activist from Accrington recalled that 'The ILP was more cultural than the Labour Party. On Sunday afternoons we had talks on Poetry, Art and Music . . .'[57]

Similar Sunday meetings took place across the city of Bradford. ILP branches had educational meetings and lectures on Sundays, similar to the Churches. Socialist Sunday Schools in Bradford had regular 'Open Sundays'. where anyone could attend a Sunday afternoon meeting, normally with a speaker and a soloist,[58] and sometimes with a full programme of 'musical items, recitals, etc. by the scholars'.[59] The meeting that most closely resembled a Labour Church in Bradford in the years immediately following the First World War was a lecture series, held during what, in Birmingham, constituted the Labour Church 'season', at the Picture House and later at St George's Hall. These venues were much larger than the elementary school halls used by Birmingham Labour Churches. Advertisements for the meetings were carried in the *Bradford Pioneer*, a weekly newspaper published under the auspices of the Bradford Trades and Labour Council, Bradford Labour Party and Bradford ILP. These ILP meetings were not given a specific name, but they were Sunday afternoon lectures – often about educational or cultural subjects rather than the specifically political. Sometimes the lecturers at Sunday meetings were well known, such as J. B. Priestley speaking at a Great Horton Socialist Sunday School 'Open Sunday' in 1919.[60]

From time to time, instead of a lecture, there would be a musical evening. Occasionally, as with the Birmingham Labour Churches, the two could be combined. In January 1919, Mr S. Midgley gave a lecture on 'Music and the People' 'illustrated by well-known local artistes',[61] and the following month Mr F. S. Howes, BA, lectured on 'Songs for Socialists' 'with illustrations by Miss Marie Howes, LRAM, and Mr George Howes of Oxford'.[62] In March 1919, and again in March 1920, 'Casey' came to perform at a Sunday meeting at the Picture House with his accompanist, 'Dolly'.

'Casey' was the nickname of Walter Hampson, an itinerant ILP propagandist and violin player, who was apparently very popular in the movement. Indeed, when he and Dolly visited the Picture House in 1920, the *Bradford Pioneer* felt the need to express their 'deep regret to the number of people who were unfortunately crowded out' and they raised £12 10s 6d for the central European famine fund.[63] Casey's performance involved playing 'music that is worthy of the worker's ear' interweaved with 'a good deal of wit and wisdom'. Precisely what music might be 'worthy of the worker's ear' is difficult to say, but one must assume that it was serious classical music judging from some of Hampson's published 'wit and wisdom', which will be considered in Chapter 6.

One has to assume that Casey was a talented violinist, since he attained the admiration of such opinionated critics as George Bernard Shaw and Rutland Boughton. They both supported his efforts in the early 1920s to purchase a Stradivarius violin which was paid for by subscriptions by labour activists.[64] In 1927, the Keighley ILP engaged Casey and Dolly to perform at the Municipal Hall on 24 October. In 1930 a testimonial fund was set up for Casey, to which Keighley ILP contributed five shillings.[65] This 'long, lean, athletic bearded man attired in velvet jacket and riding breeches' attracted a full house again at the Jowett Hall in Bradford in 1928. On that occasion his repertoire consisted of pieces by Beethoven, Mozart, Schubert and Dvorak, 'with no written music before him', as well as some folk dances.[66] Casey was also a regular visitor to Birmingham events, and being an itinerant labour musician and speaker would appear to have been his full-time job throughout the 1920s. The Labour's Who's Who from 1924 listed his occupation as a 'musical propagandist and Co-op Union lecturer (fiddleosopher)' and his recreation as 'trying to discover a Stradivarius violin'. In the past he had played first violin at the Theatre Royal in Manchester and with another orchestra at Blackpool Tower.[67]

These Sunday afternoon or evening meetings, held by the ILP across all its heartlands, could be seen as close relations of the Labour Church movement. The two phenomena co-existed before the war. In the late Victorian and Edwardian period, the ILP Sunday lecture, 'classes in singing, dancing, elocution and political economy',[68] was very much part of the 'New Life' alongside Labour Churches and the Clarion movement, either engaging in 'making socialists' or providing them with educational leisure activities. That these meetings modelled themselves to some degree on the Labour Churches is further evidenced by a request from the ILP, printed in the Pioneer, for 'two copies of the Labour Church Hymn Book (with music), now out of print' along with a volunteer pianist for Sunday evening meetings.[69]

It becomes more difficult to follow the recreational activity of the ILP in Bradford through the 1930s. Minute books are incomplete (and do not tend to dwell on such matters anyway) and the Pioneer – once considered to be an organ of the ILP – retained its allegiance to the official Labour Party in a far more partisan way than the Town Crier. Certainly in the early 1930s the Sunday lectures kept their recreational and cultural element,[70] while Birmingham's faltering Labour Church movement appeared to be losing its character of rational recreation. However, the Sunday evening meetings did suffer from low attendances at this time. When a group of musicians played the music of Grieg, Schubert and Vaughan Williams at the Jowett Hall in February 1929, the correspondent to the Pioneer asked: 'what has happened to the audiences which used to throng the Jowett Hall? Is there some other attraction in the city on a Sunday night for ILP-ers? Or is it that music is not appreciated by Bradford folks?'[71] Having said that, only a couple of weeks later an evening of chamber music, featuring a violinist, a cellist, a pianist and female vocalist,[72] was 'one of the finest concerts ever given in Bradford' and the Jowett Hall was crowded with 'a delighted audience'.[73] Either the chastisement had shamed some more socialists into attending, or there was some inevitable seasonal variation in audience sizes.

The Socialist Sunday Schools

In another area of quasi-religious, inter-war labour activity, Bradford was more active than Birmingham: the Socialist Sunday Schools. While Labour Churches, in their formative years, often had a Sunday School, the Socialist Sunday Schools themselves represent quite a distinct tradition. Formed in the west of Scotland, rather than the north of England, their primary aim was 'the conversion of a significant proportion of the new generation of British youth to Socialism for the purpose of transforming British society by political and industrial action'.[74]

A considerable amount of music was played and sung in Socialist Sunday Schools, as with church Sunday Schools, and the emphasis was on the 'pupils' making the music themselves. When Birmingham's King's Norton and Stirchley Socialist Sunday School held its 'first annual party' in 1919, the programme of entertainments was 'entirely in the hands of the children themselves'.[75] The various Bradford Sunday Schools had their own choirs and orchestras, and the choirs combined to make the 'Sunbeams' who performed at a variety of city-wide events, such as the ILP International Fair in 1925, which will be considered in more detail later. They also performed musical plays and operettas especially composed for the movement, as considered in Chapter 5.

The Socialist Sunday Schools had a hymn book that contained a variety of songs for children of various ages, and included some of the 'hymns' and anthems sung regularly by the adults. Until 1925, Keighley Socialist Sunday School used the original hymn book produced in 1910. The 1925 updated book contained a number of interesting areas of continuity and change. The 1910 hymn book announced that 'the hymns selected are non-theological, and are exclusively concerned with the spiritual and social aspirations of the human race, in regard to life and conduct'.[76] By 1925, when 'a number of entirely new songs [had] been added' and the compilers had 'taken the liberty of using a number of well-known pieces from other similar collections', other concerns had arisen beyond the theological, which show how seriously the hymn collection was taken. The editors noted, in the front of the book: 'In the case of Song No. 11 the word "England" is to be broadly interpreted. The Committee were not unanimous in reference to the inclusion of No. 70 and it was felt that this should be noted.'[77]

Number 11 was 'Praise Ye, Youth of England' and there was obviously concern that schools in Scotland and Wales might take issue with the lyric. Whether the word 'England' could be interpreted broadly enough to include the entire international proletariat, I rather doubt. The controversy around Number 70 would appear to be due to feminist opinion on the Committee: 'Onward Brothers, march still onward' referred to the future socialist state as 'man's true kingdom'.[78] No apology is made in the book for Edward Carpenter's 'England, Arise!' or various uses of the generic 'man' or 'he', so the decision to single these two out is difficult to explain. Similarly difficult to explain (other than by the fact that certain songs were 'favourites') are the decisions of which songs to repeat, omit and add from the 1910 book. 'Little Comrades'[79] is bizarre and antiquated and yet was chosen to be repeated.

> We're a band of little Comrades,
> Marching in the path of truth;
> We are marching onward, onward,
> Through the flowery land of youth;
> Marching onward up to Manhood[80]
> When we mean to join the fight
> Of the weak against oppression
> In the battle for the right.

The chorus is of particular antiquarian interest:

> And we practise as we go
> On the little things we meet,
> Carrying Granny's parcel for her,
> Guiding blind men o'er the street,
> Lifting up the fallen baby,
> Helping mother all we may,
> Thus as little duties meet us,
> We perform them day by day.[81]

These lyrics obviously reveal something about the nature of the Socialist Sunday Schools, that the younger children were given instruction in 'good deeds' as in the Boy Scout movement. This was echoed in the Schools' 'catechism', 'The Declaration of First Principles', which included the aspiration of 'cultivating the spirit of service to others'. Similarly, the 'Socialist Ten Commandments' included 'make every day holy by good or useful deeds and kindly actions'.[82] And yet there was considerable hostility towards the Scout movement owing to its alleged militaristic associations. Later in the period the 'Woodcraft Folk' were promoted as a progressive alternative to the Boy Scouts.[83] 'Little Comrades' was such a favourite that it was often the choice of song with which to close a meeting.[84]

Socialist Sunday School activists found it increasingly necessary to defend their activities from attacks in press and Parliament, and even from the concerns of Labour supporters and labour movement activists. These controversies would primarily emerge from the schools' more 'religious' ceremonies and from their determination to be legally considered a religious movement. There was a parliamentary debate about the schools in 1923 when a Conservative, Sir John Butcher, moved a bill on the subject. The *Bradford Pioneer*'s perception of the debate was that 'apparently no-one took Butcher's rubbish very seriously'.[85] During the 1922 general election, the *Bradford Argus* had carried articles attacking the Socialist Sunday Schools, especially the 'precepts' and the 'naming services'. A correspondent to the *Pioneer* from the Bradford Moor school defended their teachings and invited critics to an 'Open Sunday' to see what they did for themselves.

Whether or not the critics were right to be concerned, the schools *did* have 'naming services' that represented secular baptisms. In 1922, the Labour Lord Mayor of Bradford conducted naming services for 'a couple of bairns' and they each received a silver spoon and a bunch of flowers amidst a musical service.[86] They had their own 'Ten Commandments', which included: 'Remember that all good things of the earth are produced by labour. Whoever enjoys them without working for them is stealing the bread of the workers.'[87] They also had a catechism where pupils would learn the 'first principles of socialism' by heart. It was perhaps not surprising that the Socialist Sunday Schools were 'the butt of a great deal of splenetic splutter from Anti-Socialist organisations' and that, instead of this being 'a recommendation of us to the Labour forces', they found 'apathy and antagonism from the great majority'.[88]

In June 1933, the Great Horton Socialist Sunday School in Bradford held a bazaar to raise money to pay the rates. In the *Bradford Pioneer* they complained:

> It seems a curious thing that organisations such as the Plymouth Brethren and the Four-Square Gospellers – indeed all the religious bodies – should be exempt from the payment of rates for their premises, whilst an organisation which bases its teaching on Love, Truth and Justice should be compelled to pay. Now if the Socialist Sunday Schools opened their services with a plea to a doubtful Divinity for daily bread, instead of the statement 'we desire to be just and loving to all our fellow men and women,' their rates would be forgiven them.[89]

When trying to define the role of the Schools compared with the Guild of Youth and the League of Youth, they presented themselves as idealist and utopian. The role of the Schools was to 'teach the desire for an ideal Socialist Commonwealth', while the Guild of Youth struggled with 'actual politics'.[90] It was felt, therefore, that their roles should be complementary. A speaker at the Bradford Socialist Sunday School Union's anniversary in 1931 declared that 'Socialism is something more than politics; economics and politics are only the instruments for the creation of socialism.'[91] The Socialist Sunday Schools were increasingly marginalized, partly because of their 'spiritual idealism'. As this process occurred, they became more closely attached to the Communist Party.

Clearly there was a significant 'ethical', 'spiritual', utopian tradition in the inter-war labour movement that saw music as a fundamentally important activity. It could be the expression of its moral code, through the perceived connection between music and morals, and it could provide wholesome, rational recreation for working people whose 'spiritual idealism' was threatened by the appeal of baser, irrational, commercial pleasures. But it was not entirely a conservative, anachronistic tendency, hostile to the realities of the world around it; it embraced some new technology, such as the gramophone and the wireless, and it could become vital and controversial on occasion, particularly in the Socialist Sunday Schools. This tradition represents uses for music that do not fit neatly into the categories of 'pleasure, pennies and propaganda', but these were certainly the concerns of the less spiritual musical socialists.

Music for pleasure

Clearly trying to divide musical activity in the associational life of the labour movement into categories of 'pleasure', 'pennies' and 'propaganda' is going to be problematic. We have already witnessed part of that problem. Was the music involved in the activities of those 'religion of socialism' organizations primarily meant to entertain the members, collect money or attract new members? Clearly all three motivations played a part, alongside the specific motivations of 'spiritualism' and 'rational recreation'. Similarly, when other labour organizations employed music in their activity, the motivations were manifold. If one could find enjoyable ways to raise money or spread the word, then that was all to the good. However, one would expect pleasure (and leisure) to be the primary motivations for musical activity, especially music of a less earnest nature than that employed in the Labour Churches.

Social events

In Birmingham, the ILP had been primarily responsible for the organization of the Labour Churches, and elsewhere for organizing the Sunday lectures, etc., but it was often keen to make more frivolous use of music. The inter-war ILP tended to divide the organization of its various activities amongst numerous committees. Local groups had 'social committees' or, in the case of the Erdington ILP in Birmingham, an 'entertainment sub-committee'. An Erdington ILP concert, in November 1919, was poorly attended despite 'the varied programme provided [by] the members of the entertainment sub-committee'. The organizers were not too disheartened, however, signing off their report of the event thus: 'We hope that the next concert we arrange will be accorded more support by the Trade Unionists and Socialists of the district.'[92] A later Erdington ILP event, at the start of 1921, was far more successful and as well as the 'musical items' and 'songs' there was dancing, which 'went down very well'. This encouraged the correspondent with the *Town Crier* to note that 'it looked as if the Erdington Labour movement had at last overcome the backwardness hitherto shown in this respect'.[93] As we shall see, dancing played an important part in entertainment, fund-raising and propaganda.

Keighley ILP had a very complex committee structure. Its Sunday meetings in the Labour Church mould were not under the auspices of its Social Committee, but were handled jointly by the Executive Committee and the Lectures Committee. The branch even had a Billiards Committee, but most recreational pursuits were handled by the Social Committee. The usual non-musical social events in the years immediately following the First World War were whist drives all the year round and 'rambles' in spring and summer. The most popular and frequent musical events were dances. This would probably be true of social events organised by any provincial organization at this time, not just labour associations.

Through 1918 and 1919, Keighley ILP hosted monthly dances at the Cycling Club alongside regular concerts. Particular members of the Social Committee or the Executive Committee would be prevailed upon to arrange programmes for concerts.[94] On one occasion the committee decided to 'accept Mr Wardle's offer of two gentlemen singers and Mr Wood's offer of two lady singers and a boy violinist for Tuesday evening'.[95] Various members of the Keighley party, including senior committee members, were asked to provide piano accompaniment at the various events. Members of the party would often be asked to provide the entertainment on social occasions (particularly at concerts and small social events called 'at homes'), where people might sing, recite or play the piano. Monologues, sometimes in dialect, were also popular; the practitioners of such entertainment were generally called 'elocutionists' at this time and they can regularly be seen on concert programmes and making up the numbers of concert parties.

Much work was delegated from the Social Committee to the group variously called the ILP Women's Group, the Women's Labour League and the Women's Committee. Before and during the First World War, the Keighley Women's Labour League had been involved in serious political campaigns, such as involvement with the peace movement,[96] but when it returned to full activism in 1920 it was rather more like a sub-committee of the Social Committee. Its primary concern was actually with fund-raising, not just for the ILP or for its own funds, but also for causes such as the Russian Famine Fund and the Keighley Boot Fund.[97]

For much of the early 1920s, the Women's Group met every Tuesday with next to no political debate or considerations, concerning itself instead with teas, jumble sales and the occasional dance. Occasionally there would be some debate on these issues: on 7 February 1922 'it was decided to strike out a little different in the matter of savouries instead of so many sweets and cakes for supper'.[98] A fortnight later they decided that they would have to provide sweets and cakes as well 'for people who preferred them'.[99] Later that year it was suggested that the group could hold a concert after a jumble sale it was holding on the last Saturday in April, but it was later decided that a tea would be preferable and they decided which members would bring what cakes.[100] Such tasks were sometimes taken upon themselves – the Women's Group itself voted to take care of all refreshments for the 'at homes',[101] while on other occasions the Social Committee voted to leave refreshments to the Women's Group, such as for a Grand Carnival Ball in 1924.[102] That the women should busy themselves with the teas is a stereotypical picture that has been considered by many historians researching a woman's place in the labour movement.[103]

The Women's Group did sometimes discuss the actual provision of music at events in the same way as the Social Committee: on 25 March 1924 they 'resolved that Mr Robinson and Mrs Spencer be asked to sing and Miss Howell, Miss J. Clarke and Miss Ogden to recite and Miss Bayley be pianist' at a twelve-hand whist drive and social to be held on 8 April that year.[104] In 1925 the Women's Group decided to hold their own concert and social and the minutes for the 18 February meeting noted 'the concert to be sustained by members of the Women's Group'.

One question which inevitably arises and is not easily or satisfactorily answered is whether the choice of music, musicians or repertoires was afforded any more importance or controversy in Keighley Women's Group or Social Committee considerations than who was going to make the pies or buy the cigarettes. In other words, how much importance did ordinary activists place on music, on a day-to-day level? There is some evidence to suggest that while 'pie and fags' concerns were merely left to volunteers, there were some debates and votes on the subject of musicians. These debates did not concern the normal socials, concerts or 'at homes', where talented members who could be prevailed upon would provide the entertainments, but rather the larger public dances. What cannot be understood from the minutes are what issues led to the committee's decisions about dance bands. On 22 January 1924, during the discussions regarding a Grand Carnival Ball at the Baths Hall in Keighley on 23 February, an amendment was moved that they should engage the 'Hardacre's Band' for the dance and the amendment fell. What was not minuted on that occasion was whether another band had been engaged or proposed.

On 25 August 1924 it was decided that the choice of orchestra for another dance, to be held on 1 November, should be made by the Social Committee.[105] This clearly suggested that past decisions had been made by individuals and had not always met with approval. The committee had advertised in the *Keighley News* for tenders from bands,[106] and the meeting decided to cast out of consideration any band whose rates were higher than two shillings per hour per man. This essentially meant that they would not have been employing Musicians' Union members, although in this period, dance band performers were among the least organized, least secure and most exploited of musicians, despite popular depictions of there being a lot of money in dance music.[107] This left two orchestras: 'Schofields' and the 'Majestics'; the former received 12 votes, the latter 8. This was quite a close result. Any debates surrounding the vote were not minuted, but the result suggests that other issues were considered besides cost. One possible issue was a generational one: at the same meeting, Miss Howells made the radical proposal that the dance should continue until 11.30 p.m., but an amendment from the more mature Mrs Smith and Mrs Lightowler quickly reined the proposal back to 11 o'clock.[108]

Certainly in the early 1920s, the provision of music at labour social events was often left to the members themselves, or their children. As we have seen, as the dance-hall craze took hold in the country, it became the norm for outside bands (usually of semi-professional status) to be engaged. Keighley ILP would, on occasion, engage outside choirs, bands and performers to provide the entertainment at other events. In 1919 and 1920 the Keighley Clarion Choir was engaged for socials and, in turn, the choir booked the ILP 'rooms' for its own events. The continued existence of Clarion Choirs in the north of England will be considered in more detail in Chapter 3. A choir from Nelson in Lancashire played at the Keighley ILP rooms in 1929[109] and was regularly invited back. The Keighley Vocal Union, a non-political singing troupe, used the ILP rooms for practice space, and another local choir, the Kingsway Choir, got reduced rates on hiring the room for rehearsal in exchange for giving a concert.[110] A similar arrangement was made for a local 'Boys Band'.[111]

The fact that the room could be hired with the piano made it an attractive room for musical combinations, but playing of the piano by ILP members had to be restricted during working hours to avoid irritating nearby workers and shopkeepers.[112]

Dancing

Although dancing was used for fund-raising and even propagandist purposes, as we shall see, it was usually the case that the primary motivation for organizing a dance was to provide an enjoyable evening. Some labour organizations held regular dances, while others planned one-off events. One-off dances could be presented as rewards for activists after election campaigns or other activity.

During the 1924–5 season, the Birmingham Industrial Co-operative Society (BICS) would host dancing at the Co-operative Hall on Coventry Road on Mondays, Tuesdays, Wednesdays and Saturdays – sometimes more than once a day.[113] Before the 1925–6 season, the BICS dancing instructor and organizer, George Ray, set up his own 'academy' which kept similar hours, organizing 'Labour Dances' on Thursdays. There would appear to have been some bitterness, since his advertisement in the *Town Crier* asserted that 'he was thrown out of work, having received (while on holiday) notice to terminate his agreement at the Co-operative Hall, no reason given or asked'.[114] The sheer amount of dancing is quite staggering, especially when you consider that Birmingham was not short of commercial *palais de danse*, which were always likely to prove more popular, although perhaps more costly, than a Co-op dance and certainly an ILP dance. Having said that, a number of Birmingham ILP branches held regular weekly dances.[115] Questions about the actual music played at the dances will be considered in Chapter 6, but they were certainly very popular events.

Outings and holidays

Out of the 'season', music could still be heard at ILP and Labour Party outdoor events such as garden parties or fêtes.[116] For obvious reasons, the music employed at outdoor events was often different from that preferred indoors, brass and silver bands replacing soloists. Similarly, all branches with choirs were urged to bring them along and participate in large open-air meetings.[117] As well as the traditional musical aspects of open-air meetings, 'dancing on the green' became increasingly popular as the dance-hall craze took off. There were also branch outings in the summer. The Selly Oak ILP had a joint outing with its Labour Church

Musical Society in 1922, to Evesham. Once there the choir 'rendered a number of songs which were greatly appreciated by the audience' in Evesham's Labour Hall.[118] Even when not blessed with a choir on a trip, labour movement outings were musical affairs with lots of singing, especially on return journeys. When the Bradford ILP outing to York returned on a June evening in 1923, people loudly sang 'The Red Flag' out of the train carriage windows, from which they flew red streamers;[119] one assumes that they had enjoyed sampling some of the old city's charms! Such impromptu musical interludes were not always a source of pleasure. When an ILP group from Heaton, in Bradford, had an outing to the rural surrounds of Nidderdale, 'Miss Oldscrew performed solos which were happily inaudible' on the 'sharrabang' (*sic*).[120]

As well as the miscellaneous outings, there were various hostels, summer camps and clubhouses aimed at providing holiday destinations for labour activists. The Clarion fellowship was still active in Yorkshire between the wars. A Clarion clubhouse was situated between Otley and Menston in a rural area easily accessible from both Bradford and Leeds. It would hold various events, including sports during the day and lectures, dancing and concerts during the evenings. The idea was that people would stay at the clubhouse having a weekend in the countryside amongst comrades. The rather eccentric resident manager of the club had obviously been infected with some 'golden age' utopian imagery when he described it as a place where

> Maidens fair with golden hair,
> Do dance tra-la, and sing;
> When glistening eyes and blushes rare
> Sweet content do bring.[121]

A similar facility was located at Sheldon for visits from labour activists in the West Midlands. There were 'Concerts and balls', amongst other recreational activities and debates, at the Midland Clarion Clubhouse in Sheldon.[122] The club was advertised as 'the keen dancer's paradise'[123] and was holding dances every Saturday night in the spring of 1920.[124] Similar hostels were advertised in national publications such as the *Socialist Leaguer*, located in various parts of the country. There was a Clarion Youth Hostel 17 miles outside London that held events with concerts and entertainment.[125]

Celebrations

The labour movement sang and played for pleasure with the most vigour when celebrating; anniversaries or election victories were especially musical occasions. The big victory rallies that followed Labour's two inter-war general election 'successes' were particularly joyous and melodic occasions. The rally that followed the 1924 general election, in London, reportedly saw 12,000 people singing 'the words of the great poet of freedom, William Morris, "The March of the Workers"' to the tune of 'John Brown's Body'. Sydney A. Court, conductor of the Deptford Labour Choir, reported on the event:

> Great as would have been that meeting in any case, who can estimate the power of the music preceding it, or forget the thrill that ran through that mighty audience as the first martial strains of the 'Marseillaise' pealed out from the organ and the voices of the choir took up the opening phrase. Again, with our leaders in place and singing with us, the fervour with which the words 'England is risen and the day is here' were sung will not easily be forgotten . . .
> . . . the host of workers, still overflowing with music, sang their way through the snow homewards. Through streets or trains, 'buses and trams the songs were repeated until all London must have wondered.[126]

Clearly Sidney Court was taken with his theme and romanticized the occasion somewhat. Nevertheless, the event must have been a moving one to those Labour pioneers and the musical aspect of the celebrations can only have added to their effect.

Local election successes were similarly marked with social events, dances and concerts. Local Labour Parties would often hold a 'victory social' for party workers when a local election had been successful, such as at the All Saints Ward, Birmingham, in November 1921, where 'vocal and instrumental items' were provided by 'a number of artistes and friends'.[127] There were a large number of similar victory socials after the same set of local elections across Birmingham and the district.[128]

How many members attended 'socials' and events at branch level is difficult to estimate, but a city-wide Birmingham 'ILP Federation Social' saw only '200 ILP members and friends' enjoying 'the programme of songs, speeches, dances and orchestral music'[129] – and this was not reported as a disappointing turnout. Indeed, such a number would necessitate quite a large hall, but it would not seem to represent a very impressive combined effort from the many branches included in that 'federation'. On the other hand, the Ladywood Labour Party held a concert on 16 April 1921[130] that was considered 'a huge success . . . from every point of view, musical, social, and financial', featuring 'songs, dances and pianoforte selections' with 'no hitch anywhere'. At this early stage in the period, it was considered a 'delightfully unique experience' to have to get 'the caretaker to bring in four or five more long rows of desks to accommodate the crowd that turned up'.[131] By the middle of the 1920s, all reports of such events remarked on the large or crowded audiences. Although the event took place at a school, the image of the audience sitting at desks is a rather austere one.

Anniversaries, whether they marked the founding of a small labour organization or the transportation of the Tolpuddle Martyrs, were occasions where the movement got into good voice. During the fortieth anniversary celebrations of the Birmingham Co-operative Society in the summer of 1921,[132] there was a demonstration with 'bands and banners' on 27 August and a 'Grand Concert' at the Town Hall on 19 September,[133] featuring the 'special engagement of the C.W.S. Concert Party'.[134] The hundredth anniversary of the Tolpuddle Martyrs, in 1934, was greeted with large demonstrations (with the usual musical accompaniment – mass singing and bands)[135] as well as the Pageant of Labour, a huge musical event that composers Alan Bush and Michael Tippett worked on together.

Celebrations did not always have to commemorate anything in particular. Any excuse was often good enough for a big party. Fairs and bazaars were popular events all year round and, occasionally, there would be efforts to make them something rather more special. An example of this was the Bradford ILP 'International Fancy Fair' of 1925. A four-day event at the beginning of April and tipped to be 'the greatest social event in the history of the Bradford ILP',[136] the fair centred around stalls with international themes. The event featured well-known speakers, such as Margaret McMillan and Fred Jowett, a broad entertainment programme at the Queen's Hall and musical entertainment from a popular Concert Party at the 'Café Chantant'. The event was considered an important enough aspect of the ILP calendar for it to produce a very attractively presented 56-page souvenir programme.

The entertainment programme for the fair featured, in a different order each evening, international dances and playlets presented by a Miss Chignell and a number of infants, the local Socialist Sunday School Union's 'Sunbeams', the Clarion Concert Party and a number of dramatic sketches given by two local comrades, including a production of 'scenes from Shirley', the Charlotte Bronte novel.[137] Miss Chignell was a nursery school teacher, presenting her pupils. Much of what was performed in her section of the entertainment programme will be of interest in later chapters, including a variety of folk dances. Interesting aspects of the performance included dramatized nursery rhymes which, along with folk dancing and short musical plays, were a central part of the local infant school music syllabus to help encourage appreciation of rhythm and to keep children interested in music.[138] The 'Sunbeams' from the Socialist Sunday Schools promised 'forty minutes of melody and mirth' in the form of 'concerted items, songs and dances'. The musical entertainment at the Café Chantant, provided by Mr Joe Dixon's Concert Party, promised to be 'first class' and comprised a continuous programme from seven until ten on each night of the fair, and three until five on the Saturday afternoon. They featured a soprano, a contralto, a tenor and a baritone (Mr Dixon himself) as well as an 'entertainer' and two pianists. The soprano, Madame Alice Brewerton, was given special mention as she had lately been in the D'Oyly Carte Opera Company.

The Café Chantant was run by around thirty 'ILPers' over the weekend; all of them were women, all but four were unmarried and two of the married ones were those 'in charge'.[139] As with Keighley's Social Committee, it would appear that much business regarding social events, especially where anything like catering was involved, was handed over to the women's groups. It was certainly not unusual for committee meetings to decide to leave the refreshments 'in the hands of the ladies'.[140] The Bradford ILP continued to attempt to organize the occasional very big event like this, even after the split with the Labour Party. An example was the ILP Socialist Bazaar of 1933, which was again spread across a whole weekend.[141]

As we considered in Chapter 1, 'leisure' was deemed by inter-war socialists to be something more important than mere free time or frivolity. It was an important prize to be won and used in the correct fashion. Some would no doubt have disapproved of some of the ways labourites used their leisure, but at the same time they would rather people squander that rich prize of leisure under the auspices of labour organizations than in commercial dance halls and music halls. One reason for that was that any money spent on such frivolities was better collected by the movement than by the capitalist managers of the commercial leisure industry.

Filling the coffers

Labour organizations required funds for various reasons. One of the most pressing was the 'Parliamentary Fund' needed to stand candidates in general elections. Above and beyond this there might be rent to pay for 'rooms', club or hall, the increasing need to pay a staff member, and funds for particular campaigns or causes of the day. The raising of funds during strikes or to assist unemployment relief schemes will be considered in Chapter 4. Other causes also presented themselves. The National Union of Railwaymen dedicated most of its fund-raising activity to its Widows and Orphans' Fund,[142] regular concerts all around the country were staged for 'poor children' and the Keighley labour movement had a 'Boot Fund' to provide shoes for the poorest youngsters in the town.

Many labour organizations found themselves in permanent need of funds in this period and, as a result, the organizational motivation behind social events became increasingly geared towards fund-raising. The regular dances put on by the Keighley ILP were no exception. They were open to the general public at a cost of one shilling. Members of the ILP who wished to attend but not to dance were admitted for 6d, as were dancers who arrived late.[143] Staging the dances was not a particularly costly business; thirteen shillings were spent on the printing of 500 programmes for the 1918 dances, which would have quickly paid for themselves.[144] After one of the dances, held on 23 November, it was decided that one pound from the takings would be handed to the Parliamentary Fund.[145] The rest of the funds raised by these regular – and not unprofitable – events was kept specifically for ILP expenditure. As the period went on, fund-raising increasingly became the primary motivation behind the social events of Keighley ILP. This was primarily due to the rent that had to be paid on the ILP rooms. They hired out the rooms to labour and other organizations, on moderate terms, to raise funds. They put on concerts, 'at homes' and more and more dances, with a tendency towards 'Grand Carnival Dances' where 300 or 400 people would dance to professional or semi-professional dance orchestras.[146]

Although staging a labour social was not an especially costly business, the 'artistes' at concerts and events did not always provide their services free of charge. One ILP member announced that if they required a female impersonator then his terms were 'moderate' for 'Concerts, Socials, etc.'[147] Such a performer was not so rare an element of a labour concert as one might think. While the music hall/variety institution of cross-dressing would appear to epitomize much of what socialist commentators found to disapprove in the industry, such qualms, along with those held against dancing and 'comic' songs, would not appear to have been shared by many in the local organizations.

Many dance bands advertised their 'moderate' terms in the *Town Crier* throughout the 1920s, some because they were Labour Party supporters, others because they recognized the potential market for social events organized by the various labour organizations. However, it was more usual for concert performers to 'give' their services, especially when funds were being raised either for organizational expenses or for specific charitable collections.

Labour newspapers also found that sales alone (and what little advertising they could secure) were not enough to sustain their efforts. The 'Daily Herald League' looked to raise funds to sustain the newspaper. It had an active group within the Birmingham labour movement. At a Labour Rally at the Town Hall, under the League's auspices, with George

Lansbury speaking, there were 'Socialist Hymns from 2-30 till 3 accompanied by organ'. The advertisement instructed: 'Socialists, bring your hymn-books!'[148] without specifying a particular publication. The League planned 'Grand Concerts' for 25 April[149] and 21 May[150] in 1920. The April concert did not go ahead in the end, owing to the League's inability to secure an entertainments licence.

The League also claimed to stage 'the event of the season' in January 1922 when it held a fancy dress ball with a 'full band' providing the music. This was a more impressive acquisition than it sounds at this early stage in the dance-hall craze, as small, traditional dance-hall combinations were just beginning to adapt to the jazz sound. A photograph of this 'most successful function' was reproduced in the Town Crier, showing men and women of all ages.[151] The event was deemed so successful that it was repeated the following year and given the additional tag of 'annual',[152] although the attendance on this second occasion was disappointing.[153]

A social and 'at home' was organized at Britton Hall in Bradford in 1923; it was entitled 'The Daily Herald must live' and featured music from a local combination, the Lyric Quartette. A more unusual advertisement for the Daily Herald was included in the Bradford Pioneer, asking 'Have you seen the Pioneer Choir's advert in the Daily Herald? If not, have a good look at it.' The Pioneer Choir will be considered in Chapter 3.

Along with a number of other organizations, local Labour Parties would sometimes provide entertainment for 'poor children'.[154] One such entertainment in January 1922 under the auspices of the Duddeston and Nechells Labour Party featured 'the "Merry Nibbs" Concert Party', who apparently provided 'a very pleasant programme' for 500–600 children.[155] Sometimes the children's entertainment would feature modern, popular music such as 'Mr Rawlings, with his Jazz Band', who 'nearly took the roof off' when entertaining 500–600 children (a popular number!) at Saltley ward in January 1922.[156]

Although, as we mentioned in Chapter 1, the idea that art should pay was anathema to some musical socialists, it was essential to the day-to-day existence and business of the labour movement, as well as beneficial to some 'good causes' that the movement chose to sponsor. As with so many other aspects of socialist thought about music – opposition to dance and jazz music, musical comedy and variety – concern about 'selling' one's art was not felt particularly deeply by general activists, or considered important in the face of day-to-day practicalities. At the same time, trade union principles were not always kept to the fore when organizing fund-raising events: artists who 'gave' their services were preferred to those who charged Musicians' Union rates.

Spreading the word

> Dare to be a Tory,
> Dare to wear the blue,
> Dare to say 'I love my Boss',
> And swear to heaven it's true.
> Dare to be a Tory,
> And say my life's my own,
> When but the dirt around my face.
> Is all the land I own.[157]

Parody and humour were the literary and musical tools in the hands of the musical propagandists, as we shall see. How such propaganda could reach the desired audience in the day-to-day life of the labour movement was more problematic. The era of touring street speakers, Clarion buses and ILP propagandists was drawing to a close. It had sometimes been the theatre of such activity that had attracted the crowds and there were new diversions now. Exploiting those new diversions – dancing, the wireless, etc. – was the challenge for inter-war propagandists and so music remained as important as when the socialist hymn singing drew crowds to a Clarion cart.

Co-operative societies and Labour Parties

The Birmingham Industrial Co-operative Society (BICS) held regular concerts alongside its very busy programme of dancing and dancing instruction. BICS musical evenings, such as those held in March 1921, would feature various 'artistes' and one of the Birmingham Co-operative Choirs (there were 'Senior' and 'Junior' Choirs).[158] The small print on advertisements would invariably reveal that a member of the BICS Education Committee would deliver a 'short' address. These evenings were held on a regular basis from 1919 to 1922. Similarly, when the Soho Co-operative Society held a large public meeting in May 1920, also in Birmingham, its Co-operative Choir sang selections at intervals throughout.[159] More importantly, it was advertised as doing so; a musical aspect to a programme was considered likely to attract more people to political meetings. Music and social events generally were also considered to contribute to recruitment for co-operative guilds. When the Co-operative Central Women's Guild held a social to celebrate their twenty-ninth birthday, featuring 'songs' 'ably rendered', it was considered 'a nice evening that ought to bring new recruits'.[160]

There is some evidence that local Labour Parties incorporated music into ordinary meetings. There were musical selections and songs at the meetings of St Bartholomew's Ward Labour Party, Birmingham, in May 1920,[161] and an advertisement for Duddeston Labour Party meetings in the *Town Crier* in July 1922 appeared to be appealing to Labour Church enthusiasts by promising 'local speakers, music, songs'.[162] To describe this as a propaganda role for music is possibly slightly misleading. The aim was clearly to encourage Labour members or supporters to attend meetings – such attendances, even during the 'heroic' early 1920s, could be rather thin on the ground from time to time. Some concern was expressed about the use of music during meetings dedicated to political business, that it might get in the way or attract people who were not serious enough about their politics. On the other hand, some recognized the benefits of some musical entertainment, or mass singing, to end a lengthy oration or reunite the room after a hostile debate.

Even dances could act as subtle propagandist activity. ILP dances were often well attended and were aimed at a wider audience than just their own younger members. Smethwick ILP was organizing weekly dances in 1925, and one of these was reported on in the 'Smethwick Notes' section of the *Town Crier*. According to the correspondent, 'quite 200 dancers were present'. While the writer lamented the passing of 'the old fashioned dances' ('why some of these youngsters can't even waltz!'), he asserted that 'the great thing is that young people enjoy themselves on the finest dance floor in the borough under the auspices of the ILP'.[163] The primary function of 'one-off' dances or similar events would appear to have been a reward for members, the entertainment aspect being placed a long way above any political benefits. These weekly dances, operated by a small number of ILP branches, were combining that role with one of subtle recruitment and propaganda. The dances looked to demonstrate the ILP's vitality in embracing the latest fads, and thereby hoped to attract more young people to identify with the party and to be aware of it. Most notable were the activities of groups like the Witton branch of the ILP, in Birmingham. In 1926 it was holding weekly dances[164] along with regular concerts.[165]

Bradford Guild of Arts

The ILP was certainly at the forefront of music making in Bradford and nearby towns. As well as the Sunday lectures, the dances, the fairs and bazaars, the Bradford ILP instituted a Guild of Arts in line with national ILP plans at this time, interestingly coinciding with the plans for a National Labour Choral Union in the Labour Party. At the institution of the Bradford branch of the Guild, the *Pioneer* considered two justifications for its existence. The first was to retain those members who were less serious about the political activity, keeping them 'amused' while the 'earnest' got on with the 'proper job'. This reason was clearly presented as an unattractive or unacceptable view. Rather, it was suggested, socialists had cultural 'duties' to perform.[166] This was not explained or expanded upon, but similar language echoes through much inter-war socialist writing on culture and the arts.

There is a discourse of 'doing one's bit' and demonstrating the power of labour in all fields of life. If it was deemed that art could be used in the service of the movement, then the artistic socialist had the same 'duty' to direct his or her talents for the services of the movement as had the politically astute or well educated. What is not clear is how art – other than that of a propagandist nature – could be of service to the movement except in those most prosaic of ways: fund-raising and entertaining. If that was the only service of the Guild of Arts, did it have any more pressing a duty than those who made the pies for a bazaar or outing?

Some of the sections might have considered propagandist art, but the only musical aspect in Bradford, the Operatic Section, did not stray from the well-trodden path of popular comic opera. There was certainly some disagreement with the choice of musical activity that was proposed within the movement. An article in the *Pioneer* (bearing no name, suggesting it had editorial support) recorded the formation of the Operatic Section thus: 'without wishing to discourage this, one feels rather that light opera is not quite in the special direction of the Guild, unless new ground can be broken. One hopes that other musical developments will be considered.'[167] Five years later (the Operatic Section had had some successes), a reviewer in the *Pioneer* still followed up a good review of *The Mikado* with the suggestion: 'having got thus far with some good singers and actors in the company, branch away from Gilbert and Sullivan and try something new and different'.[168]

The contradiction with the Guild's 'special direction' was not, one feels, because of the (at best) political neutrality of light opera, but merely because of its lightness. The ILP Guild of Arts was a national movement, getting under way in 1925, and its 'special direction' was quite specifically not 'a desire to make propaganda more attractive', but an 'expression in the modern Socialist movement of the spirit of William Morris'. It was, in other words, 'a revolt against the ugliness and monotony of modern industrialism', a 'seeking after beauty and a fuller life'.[169] It represented the continuity of the 'golden age' utopianism or socialist romanticism of Edward Carpenter. It is perhaps understandable, therefore, that the Operatic Section's series of Gilbert and Sullivan productions over the following years were not really considered to be in the right spirit.

One of the national figures in the Guild of Arts, the actor Arthur Bourchier, expanded on much of this in an ILP pamphlet in 1926. He firmly placed 'seeking after beauty and a fuller life' at the centre of the socialist project: 'It is only cowardice, stupidity and apathy that prevents us from organising our economic and social affairs in a manner that would give ample leisure for artistic and cultural enjoyment for everyone.'[170] Bourchier's desire was to 'enliven and enlighten' workers' 'sordid, toilsome and monotonous lives'[171] with the 'pure' and 'beautiful'. It is interesting that in this intensely political view, art itself is stripped of any political character. Bourchier would have been hard-pressed to approve of the Bradford ILP Operatic Section's Gilbert and Sullivan productions, whatever he felt about the politics of their satire, because they did not seek 'purity' and 'beauty'.

While the ILP Guild of Arts Operatic Section could clearly be considered as using music for pleasure, its purpose seeming to have been to entertain its own members and others, the Guild itself is rather more difficult to place in the 'pennies', 'pleasure' and 'propaganda' framework. It would appear to represent a peculiar kind of propaganda, returning to that Clarion Vocal Union aspiration of providing a glimpse of what was to come. The ideas of Bourchier and the Guild of Arts will be considered in more detail in Chapter 5.

Campaigning organizations

Music was incorporated into the work of specific campaigning organizations such as the 'Hands off Russia' Committee. This group attracted quite broad labour movement support, although there was obviously a strong communist contingent. There were organ recitals at the Birmingham meeting of the Committee in March 1920 – organ recitals were commonplace for half an hour or so before any big, civic meeting.[172] Sometimes there would be a larger-scale musical contribution to meetings organized by the 'Hands Off Russia' Committee: at a 'lantern lecture' on 'Russian labour' on 13 February 1921 at Birmingham Town Hall, musical items were provided by 'the "Internationale" and Rotton Park Labour Choirs'.[173] The 'Internationale' Labour Choir was not referred to elsewhere in the Town Crier in the 1920s and so was either a short-lived outfit (at least under that name) or a visiting choir from outside the city. The 'Hands Off Russia' Committee had occasional social events[174] as well as propaganda meetings, and supported the showing of a Russian film about the famine at the 'Futurist cinema' in 1922, where one of the features was Russian music.[175]

Explicit propagandist use of music became more commonplace later in the period, employed by groups such as the Workers' Theatre Movement and eventually the Workers' Music Association. Their activities will be considered in Chapters 5 and 6, as will the reasons for the changing form of musical propaganda through the period.

Conclusions

It is clear from this limited survey that labour activism in this period had a varied and ever-present musical soundtrack. This presented itself in a variety of ways. There were traditional hymns in Labour Churches and Socialist Sunday Schools, massed voice anthems at large meetings and rallies, and a variety of 'serious' vocal and instrumental music performed at social events and musical services. There were comedy songs at less formal social events and jazz music at many labour movement dances. While most examples of music in the service of the labour movement in inter-war Birmingham and Bradford could be slotted into the headings of entertainment, propaganda or fund-raising, music also played a more sombre role, particularly in the ILP, such as at memorial services for activists. In May 1922 the Birmingham City branch of the ILP held a benefit concert 'in aid of the widow and family of our late comrade F. E. Sedgewick' at which the Amalgamated Engineering Union Choir provided the music.[176]

Looking at the *Town Crier* over the twenty-year period reveals a convincing narrative of the changing place of music in the official labour movement between the wars. Through the 1920s, there was feverish musical activity at meetings and concerts, with the emphasis being on activists making music themselves. By the end of the decade, the official labour movement would appear to have stepped back somewhat from this activity, taking a broader interest in popular culture and accepting that its supporters were more interested in popular leisure opportunities than anything the labour movement could produce for itself. Pages of reports on musical evenings and concerts were replaced with reviews of variety performances and gramophone records; amateur poetry in every issue was replaced with book reviews. One could speculate about why this might be the case, and the mass appeal of popular leisure activities might be as big an influence as Labour's electoralism. However, although this narrative is convincing, it requires a stronger foundation than that provided by the identification of changes in the *Town Crier*.

The *Town Crier* was a small newspaper run by very few people at any one time, and the personalities behind it changed over the period as well. Through the 1920s it was edited by Will Chamberlain, an enthusiastic writer and devotee of Robert Blatchford; he pushed for the paper to be lively and vital. Through the 1930s the *Town Crier* was in crisis and was permanently in fear of stopping publication; this could have been a major influence on the increase in popular culture pieces and gramophone, football and variety-hall reviews as well as the reduction in reports of meetings. Right at the end of the period, despite still officially being the Labour Party's paper, the *Town Crier* was edited by a communist, Philip Toynbee. During his short tenure as editor, Toynbee's intellectualism was probably a bigger influence on the *Town Crier* than his communism. He brought in W. H. Auden to write literature reviews and Richard Crossman to write on foreign affairs. But Toynbee's style did not prove popular with the long-term readership of the *Town Crier* and did not attract new readers; having taken the job in 1938, he left it again in 1939.[177]

As we can see, one cannot simply read across from the pages of the *Town Crier* – what was included and what was not – the spirit and passions of the inter-war official labour movement, even just in Birmingham. Yet the narrative remains convincing, and it is backed up to a certain extent by other evidence. Through the 1930s, reports in the *Bradford Pioneer* moved from specifically Labour concerts to concerts in working men's and other social clubs, and the paper reported far more regularly on variety concerts. There would appear to have been a change from labour activists as producers of music towards them as consumers. This change seems to be contemporaneous with a very different trend in communist politics, from having but a passing interest in the arts to seeing them as a 'weapon in the struggle'.

For most of the inter-war period, labour activism went hand in hand with musical activity whether that activity was performance, dance or appreciation. Related to this activity was a growing desire to form musical associations, particularly choirs, bands and orchestras. This was built on the older tradition of labour movement choral activity, but as we shall see in Chapter 3, it branched out into other, occasionally very ambitious areas.

3

Choirs, Bands and Orchestras

Before the First World War, in that period when music was apparently the main cultural thrust of the labour movement, there was no genuinely national labour musical movement. The Clarion Vocal Unions (CVUs), established in 1895 with their slogan of 'let us Work and Sing our way to Socialism',[1] arguably came quite close. However, although there were twenty-three choirs by 1910, they were still concentrated largely in Yorkshire and Lancashire. They tended to sing the standard choral pieces that would be heard in non-labour choral festivals of the north of England, with the occasional rendering of 'The Red Flag' or 'England, Arise!' By 1914, they were beginning to sing some pieces written especially for them, such as 'The City' by Rutland Boughton (who, by that time, was running the movement) and '1910' by the radical suffragette composer Ethel Smythe.[2] The Clarion choral movement appears to have declined with the paper that spawned it, despite some rallying of efforts during the 1920s. Boughton's efforts were eventually to be redirected to a new musical movement: a choral organization based in London which was, for a time, to expand to a national scale and was more specifically connected with the official Labour Party: the National Labour Choral Union.

The National Labour Choral Union movement

By 1926, there was, 'all over the country, a movement amongst Labour folk for forming choirs and orchestras',[3] which inspired national figures to try and co-ordinate such ventures. On 14 August 1925, the *Town Crier* in Birmingham reported on these National Choral Union plans under the headline 'An "Eisteddfod" for Labour'. The report mentioned that a plan including a National Choral Festival for Labour would be outlined to local organizations by the National Executive Committee (NEC), which had been discussing it that year. The report went on to say that the plan was prompted 'by the remarkable success of existing choirs and musical societies within the movement', which those planning the Festival felt had 'proved of immense value in nurturing Party enthusiasm'. The scheme would include local choirs, in association with local Labour Parties; Labour Choral Unions, which would co-ordinate the activities of local Labour, Socialist and Co-operative Societies; and a National Labour Choral Union, which would link together all the other unions. The plan envisaged annual local, municipal competitive festivals as well as a national festival for the winning choirs. Rutland Boughton and Herbert Morrison had drafted a constitution for the National Union, which declared the scheme's object to be 'to develop the musical instincts of the people and to render service to the Labour movement'. The report concluded that the NEC had appealed to all Divisional Labour Parties (DLPs) and local parties to try and start choirs.[4] Although, as we shall see, some efforts were made in the provinces to help build the national choral movement, the London Labour Choral Union was the most successful and long-lasting constituent of the movement.

The London Labour Choral Union

The London Labour Choral Union (LLCU) was made up of a number of local choirs. Some of these were conducted by well-known people in the musical world, such as Rutland Boughton, Alan Bush and Michael Tippett. Some of the choirs were newly set up as part of the Union; others had existed for some time. There was quite a revival of choirs in the London area and the south-east in the years immediately preceding the formation of the Union. New choirs had been set up at Slough and Bellingham, and many old, defunct choirs had been revived, such as the Woolwich Pioneer Choir. The Deptford Labour Choir, conducted by Sydney Court, had had an unbroken existence since it was founded in 1913.[5] Court, like Boughton and others, helped to spread the choral movement by writing magazine and newspaper articles that aimed to assist and inspire the organizers of new choirs.

One of the first occasions when the massed choirs sang together was at the 'Great Rally for the *Daily Herald*' in 1924. To give some flavour of the repertoire of these choirs, this performance included the 'Marseillaise', 'England, Arise!', 'Jerusalem' and 'The Red Flag' on the political front, while Elgar's 'My Love Dwelt in a Northern Land' and Boughton's own 'Pan' would appear to have been included entirely for their musical worth.[6] Alan Bush later recalled that 'the use of music by the Labour Party was political' and that 'politically progressive musicians didn't concern themselves in general with awakening the interest of the working class in the traditional classical heritage of music'.[7] This was not always the case.

Certainly in some of the provincial choirs and bands considered in this chapter, political music made up only a small part of repertoires. Even in the London movement that Bush was describing, 'music as a political and agitational weapon' would appear to have been only part of the story. Sydney Court's description of the musical aspects of the Deptford Choir show the persistence of a different approach:

> In the first place the music we attempt is of the best. While always prepared to lead the audiences at meetings with the well-known Labour songs we are keeping abreast of the times by studying the unrivalled music of the Elizabethan period, which is just coming into its own, and which apart from its intrinsic value as music is unsurpassed for choir training.[8]

This was meant as advice to other choir organizers: to strive for the best. As we shall see, this was very much the driving force behind the efforts of some of the choirs elsewhere in the country. 'Keeping abreast of the times' here had nothing to do with making any capitulation to popular or mass culture, but merely meant that they were attempting to keep up with trends in classical music appreciation. Indeed, the Deptford Choir competed at 'the first Elizabethan Festival': a music contest entirely unconnected with the labour movement that took place in 1923, adjudicated by Vaughan Williams amongst others.[9]

On the other hand, the Deptford Choir did sing some 'popular' songs. At least, when they went to 'Poor Law institutions' in London they would sing 'old familiar songs' (not twentieth-century popular music) to 'the very old people'. This philanthropic aspect of the choir's efforts appears to have been a strong motivation for Court, rather than the campaigning, agitational motivation preferred by Bush. Court ended his message to other choir organizers with the evangelical statement:

> We pass on our greetings to the new choirs being formed and a message: work hard, work together, work for those who need you, take music into the lives that need it most, and you will realise the joy of service and that it is 'more blessed to give than to receive'.[10]

This would certainly suggest that there was not an absolute unity of purpose in the burgeoning Labour choral movement; the aims of Court and Bush were very different, and both were distinct from the old Clarion agenda. The London choirs continued to flourish through the 1930s, after the national movement had fizzled out, and they took part in international festivals, sharing the first prize in the choral section with the Choir Populaire de Paris in Strasbourg, 1935.[11]

However much Morrison and others might have wanted the National/

London Labour Choral movement to be firmly in the bosom of the Labour Party, Boughton's decision to join the Communist Party in 1926 complicated things somewhat. Similarly, his successor, Alan Bush, also joined the Communist Party while at the helm of the LLCU. Although Boughton gave many reasons for deciding to join the Communist Party, his biographer Michael Hurd suggests that the Labour Party's lack of enthusiasm for the National Labour Choral Union plans was a contributory factor.[12] Yet the choirs continued to be sponsored by the Labour Party while Boughton, Bush and others were promoting 'working-class songs . . . of the Soviet Union'.[13]

The Workers' Music Association (WMA) was eventually to emerge from the LLCU, initially with aims similar to the short-lived National Labour Choral Union, only less specifically connected to the Labour Party, and later more explicitly connected with the Communist Party. In forming the WMA, the LLCU joined forces with another socialist musical tendency that had grown out of the Workers' Theatre Movement (WTM). The WTM always had a musical aspect – Rutland Boughton was one of its founders in 1925.[14] This was to become a movement very much under the control of the Communist Party, eventually transforming into the Unity Theatre. The sketches that were performed by Workers' Theatre groups always involved music, but there was also a movement within the WTM specifically to set up music groups. There was some debate and conflict as to whether such groups should attempt to attain the aesthetic standards of some of the other labour movement musical associations, or instead retain the first principles of agitation and propaganda which drove the theatre groups. What sort of music should be performed was also an area for concern, as we will see in Chapter 6. The musical associations that were formed were an integral part of the WMA, which was itself to come into its own in the post-war period.

Although Alan Bush argued that labour music was 'only important in London'[15] and the LLCU certainly had its successes, as Elgar once said, 'the living centre of music in Great Britain is not London, but somewhere further north'.[16]

Birmingham and district

The nationally directed plans of Morrison and Boughton affected the city-wide musical adventures of the Birmingham labour movement in 1925, but they did not initiate them. Attempts at communal music making under the auspices of the Birmingham Labour Party began during the winter 'season' of 1920–1 with the Birmingham Labour Party Brass Band.

The Birmingham Labour Party Band

In January 1921 the organizers of the new band advertised for players to make up the full complement.

> Wanted, urgently, the following players:- 1 Monster Bass, 1 Baritone, 1 Trombone, 1 Tenor Horn. Instruments waiting for the foregoing. Applications will be welcome from any other brass instrumentalists with own instruments. Bandmaster: G. Sullivan.[17]

Purchasing those instruments was the first of Mr G. Sullivan's mistakes: the story of the ill-fated band contains quite a catalogue of them. The aforementioned advertisement was repeated in the *Town Crier* on numerous occasions. By May, Sullivan was appealing to the Executive Committee of the Birmingham Labour Party to help raise more funds for the band, which was 'in financial difficulties'. Money was needed to help pay for 'hire of room, purchase of music, etc.' to help to make the band 'second to none in the city'. The *Town Crier* reported that the Executive Committee made a number of suggestions including occasional fund-raising functions, collections at open-air performances and a fund to which activists could subscribe. A number of Executive Committee members guaranteed one shilling a month to the fund.[18]

The band made some public appearances in 1921. It played for half an hour at the start of the 'Great Midland Conference Demonstration on "British Labour and Irish Peace"'.[19] Shortly afterwards it played a similar role at a meeting on 'The Spirit of Revolution' organized by the National Guilds League (Birmingham Group).[20] The band also played at the Free Speech Committee social at the Bull Ring in April that year,[21] as well as being one of the bands in the Birmingham May Day procession.[22]

It was not until August 1922 that the Labour Party Band first tentatively advertised the possibility of further public performances, including making its services available to the Labour Churches. The advertisement in the *Town Crier* read: 'the bandmaster is prepared to send a representative band to any Labour Church or other Labour function'.[23] Sending 'a representative band' was not due to a full band being too big for such events, but because a full band did not exist, and what did was not quite what Sullivan and others had had in mind. Sullivan's strategy was rather different from the Clarion strategy of 'making socialists' by encouraging people from outside the labour movement to join choirs, cycling clubs and the like, in the hope that they would be brought into the political side of things later on. Sullivan had intended the Labour Party Brass Band to be made up exclusively of Labour Party members. This desire to make musicians out of socialists rather than the other way around was a stumbling block for most of the city-wide musical adventures.

One of Sullivan's colleagues got to tell the particularly tragic story of his efforts in an interesting exchange in the correspondence column of the *Town Crier*. Firstly a letter headed 'wanted: a Labour Brass Band' appeared in August 1923 by Mr W. A. Hay, chairman of the Rotton Park Unemployed Committee. He believed that 'there must be dozens of musicians in the movement who could form such a band' and suggested a 'joint committee, drawn from the Labour Party, Trades Council, ILP, etc. be set up to get the band together'.[24] J. Thompson wrote the angry reply under the heading 'A Labour Brass Band'.

> Sir, – Mr Hay's letter on the above subject, in last week's issue, is a little behind the times. It is a great pity Mr Hay did not take in the *Town Crier* two years ago or we may have had in Birmingham the Labour Band of which he now talks. For a period of six months an advertisement appeared in the *Town Crier* asking for players (with or without instruments) and only one application was received. In addition appeals were constantly made at Labour Party meetings, and it seems strange that none of the 'dozens of musicians' came forward to help. Members of the Party came forward with money to buy instruments and at the present time I believe they are still lying idle.
>
> For a period of six months the Labour Party Band flourished with non-Labourites, and then passed away as quickly as it came. Should any Labour organisation require a band, they will do well to communicate with . . . the NUR Orphan Fund Band. Their terms are as reasonable as any other band, Labour or otherwise. In the meantime, I think the suggestion of Mr Hay can 'lie on the table'.[25]

But Mr Hay was not to be so discouraged. He responded the following week in a letter full of optimism and old adages:

> Sir, – I am sorry to learn from Mr Thompson that an attempt has been made to organise a band. But that should not deter us from making a new attempt. Presumably Mr Thompson does not believe in the old proverb, 'if at first', etc., but I should advise him to give up his pessimism. He should remember that a defeat should only make us more determined than ever. But, anyway, Mr Thompson states that the instruments were obtained, and are lying idle. If that be so, let them be handed over to a new committee, and let him co-operate in a new attempt. I may be a trifle late, but 'better late than never'. Nothing was ever gained without a struggle against adversity, and this venture would be no exception. The scheme can go through despite Mr Thompson's assertion to the contrary.[26]

Nothing came of Mr Hay's optimism and the scheme was not heard of again. But two of the statements made in the exchange bear closer examination, as they would appear to be quite true. The band *did* flourish for at least six months with 'non-Labourites', and there *were* dozens of musicians in the local labour movement, to which the various Labour Church and concert programmes bore testimony. There were plenty of reasons why those 'dozens' did not join the band, the most obvious being that while the labour movement was blessed with musicians, most of them were pianists or singers. Very few of the instrumentalists mentioned at Labour concerts and musical evenings were brass players and there would certainly not be a full complement of the brass instruments that make up a brass band. Many of the instruments in the band are not really solo instruments and would only be learnt with joining a band in mind. There were plenty of works bands and one trade union band in the city, but a brass instrument would not necessarily be the first instrument of choice for an aspiring musician of limited means.

Furthermore, many of the 'dozens' of musicians in the movement were women. Although none of the advertisements for players in the Labour Brass Band specified that applicants would have to be male, brass bands were a masculine phenomenon. Indeed, the great pillars of traditional British working-class music making – the brass band and the male voice choir – were entirely male domains. The Birmingham labour movement sensibly moved in the direction of full choirs and orchestras later in the decade, which meant that women singers and instrumentalists could be brought in.

The reason for the band folding despite having 'flourished' was not given by Thompson in his letter, but one factor would certainly have been the persistent desire to have a Labour Party Brass Band made up of Labour Party members. By restricting themselves to a small number of people – male party members who played brass instruments – they rendered their task impossible.

The Smethwick Labour Male Voice Choir

Smethwick had a civic identity independent of Birmingham and therefore the *Town Crier* had a 'Smethwick Notes' section written by its Smethwick correspondent, not dissimilar to the 'London Letter' that it also carried. The writer of the Smethwick Notes was one 'W.A.E.', an elderly stalwart of the Smethwick labour movement. In January 1921, W.A.E. made the first request for a Smethwick choral association which, over a number of years, eventually emerged as a male voice choir. Under the heading 'Why not a Labour Choral Association?' he insisted: 'surely there's enough musical talent in the movement to form the nucleus of a really fine choir . . . it only wants a few enthusiasts to put their heads and voices together and the thing would be done'.[27] Of course, the formation of a choir was always an easier proposition than the formation of a band or an orchestra – everyone came with an instrument and a reasonable result could be achieved without very much technical training. As long as there was a core of singers who could read music or follow 'sol-fa' instructions, others could follow the leader of their 'part'. Many choral pieces also followed quite a predictable four-part arrangement.

Included in the appeal from W.A.E. was the question: 'what has Mr F. Adams to say on the idea?' Fred Adams, the music enthusiast, was not slow to answer. On 11 February he wrote to the *Town Crier* expressing his view that 'there is any amount of scope for a really good combination, either purely male voice or mixed, and I am prepared to do anything in my power to get such a choir started and help it to success'. But Adams could not resist a swipe at the competition. While most correspondents to the *Town Crier* were invariably polite about the musical combinations that were emerging at this time, Adams took a different approach:

> I must say, however, that none of the Labour Choirs I have heard locally have ever roused any feeling within me other than a desire to go out and get a drink as soon as it was decently possible – and even the chairmen (callous old ruffians as most Labour chairmen are) have looked ashamed of themselves when proposing votes of thanks to 'our young friends who have done their best to entertain us this evening'.
>
> Believe me, sir. I don't wonder at the chairmen looking ashamed. If they had done their duty they would have sent for the police to put the whole lot in a place of safety.[28]

He did eventually return to the point and offered to arrange a preliminary meeting. But by this stage, Adams had caused considerable offence. W.A.E. made a few wry references to Adams in his notes on 18 February, but on 4 March the conductor of the Rotton Park Labour Choir wrote to the *Town Crier* in protest:

> Sir – I was rather amused at our friend Fred Adams' letter re: Labour Choirs and the reply in last week's issue by your Smethwick correspondent. I agree that a choir in that area would not only be an asset to the cause but would be a source of rivalry for the only other Labour Choir I know of locally, to wit, the Rotton Park Labour Choir. And as one who has striven might and main to make that a success against all odds, I should have been glad of his help to further the interests of same.
>
> At the same time I hope he will meet with huge enrolment and that when they get going, 'ruffianly' chairmen may only call in the police to quell the tumult of applause which will greet their efforts when they are ripe enough to appear in public. Anyway, I shall deem it a boon to a

musically starved Labour community, who appear too sleepy and lethargic to be awakened by the Archangel's Trump, let alone by 'those
who do their best to entertain' without any sneering remarks from one
who has only just awakened to a sense of 'doing his bit'.

May that bit be a good'un, and achieve the results it will merit in
making Smethwick and locality resound in praise for Fred Adams'
choir, is the sincere wish of yours, etc. WILLIAM MACBEATH.[29]

There are two interesting points amongst the indignation. The first of
these is that Rotton Park Labour Choir was the only local labour choir in
1921, which demonstrates how the number of these choirs grew later in
the 1920s. The other point is the image of a 'sleepy and lethargic' 'musically starved Labour community', which does not seem to square at all
with the picture of the associational life of the Birmingham labour
movement painted elsewhere. People like MacBeath and, later in the
period, H. G. Sear seemed almost to forget that the labour movement had
a role outside producing and understanding 'good' music. The problem
was not so much that the music became more important than the labour
movement in the minds of these people, but that they became almost in-
terchangeable. MacBeath commented that Adams had 'just awakened to
a sense of "doing his bit"' – Labour musical adventures were considered a
cause in themselves.

But the Smethwick Choir took a long time to get off the ground. Under
the heading 'Labour and music', W.A.E. wrote in response to
MacBeath's letter mentioning a pre-war socialist choir that sang at
Smethwick Town Hall (which 'was music, too, Fred Adams!').[30] He then
went on to suggest that there should be a meeting to discuss the idea 'so
that in the very near future Labour will be able to hold its own in the musical world, and we in the Labour and Socialist movements must have it as
quickly as possible. Now then, start shouting, somebody.'[31] But, this
time, nobody did – at least not through the pages of the *Town Crier*. That
Labour should be able to 'hold its own in the musical world' was a peculiar goal in some ways; after all, neither the Conservative nor the Liberal
Party attempted to form great choirs, bands and orchestras.[32] Labour
wished to 'hold its own' with musical organizations, not political organizations, perhaps demonstrating once again its apparent confusion of
causes.

Other parts of the Birmingham area quickly began to overtake
Smethwick. East Birmingham began planning its Labour Choir in May
1924,[33] and many branches, wards and Labour Churches were setting
such groups up throughout the decade. Indeed, the Birmingham Labour
Musical Society[34] (later the Musical Union) was established before the
early plans in Smethwick came to fruition.

The Smethwick Choir's first mention in the *Town Crier* was not too auspicious. In the Smethwick Notes section, under the headline 'Our choir', W.A.E. asserted: 'notwithstanding all that has been said to the contrary, the Unity House Male Voice Choir has come to stay'. This was not the most emphatic introduction to Labour supporters outside Smethwick, as there was no clarification of 'all that has been said to the contrary' either following this statement or at any time before or after in the pages of the *Town Crier*. Unless criticisms of the choir had already been spread widely by word of mouth, this was the first warning that the choir was not as good as it could be. The quick advertisement that W.A.E. gave for its opening concert would not really have instilled any more confidence:

> As evidence of their desire and ability to contribute their quota to the movement they are giving a concert at the club. Unfortunately, I shall not be able to listen to it, but I sincerely hope that all who are interested in music and singing will come along if only to show their appreciation of the efforts the choir is making.[35]

The choir clearly made some slow progress. Its first concert was given to a 'crowded audience' according to W.A.E., although he admitted (as he had predicted) that he was 'unable to be in the room' despite being 'on the premises' and was only able to hear 'snatches of various items'. He primarily used this section of his column to lobby for a new concert hall, stating that the Smethwick Labour Club room was 'totally unsuitable for a concert. In addition to being small, the ceiling is much too low to allow the beauty of the singing to be revealed as it ought to be.' On this occasion the choir did not 'go off the beaten track', performing male voice choir standards: 'Sweet and Low', 'Loch Leven Love Lament', 'Old Farmer Buck' and 'Comrades in Arms'.[36]

By February 1927, W.A.E. was writing about the choir 'getting into its stride, and breaking new ground', and, indeed, at that time it was visiting Labour Clubs in the Midlands and providing an evening's entertainment. That month it had visited clubs at West Bromwich and Rowley. The repertoire had altered a little since its first performance: 'Sweet and Low' and 'Comrades in Arms' were still performed, but 'Little Heather', 'The Wanderer' and 'The Policeman' had joined them. The choir took more musicians around with them, acting more like a concert party then a basic male voice choir. These performances included 'a violin solo by Mr Dudley, a monologue by Mr Guest, and two solos by Miss Bastock'. W.A.E. also mentioned that at both events 'the choir and artistes received – and merited – rounds of applause'. He even attended at least the West Bromwich performance, where he was called upon to give 'a few words' and declared his wish for 'every local Labour Party to organise their own choir, so that eventually, we might have our own massed choirs contest, and so on'.[37] This aspiration was clearly inspired by the Boughton and Morrison plans, but the visit to the Birmingham area of the Welsh miners' choir known as the Apollo Concert Party also appears to have influenced the nature of the Smethwick Choir's performance. The Welsh visit, in 1926, will be considered in Chapter 4.

The choir made a return visit to its 'home' club in April, which W.A.E. declared to be 'undoubtedly, the best concert yet given at the club'. The Smethwick Notes had included some enthusiastic receptions to visiting choirs and bands in the past, so this was praise indeed, although W.A.E. did add that 'none of the items given were difficult from the musical point of view, but all of it was done as it ought to be done'. He tried a more subtle approach to having the room altered this time: 'If all the concerts at the club maintain the standard set by the choir, I can visualise a bigger room being required very soon.' The repertoire was similar again, 'The Mulligan Musketeers' and 'Rolling down to Rio' being added, as was 'a humorous turn' by Mr H. Leighton.[38]

The Smethwick Notes got even more excited by a later concert by the choir under the headline 'The concert'. However, as the concert was organized in order to raise a testimonial fund for W.A.E. himself, it would have been a little ungracious to criticize it.[39] The Smethwick Notes continued to report on the occasional performance by the choir, sometimes on second-hand information where 'according to information received' 'everything went off very well indeed'.[40] The choir increased the number of solos, and inviting local singers to contribute sometimes led to 'exchanges' with other clubs.[41] It had its first annual outing in July 1927 and was clearly all set to become a long-standing organization.[42]

With the success of the choir, the Smethwick labour movement also looked to form an orchestra, rehearsing for the first time in March 1927. The wish for Smethwick's labour movement to have a choir and an orchestra was clearly inspired by the Birmingham Labour Musical Union.

The Birmingham Labour Musical Union

> Labour has always gone in for brass bands and male voice choirs and has done most admirable work. Now, the tendency is to get the women to join up with the men, and mixed choirs and orchestras give both sexes more scope.[43]

Of course, mixed choirs and orchestras were also easier to fill than all-male ventures, and after the disaster of the Labour Party Band, the Birmingham movement would want to see some return for any further investment in musical ventures. The foundations of the Birmingham Labour Musical Union probably stem from the Birmingham Brass Band and the many local choirs that were set up during the early 1920s, but an article in the *Town Crier* at the beginning of 1925 (reproduced from the January *Socialist Review*) would appear to have actually got things under way. The article was entitled 'Socialism and song' and subtitled 'A plea for music: make meetings merrier'. It looked at the power of music when used by religions or the military, suggesting that the labour movement could reap similar benefits. The author, C. Salway-Wallis, concluded by saying, 'Socialists should think twice before considering this question as of secondary importance, and I believe after due consideration we shall realise that music and melody cannot be relegated to the background, but [should be] put in its rightful place at the front of our programme.'[44] The article clearly expounded one of the traditional arguments for the labour movement to take an interest in music: namely, that music had a power to draw people, as shown by music halls, churches and armies. What the article did not explain (and nobody ever explained it satisfactorily between the wars, despite many attempts) was *why* music and melody had a rightful place at the front of the socialist programme. It seemed that this was too obvious a point to merit further exposition.

The article inspired a member of the Handsworth ILP, Edward Wright, to write to the *Town Crier* with a plan for forming a Labour Orchestra: 'it would not be difficult to organise an Orchestra to perform at some of the Labour Churches and at the different functions that take place', he wrote. 'Get a small committee together and appoint a secretary' and 'secure a room in which to hold a weekly practice, with piano, as centrally placed as possible'. Wright also considered the details of how to borrow or pay for music stands, etc.

> There must be a number of amateur and even professional musicians in the movement who would join such an orchestra. If the *Town Crier* would insert notices asking for the material and players wanted, and generally take an interest in the concern, I feel sure such a venture would be a success, and that without a lot of expense. Of course all services would be voluntary.
>
> If my services as conductor are acceptable, I would be pleased to help. –
> Yours faithfully, etc. Edward Wright (Member Handsworth ILP)[45]

The plan was quite clear – rather similar to the plans behind the brass band, only without the suggestion that instruments should be bought.

The following month saw the first meeting of the Birmingham Labour Musical Society. The meeting was well attended and it was decided that membership would be open to all Labour Party members or members of affiliated bodies. Once again it was organized along the lines of activists getting involved in music rather than presenting a possible path for musicians to get involved in politics: the aim was to 'bring out the latent talent that exists in the Labour movement'. From the beginning the plan was to have a central choir and orchestra with the aim of developing ward-level choirs and orchestras later. The membership fee was one shilling a quarter when the movement first came into being.[46] It took some weeks of hard recruitment before the Society held some rehearsals. It had forty members by this time, and its correspondent to the *Town Crier* was very enthusiastic, declaring 'if progress continues at this rate, Birmingham should soon have a Labour Orchestra and Choir second to none in the country'.[47]

Unknown to the organizers of the Birmingham Labour Musical Society, plans were afoot on a national scale that would fit in with their venture rather well. This was first brought to their attention by Lionel Field (Mus. Bac. LRAM), who offered his services to form a Birmingham Labour Musical Union when he moved to the area in July 1925. He wrote to the *Town Crier* at the beginning of May that year to explain his association with national leaders and to explain his plans under the headline 'Music in the labour movement'. He was not, unfortunately, entirely up to date with recent developments in the Birmingham labour movement's musical activities.

> Sir – I have lately had the pleasure of conversing with Mr Herbert Morrison, of London, on the subject of the Labour Musical Movement. This gentleman, in connection with Mr Rutland Boughton, the eminent composer, has outlined to me a very powerful and comprehensive scheme for developing the aesthetic side of Socialism through music.
>
> I believe I am right in assuming that the musical activity of the Labour Party in Birmingham is confined to the efforts of various choirs and orchestral bodies which function individually. This in itself is a very excellent and praiseworthy thing, but to my mind the whole secret of power in the musical movement must lie in the direction of co-ordination. The scheme of the London Labour Choral Union, to which Mr Boughton is musical adviser and Mr Morrison secretary, is briefly this: A central committee is set up to decide the policy and arrange the activities of a central musical body, to which a definite programme is allotted. Musical demonstrations are given in the outlying districts of the suburbs and the formation of new choirs, etc. is thereby encouraged. The ultimate aim is to cultivate the spirit of local musical festivals (not necessarily competitive), bringing in representatives of all the Labour organisations within a certain area, and from that point, a National (and perhaps International) Labour Musical Festival is contemplated.

> I should be glad to hear from any of your readers who are interested and prepared to do some of the spade work in forming a Birmingham Labour Musical Union. I shall be taking up residence in or near Birmingham in July next, by which time I shall have a definite progressive musical scheme for consideration.
>
> The London office has given the proposed venture its blessing, as have those officials of the Labour Party in Birmingham whom I have been fortunate enough to meet.[48]

The organization eventually changed its name to the Birmingham Labour Musical Union, but Lionel Field was never incorporated into the project.

On 27 June 1925, the Society (it was still called the Society not the Union at this stage) held a 'grand social and dance' with 'musical items by the Choir, the Orchestra and our own Soloists'.[49] Twelve new members were recruited at this event, bringing the total membership up to seventy. The event included 'orchestral and choral items, violin solos (Mr T. Walton) and contralto solos (Mrs G. Morris)', 'addresses by Mr Ager (President of the Borough Labour Party) and Mr H. G. Sear (President of the Birmingham Labour Musical Society)', and 'dancing to the music of the Society's Dance Band'.[50] The main difference between this event and most of what was heard from the Society over the next twelve months or so is that there was a dance band (this was not heard of again), and that the orchestra actually performed. A change in the guiding philosophy behind the Society led to a major change in its activities. The move of H. G. Sear from the presidential role to conducting the orchestra later in its history also contributed to this change.

When the *Town Crier* published Boughton and Morrison's plans for a National Choral Union in August 1925,[51] the Birmingham Labour Musical Society was already considered to be part of Birmingham's efforts in this area. The new-look Society was unveiled in February 1926. The name changed on a regular basis, but the permanent change at this stage was from 'Society' to 'Union' to tie in with the National Choral Union plans. Another change was for the orchestra to be rearranged 'on symphonic lines, under the directions of Mr H. G. Sear'. This was immediately problematic. Although the orchestra had 'an interesting, and, if appearances count, enjoyable rehearsal', where it attempted part of Handel's *Water Music*, two movements from Haydn's 'Surprise' Symphony and Beethoven's *Coriolan* Overture, the conductor did not 'yet feel justified in accepting [the] many offers of engagements received'. The orchestra needed to make up a 'full complement of strings (violas and cellos in particular), flutes, oboes, clarionet, bassoons, trumpets (or cornets), horns (or euphoniums), trombones and drums'.[52] Therefore, the movement's ambitious, musically minded activists had once again developed from the possible – the formation of an orchestra of sorts that could perform special arrangements – to the unfeasible: a full symphony orchestra. Once again the musical talent in the movement was having the impossible asked of it – they were to find players of some of those instruments, but searching for a full complement of them was just a hopeless undertaking.

The basis of the problem that necessitated this search was H. G. Sear's avowed objection to musical arrangements, which he made clear in his music column in the *Town Crier*. His imagery is peculiar from a socialist perspective ('an arrangement is like . . . a duke taking up his abode in a miner's hut')[53] but it certainly made it difficult for him to be the President of an organization that arranged music for a hotchpotch orchestra. Exactly when Sear took over the baton is difficult to say, but he was definitely conducting before the end of February 1926. He continued to make pleas for all the extra instrumentalists so as 'to play the works of Handel, Haydn and Beethoven as they wrote them'.[54]

At this time the name of the organization appeared to settle as the Birmingham Labour Musical and Dramatic Union. It did not incorporate the embryonic Birmingham People's Theatre Movement, and the inclusion of 'Dramatic' would appear to have been in case it decided to tackle opera at a later stage of its development. Requests for instruments seemed to get increasingly desperate:

> Richard III once offered his kingdom for a horse. The orchestra is in such dire need of 'cellos, violas and bassoons that it might even offer a Republic? That is not to say that it no longer needs players in other branches. There are still vacancies for violinists, flutes, oboes, horns and trombones; and, if this paragraph should meet the eye of a Timpanist (with his own drums) he would do well to meet the conductor (Mr H. G. Sear) next Wednesday.[55]

A postscript mentioned that Mr Bird, the conductor of the choir, needed more singers at the choral rehearsals as well, but it was clear that a choir was easier to assemble than a symphony orchestra. The chances of a timpanist with his own drums being amongst the small number of readers[56] of the *Town Crier* that week seem particularly low. Later the Union's correspondent (it could be Sear, it is difficult to be sure) remarked:

> One thing puzzles me. The conductor of the City Orchestra who, in all probability, does not sympathise with our politics, in a pure and disinterested love of music lends us music which we could never afford to buy. Yet amateur string-players, belonging and subscribing to the movement, will not sacrifice two or three hours a week for orchestral practice in their very own band.[57]

The next request for new players took a slightly different tack: 'General enjoyment seemed to be the order of the day at the orchestral rehearsal last week. Everything went with a swing.' Of course, the writer's mood may have been improved by the addition of two new players, a viola player and an oboist. The assertion that 'there really was an excellent sense of orchestral colour' and 'a notable improvement in the string tone' certainly gave a more positive feel to the brief article, but it still concluded that 'flutes, trombones, horns, violas, and 'cellos are sorely needed'.[58] These weekly crisis reports and appeals for members hardly showed the orchestra in the best possible light. From time to time the appeals would stop and concern about how their desperation looked to observers would appear to have been the primary reason.

A headline appeared in the Town Crier on 16 April 1926 that read: 'Birmingham's Labour Orchestra is making good'. This title appeared to refer to the arrival of a new trombone player and an eleven-year-old cellist ('a real inspiration for he laboured joyously like a young god'), and that they had finally succumbed to the temptations of arrangements. Two members of the orchestra had provided them with arrangements of Beethoven's 'Moonlight' Sonata and Schubert's 'Serenade'. The article also included a request to parents to encourage their children to take up instruments,[59] demonstrating that they were in for the long haul in developing this symphony orchestra. The following week there was a complaint at 'a falling off in members' despite a promise of two extra cellists. The repertoire the orchestra was working on was listed again (with no mention of the arrangements the two orchestra-members had worked on – hardly the way to keep the members they had), which was 'a programme that the finest orchestra in the world could tackle without any fear of losing caste. On the other hand it is not so high-brow that the loyal members of the band get tired of it.'[60] The orchestra and choir were finally, at this stage, starting to discuss a joint work that could be performed.

There were to be more problems, however, before they were to make that public appearance. The Town Crier carried 'An appeal to labour musicians' on 4 June 1926, declaring: 'Eleven! That was the total attendance at the last rehearsal of the Labour Orchestra.'[61] There was a problem that societies (especially social or 'cultural' functions) in the Birmingham labour movement generally came to a standstill in the summer. Most of the associations, like the Labour Churches, worked in seasons, and the summer months were left for outings, demonstrations and open-air meetings as well as non-political activities such as gardening and holidays. Organizers of the orchestra realized that this was a contributory factor to the falling-off in active support in late June, declaring in an article: 'There seems to be an impression that the weekly practices are not held in the summer. It is a mistaken one. The same enthusiasts turn up week by week, no matter what the weather.'[62] Sear clearly became more and more discouraged by poor attendance. 'Are there no fiddlers, violinists, 'cellists to be found in the movement? Or are they shy, superior or ashamed? Then they cannot be true music lovers or they would turn up weekly.'[63] Through July and August the orchestra received quite a few new instrumentalists in the areas where they were required: 'a new flute, clarinet and bassoon' were welcomed in the pages of the *Town Crier* on 6 August, but the orchestra was losing violinists. They gave in to the seasonal nature of the Birmingham labour movement by noting that 'after the holiday the Labour Orchestra recommences serious practice'.[64]

The organizers of the orchestra were fully aware that it was a long time since it had made a public appearance, and that it never had since they had announced their intentions to make the orchestra 'symphonic'. 'The winter season is now setting in, and the choir will have to do some public work if only to justify its existence.' But they continued to dress down unreliable players through the columns of the *Town Crier* and it can hardly have presented the most welcoming picture to musical Labourites considering joining in. A horn player from Derby had announced that he was going to travel down to Birmingham and join the orchestra once he had returned to full-time employment. 'That is a piece of news that should shame those who lag behind', the Labour Orchestra column chastised. 'It is a costly business, it is a tiring business, it is laden with difficulties. The most certain way to overcome these things is to turn up in numbers, regularly, with the will to work patiently and hard.'[65] This was rather different from providing a couple of solos at a Labour Church meeting or providing some entertainment at a social evening. The amateur players in the movement, whom Sear and others were appealing to, in many cases might not have shared their zeal for the 'Labour musical movement'. The motivation behind the Labour Orchestra was not to provide entertainment for the movement, or recreation for the players, but to compete with professional orchestras. It is perhaps not surprising that this goal appealed to a limited number of enthusiasts, but not to the majority of labour instrumentalists in the city.

In October 1926 the Union finally announced its intentions as far as a public appearance was concerned. The two reasons given for their 'pledge to a public performance in January' were to provide 'an incentive to players and singers' and also 'to justify their existence'. The choir was working on Mendelssohn's *Hymn of Praise* and the orchestra would back it. To do so to the standard to which the Union aspired, however, a 'well-balanced' orchestra was required and so there was a repeated request for 'strings, flutes, oboes, clarinets, bassoons, trumpets (or cornets),

French horns, trombones and drums'. At this stage it was also pointed out that the orchestra made no test of proficiency before accepting new members: 'players first, reasonable proficiency afterwards'. They even announced that they would perform 'two or three light orchestral numbers' at the proposed concert, in case prospective players were worried that the standard would be too high. The correspondent to the *Town Crier* was quick to point out that 'on principle, however, the aim of the band is nothing less than the best'.[66] Clearly, once the orchestra was opening its doors to the paying public a certain standard had to be striven for, although certain allowances would be given to an amateur orchestra, especially if the bulk of the audience came from within the movement, as seemed likely.

At this stage, H. G. Sear was not interested in people making allowances for a Labour Orchestra. This was based on a more general opinion of his that 'Labour must mean the very highest, whether in every-day efficiency, or science, or art or craftsmanship.' It was this view which led him to believe that 'nothing less than the very best was good enough for Labourites'.[67] It was a peculiar variation of a more usual socialist view of the arts – that the working class should be provided with the best art available, rather than 'the best' being hoarded as a plaything of the wealthy and powerful. Clearly Sear was more interested in that theory than in the possibility of an alternative working-class art that could be encouraged and used by the labour movement. But Sear's position *was* a variation. The essential point of his labour theory of music was that the labour movement must be seen to be 'the best' at whatever it turns its hand to in order to demonstrate the power and importance of labour. Really, there was nothing in these statements to make the prospect of joining the orchestra any more attractive to the casual performer whose goal was more modest than 'the best'.

In the following week's *Town Crier*, H. G. Sear decided to devote his music column to 'Labour Choirs and Orchestras', and although he began in general terms, it quickly became clear that he was dealing with the specific problems thrown up by the Union. 'There seems to be no difficulty with choirs', he asserted, but forming an orchestra was much harder. He wrote of a meeting he had attended where somebody insisted that forming an orchestra had been no difficulty in their district: 'when I enquired as to the constitution of his orchestra, it turned out that he meant a piano, a handful of fiddles, a 'cello and some cornets'. Sear recognized 'the difficulty of the orchestra' to be that it was 'impossible to make up a complete body of violins, violas, 'cellos, basses, flutes, oboes, clarinets, bassoons, horns, trumpets, trombones and drums' – but his solution was not to make do with what he had, but instead to propose an elaborate system of suburban orchestras and 'what musicians we lack we must breed, borrowing meanwhile'. That is, youngsters born into the labour movement would have to be taught to play a wide range of musical instruments, and in the meantime non-Labourites could fill the places in the orchestra – not with a view to recruiting them, but simply to fill the gaps in the traditional symphonic orchestral structure. The plan also included suburban orchestras that could 'play light music as light and rubbishy as they like, though I should deplore it and decry it strenuously. But then, they could contribute their best players to a central symphonic orchestra.'[68]

The desperate search for musicians to make up the missing places for performing *Hymn of Praise* continued with a plea to Labour Church members:

> Labour Church advertisements show clearly that there are several groups of orchestral musicians regularly performing in Labour circles. Labour orchestra statistics prove equally clearly that these bodies do not reinforce their efforts. Orchestral players who can spare a Wednesday evening every week are asked to report to H. G. Sear . . . to work towards a concert to be given in January.[69]

It was clearly thought that the prospect of a performance would be an incentive and the orchestra's leaders would appear to have calculated their tactics correctly. The membership of the orchestra expanded considerably over the following fortnight. The rehearsal on 3 November was described as 'an excellent muster' and the list of instruments still required was depleted considerably (the *Town Crier* still carried a request for more brass and string instruments, a second oboe and some bassoons). Despite these encouraging developments, the notes in the *Town Crier* still urged people to 'put aside personal convenience and turn up regularly at the Wednesday practices'.[70] Even the Labour Choir organizers were worried that they were not quite at their optimum strength. The William Morris Choir of Glasgow challenged them to a competition in December 1926,[71] which they did not feel able to accept,[72] and the chairman of the Union's Executive Committee, Jabez Hall, wrote 'An appeal to labour vocalists and musicians' to the *Town Crier* that same month. Hall also gave a version of the history of the Union in his letter:

> Sir – The Birmingham Labour and Dramatic Union has been in existence for the last twelve months, and is destined to be of valuable assistance to the great Labour and Socialist movement of this city and district. Under its auspices the committee have decided to give a concert on the last Friday in January, 1927, during which Mendelssohn's 'Hymn of Praise' will be rendered . . .
>   . . . The Committee are anxious that the work should be rendered

with the efficiency all music lovers could desire, and to obtain that it is necessary that all in the Labour movement that know the work should give their assistance. We could augment from other sources, but our object is to demonstrate to the musical life of Birmingham that the Labour movement has the talent and ability in its own ranks to render such a work. We are convinced that in Birmingham, Labour has the power to build up a Musical and Dramatic Union equal to any such organisation in the country.

Since the formation of the Union, progress has been made in spite of difficulties, financial and otherwise, and the members have made sacrifices to accomplish what has been done. It is to the music-loving of the Labour movement of the City to determine whether Birmingham's Musical Union shall attain the success and proud position as attained by the Glasgow Orpheus. We believe this can be done – the Labour movement possesses the talent, and we appeal to all vocalists and instrumentalists in the movement to come and help us to accomplish our idea of a Labour Musical Union in Birmingham second to none in the country.

Yours faithfully,
JABEZ HALL (Chairman of Executive)
E. P. MARLEY (Secretary)
D. H. MARTIN (Treasurer)[73]

The very popular, well-known and respected Glasgow Orpheus Choir was conducted by Hugh S. Roberton, a member of the ILP and the '1917 Club' and an adjudicator at many musical festivals, including some Clarion Vocal Union festivals.[74] The editor of the *Town Crier* inserted a short response to the letter expressing the desire that the Union could soon accept the challenge from Glasgow.

The chairman, Jabez Hall, was a well-known character in the Birmingham movement. A 57-year-old ex-councillor who considered himself to have been 'brought up in the hard school of experience' and a 'life-long worker in the religious and social movements',[75] he was occasionally known to demonstrate his singing talents at Labour Church meetings, and party 'socials'. His letter underlined the goal of the Union once again – to show what existing Labour members could do. The recruitment possibilities of this organization just did not appear to occur to these activists. The possibility of *competing* with the labour musical ventures in other cities and areas had very clearly been established by this time and things had moved on a long way from when Lionel Field remarked that labour musical festivals would be 'not necessarily competitive'.[76]

As the first concert came closer, notes in the *Town Crier* about the orchestra became increasingly positive: 'it is meeting its task with courage and even conviction'. There was also the need, especially after the frankness of some of H. G. Sear's musical criticism in his column, to prepare the way for the performance to fall somewhere short of perfection. 'In attacking a work bristling with difficulties such as Mendelssohn's "Hymn of Praise", the Labour Orchestra is assuming a great responsibility. It should be remembered that it is an amateur band.'[77] This was clearly an excuse that Sear would not have liked to make earlier in the history of the Union, and had it been possible, he might well have shielded his orchestra from the public eye for even longer.

When advertisements for the 'Grand Concert' appeared, they highlighted the numbers of those involved – the 'combined choirs and orchestra of 100 performers' – and promised 'glees, duets, solos and orchestral items' as well as the *Hymn of Praise*. The concert cost 6d to enter.[78] The editor of the *Town Crier*, Will Chamberlain, appealed to readers to support the concert, insisting that 'there should be no vacant seats'.[79]

He, for one, was thoroughly impressed with this first performance from the Union. After confessing that he 'went to the concert trembling', he expressed his enjoyment in unreserved terms. He wrote of the 'fine orchestra' and 'the glorious final chorus by the combined choir'. He declared that the 'wonderful performance' made him 'proud of the good comrades of both sexes who have reached such a state of efficiency' (they always made more of 'efficiency' than 'proficiency'). He looked forward 'to the time when the Labour Choir and Orchestra will be popular attractions at all our central meetings – and even be sought after by the BBC!'[80]

The *Town Crier* carried a more balanced criticism later in the same issue. The article was anonymous, although it was made clear that it was not written by the usual *Town Crier* critic – the conductor, H. G. Sear! The headline was 'A successful concert', but the article was rather more critical than most 'reviews' of home-grown entertainment in those pages. While initially saying that the concert was 'a great success' and 'a real artistic achievement', the critics[81] went on to suggest that Sear had 'not yet imposed upon his band an exact observation of note values. A finished performance is impossible if each member of the ensemble does not agree as to the length of a crotchet or a quaver.' This suggested that the orchestra failed at the most basic of levels. The 'string tone' of the orchestra was also criticised. As for the choir, these critics suggested that 'attack was often a bit wobbly; particularly amongst the men we noticed a sliding up and down in searching for the right note, and it was not always possible to follow the words'. 'Enthusiasm' and 'improvement' were the virtues praised by these friendly critics, despite the initial suggestion that it had been 'a real artistic achievement'.

The soloists did not escape the basic criticism either. Madame Emilie Waldron received one of the best write-ups: she 'sang the first soprano part beautifully' and 'her voice is a lovely one, well produced'. However, the line 'her feeling for the work is true, if not deep' would appear to be rather unnecessary. Other singers were criticised: Mr Philip Taylor fell foul of 'a little lack of understanding as to tempos'. When considering individual orchestral pieces the reviewers asked 'where were the trumpets in the March?' However, the review ended 'we look forward eagerly to the next concert'.[82]

Sear's earlier appeal for people to remember that the orchestra was 'an amateur band' would suggest that he was prepared for the possibility of less than positive reviews – but maybe not from the columns of the paper for which he was the reviewer. His defence – and it can only really be seen in that way – appeared on the front page of the *Town Crier* the following week, on 11 February 1927. He began bitterly:

> no-one who has not actually participated in the organisation of a serious choral and orchestral concert such as that recently given by the Birmingham Labour Choir and Orchestra at the Priory Rooms, can form any idea of the immense labour and arduous attention to detail that have to be undergone.

Most of the article sought to defend the conductor at such a concert, who 'sighs for perfect phrasing, moving expression, correct enunciation'. It pointed out that

> he has a score before him demanding four horns and he has but two, or even one; three trumpets and he has but one; two oboes, two bassoons, and he has but one of each; drums and he has none. There are holes in his canvas and he knows it; knows it acutely.

Sear also gave a spirited defence of the choristers and his players. He pointed out the difficulties of getting singing or instrumental lessons while also working full time, as well as the possibility of stage-fright: 'even an orchestra of professional musicians, the City of Birmingham Orchestra, for instance, takes years to acquire [the] necessary perfection, and even then they are regularly admonished by the critics'. As well as being a defence of the performance, this was another appeal to swell the ranks of the choir and orchestra. 'The choir needs to be trebled', he declared, and there were still many gaps to fill in the orchestra. Indeed, he hoped to have *more* instrumentalists than required to 'put players to the test of merit'. The Union *did* receive assistance from outside the movement in spite of its aims. Music teachers 'sent their pupils along', 'professional players have given their services to fill up weak spots' – 'it remains for the players and singers in the movement who are holding back to come forward and offer their services'. Why were professional musicians 'giving' their services to the Labour Orchestra? Followers of the Clarion, Blatchford philosophy of 'making socialists' through such ventures would surely have been encouraged by the outside assistance they received, rather than embarrassed by it.

'If you can't sing, learn to play. If you are too old, or tired, encourage the youngsters. If you can't do that, learn to listen.'[83] Sear's evangelical zeal was still at its height, but with the concert under their belt the incessant crisis reports and appeals for new members ceased, despite Sear's assertion that the Union would not 'rest on its oars'. Their next appearance was in April 1927 at the Young Socialist League's 'Labour Community Singing Night', where the orchestra 'played selections from Beethoven, Berlioz, and others of the great composers' and 'community singing was led by Mr J. Bird and the Birmingham Labour Choir'. The songs sung included 'The Old Folks at Home', 'The Londonderry Air', 'Poor Old Joe' and 'The Ash Grove': all sentimental, standard community singing material. The *Town Crier* did not report any socialist or labour songs and anthems being included in the programme.[84] The choir performed a similar duty at the May Day celebrations in 1927.[85]

After all the appeals for new members that had emanated from the orchestra, Jabez Hall wrote to the *Town Crier* in the summer of 1927 to make a similar request on behalf of the choir. The purpose of the letter was nothing more than asking for some more tenor singers to join the ranks. The letter was written as if the choir would survive or fall on this issue alone. This was one major aspect of the history of the Birmingham Labour Musical Union – that it was always discussed by its organizers in the language of perpetual crisis.

> The Choir is in urgent need of tenor voices, and it is to these we appeal to come and help to make the Choir the success worthy of the movement. It may mean the sinking of one's individuality, but in the success of the whole this ought not to be a sacrifice.

Why both Sear and Hall felt the need to wrap their simple requests up in such dramatic language is impossible to say. One explanation is that they felt that asking 'is the Choir to succeed or is it to fail?' might have troubled the conscience of tenors who had limited their performances to solos at the Labour Churches. The pathos of the letter's conclusion demonstrates this over-dramatization of the mundane rather well:

> To this side of the movement the National Labour Party has given serious consideration, with the result that similar organisations are springing up throughout the country. The Birmingham Labour movement is in possession of the talent. Shall we let the opportunity pass, or rise to the occasion by demonstrating to the musical life of this city that this side of the movement is not to be neglected? It will be a success if a few tenor voices rally to the cause ...[86]

The Union's annual meeting in 1927 was reported in the *Town Crier* and the feeling of the meeting was that they had made 'excellent progress'. They welcomed the formation of a new constituent choir at St Martin's and Deritend ward and had a plan for persuading existing choirs outside the Union to get involved: a competitive festival was to be held in the autumn of that year.[87]

Indeed, it was the choral section of the Musical Union that was to remain active through the 1930s. It is perhaps inevitable that the orchestra was unable to sustain its efforts, depending so much as it did on the largely vain labours of a single man. The orchestra, especially its struggle to be 'symphonic', was certainly the most singular and interesting aspect of the Birmingham labour movement's attempts at musical combination. But choral associations had not been the most successful labour musical organizations for no reason: even works-sponsored brass bands required regular and considerable funds to keep them going. Music was very important to socialists between the wars, but what some enthusiasts did not really understand was that the music had to pay for itself. It could not be robbing funds that would otherwise be spent on fighting elections or running campaigns: it was better by far if those groups could do more than pay for themselves and raise money for the movement. The Birmingham Labour Party Symphony Orchestra was never going to manage that.

There were many other labour musical combinations in Birmingham between the wars: choirs, quartets, concert parties and bands organized by local Labour Parties, Labour Churches and trade union branches. By the middle of the 1920s a sizeable list could be compiled, although they did not all prosper for long. These included the Ladywood Labour Choir, the Stirchley Co-operative Choir, the Plebian Trio, Tom Osborne's Choir, Mill's Male Voice Choir, Rotton Park Labour Church Choir, Bordesley Labour Male Voice Choir, the AEU Choir, the NUR (number five branch) Orphan Fund Band, Mrs Lilian Green's Ladies' Choir, the West Birmingham Labour Band (who played dance music), the Sparkbrook Labour Jazz Troupe, the Orpheus Band (also a dance orchestra) and many others. The Birmingham labour movement was far from 'sleepy and lethargic' or 'musically starved', especially in the second half of the 1920s.

Bradford and district

The Clarion Vocal Unions (CVUs) were always at their strongest in Yorkshire and Lancashire, and the West Riding of Yorkshire, in particular, was the real heartland. While the work of the CVUs after the First

World War has not been considered by historians, a number of choirs were still operating in the years immediately following the war and the National Clarion Vocal Union regained its strength through the 1920s with an annual national contest as well as regional contests. The focus of labour musical combinations in this area was centred on these enduring older organisations.

The Pioneer Choir

At the end of the First World War, the CVU in Bradford was meeting on Tuesday evenings at its own rehearsal rooms. Occasionally it would open the doors on a Tuesday night, bringing in the public and embellishing the programme with instrumental music – in November 1918 the programme for the 'open night' included violin solos.[88] By February 1919 the choir had changed its name to the Pioneer Choir, although it still advertised itself as the Bradford branch of the Clarion Vocal Union. The Clarion movement in general was still alive and well in Bradford, with Clarion cycling clubs in operation there and in neighbouring Keighley, and a Clarion Clubhouse between Otley and Menston in the rural area to the north of the city. However, the *Clarion* as a newspaper, and Robert Blatchford – the man behind the movement, credited with making many socialists – were both intensely unpopular in the Bradford labour movement, and the ILP in particular. Therefore, it is reasonable to assume that there was a political aspect to the decision by the choir to exchange 'Clarion' for 'Pioneer' in the name of the choir.

The *Bradford Pioneer* at this time made strong attacks on the *Clarion* and its editor on an almost weekly basis in 1918, 1919 and 1920. This was primarily due to Blatchford's criticisms of the ILP's support for conscientious objectors and later Blatchford's support for intervention in the Russian civil war against the Bolshevik government. These criticisms coincided with a low-point in the history of the *Clarion* with its editor complaining that the circulation had fallen to little above zero and, in the summer of 1919, was in danger of collapsing. The *Pioneer* made it very clear that it would not mourn the *Clarion*'s passing.[89]

It does seem strange that somebody who had played such an important role in Victorian British socialism as Robert Blatchford should meet with such venom from a provincial Labour newspaper, and from two editors, but his popularity had been waning in some areas since his support for the Boer War.[90] The 'condition' of his mind was even questioned by the *Pioneer*, which, considering his age, might have considered the issue more sympathetically.[91] The *Pioneer* would even recommend the choir to its readers 'whatever be Blatchford's present failings', recognizing the 'fine legacy of choirs founded under the inspiration of him and the good fellows who used to write for the *Clarion*'.

Whether or not the Pioneer Choir's change of name can be put down entirely to this, it got down to considerable activity and looked to expand its numbers. It was not just a relic of a past age. As well as the open nights at the rehearsal rooms it hosted musical evenings in larger halls[92] and in September 1919 it began 'an elementary singing class' on Tuesday evenings to help swell the ranks.[93] Members of the choir sometimes appeared as the Pioneer Quartette (or sometimes the Clarion Concert Party) at large labour meetings or rallies, the quartet consisting of a soprano, contralto, tenor and bass.[94] The choir sang at a large number of socials and bazaars in most ILP and Labour Party branches in the city throughout the period.

To demonstrate further that it was not merely a monument to a historical movement, the choir began putting on an annual 'great event': a large concert at the Mechanics' Institute. The first of these was in the spring of 1922 and the main attraction was a 'concert version' of Edward German's popular opera *Merrie England*.[95] 'The Bradford ILP turned up in large number' and 'every song was received with delight and acclamation' according to the review in the *Bradford Pioneer*. The concert also included a 'rustic dance and jig', which 'caused quite a sensation'. The reviewer, 'E.M.S.', put most emphasis on the enjoyment of the event displayed by choir and audience alike, remarking that 'if our own Lord Mayor had not been there to remind us to behave ourselves, the odds are we should have gone entirely mad'. The choice of music was popular with the ILP/ Clarionette audience because of the 'breezy Robin Hood touch' to the lyrics and, no doubt, because it shared its title with Blatchford's popular propaganda book.[96]

Merrie England was a popular choice for the choir's regular concerts in February or March. It was, however, a light comic opera popular amongst Gilbert and Sullivan enthusiasts (less satirical but with 'crisper orchestration')[97] and so the concert was not made up of a political programme at all. In the mid-1920s, comic and light opera was almost as ubiquitous as dancing in the recreational life of Bradford. It was remarked in the *Pioneer* that 'today, the Bradford citizen, if he wishes to escape from comic opera, and the non-musical inanities provided for his consumption by an all ruling providence, must flee his native city and seek the drama in (horrid thought) Leeds, and other lesser towns in the neighbourhood'.[98] In 1925 an estimated 800-strong audience saw the choir (with the soloists or 'principals' as three years earlier) perform *Merrie England* and a song-cycle called *Flora's Holiday* which was 'quite a success'.[99]

The Pioneer Choir numbered thirty members in 1925, which was considered 'on the small side for a Bradford Socialist choir'. This would appear to be in terms of how large 'Mus. Bac.' (a reviewer in the *Pioneer*) would wish Bradford socialist choirs to be rather than a suggestion that there were other, larger socialist choirs in the city. The only other combinations that might have fallen into that category were the adult and junior Co-operative Society choirs and the various Socialist Sunday School choirs, who restricted their performances to their services.

Like its Birmingham counterparts, the Pioneer Choir entered into a protracted recruitment drive to expand on that base of thirty. As with the Birmingham Musical Union, these recruitment efforts tended to centre on the affirmed belief that 'Bradford musical enthusiasts with real good voices must be in plenty'.[100] Although the *Pioneer* did not have the Labour Church reports to add weight to this assertion, the large number of concerts in labour clubs across the city provided similar evidence.

While Birmingham musical combinations were unwilling to enter competitions until they had reached a higher standard, the Pioneer Choir came from the competitive Clarion tradition and continued to enter the CVU national contest, which had continued as an annual event and was beginning to return to its former importance in the Clarionette calendar by the middle of the 1920s. In November 1925, when the contest took place at Leeds Town Hall, the choir was victorious (though only twenty-seven strong), taking home the 'Clarion Challenge Baton'. Mr Boddy, the conductor, reacted with gleeful triumphalism: 'The Bradford Pioneer Choir has been after this stick for twenty years,' he said, 'and you can imagine with what joyful hearts we shall return tonight, because it is at last in our possession.'[101]

The Clarion choir contest was judged on a 'test piece' selected on the day from a large number of possibilities. That year it was a 'delicate, almost mystic' song by Rutland Boughton called 'Early Morn'. However, the concert of the massed choirs was generally presented in both the *Pioneer* and the *Clarion* as the most popular aspect of the contest,[102] which is perhaps surprising when one considers the suggestion in some secondary literature that pre-war contests were extraordinarily competitive, particularly amongst the 'supporters'. Certainly the *Pioneer* suggested that more sentimental emotions held sway at these inter-war contests. The Bradford victory was reported as being 'popular' amongst the 'rival choirs'.[103] That is not to say that people did not take the competitive element seriously; they clearly did, as Fred Boddy's victory speech demonstrates. However, winning the contest was not the be-all and end-all of the festivals: they were popular because of the fellowship, the chance to see old friends and the quality of the music performed as well as for the competitive spirit. Besides the annual national contest there were local contests (a Lancashire one, for example), although the national contests were often unable to draw choirs from further afield than Lancashire and Yorkshire.

Through the 1930s the Clarion Vocal Union tradition was on the wane, and the choirs did not get involved with the Workers' Music Association, just as they had failed to be a part of the National Labour Choral Union. That is not to say that one or two choirs that were involved in the early stages of either of those ventures had not begun life as Clarion choirs, or developed out of a Clarion choir. However, the CVUs were keen to maintain their organizational distinction even when in decline, and the metropolitan-centred nature of both the NLCU and WMA was not conducive to bringing provincial combinations into the fold.

The Pioneer Choir maintained its Clarionette connections in more ways than just the regular contests. It would sing at the national Clarionette 'grand meets', such as at Hardcastle Crags in 1923, which, 'by happy chance', coincided with the Sowerby ILP Federation Rally.[104] Furthermore, it made regular trips to the Clarion Clubhouse near Otley. When the choir was performing in July 1923, the Clubhouse's advertisement in the *Bradford Pioneer* included a 'WANTED' poster for an audience of 300 strong to hear the choir the following Sunday.[105] Whether they reached the requested number in the audience or not, the concert was warmly appreciated by the fellow Clarionettes who ran the Clubhouse: 'Now and again the golden sun peeped through the clouds last Sunday; but what care we when our good friends the Pioneer Choir are out to charm? Trouble goes by the board, hearts are free and it is real good to be alive.'[106] The choir gave plenty of service to the labour movement more broadly. As well as performing at regular social events, bazaars, rallies and meetings, it provided the musical entertainment for the Labour Party on occasions such as awaiting local election results.[107]

Bradford and the surrounding district had other choirs and bands, but the Pioneer Choir in Bradford and the Keighley Clarion Choir (both part of the 'national' CVU movement) would appear to have been the main local inter-war organizations. There were many Socialist Sunday School choirs and orchestras (and their combined choirs, the 'Sunbeams'), the Lyric Male Quartette, the adult and junior Co-operative Choirs, the Guiseley Labour Party Band, the West Ward Labour Club Orchestra[108] and a variety of other short-lived or small combinations, all of which gave good service at social events and propaganda meetings.

Conclusions

'There is something particularly fitting for the Socialist movement about choir concerts, where the music seems to say "we do enjoy singing together".'[109] What that 'something' was, however, appears somewhat intangible. Sponsoring choirs, bands and orchestras was deemed to be a useful or worthwhile practice for labour movement organizations, but there does not always seem to have been agreement as to why that should be. Primarily, it was those functions considered in Chapter 2 that drove the desire to form specifically Labour (or Communist or 'Workers') choirs, bands and orchestras: socializing, fund-raising or propagating the socialist message. There was probably a good deal more of the first two than the last in all cases except the Workers' Theatre Movement combinations and possibly the London Labour Choral Union, under Bush, in its last period before transforming into the Workers' Music Association.

But there would appear to have been another motivation: to produce 'the best' music, to the best of the players' or singers' abilities. The reason given for this was always H. G. Sear's desire to show that Labour could 'hold its own' in the musical world. This clearly was deemed important by some individuals, but it would also appear that the labour movement gave some individuals the opportunity to try and realize their dreams of producing or conducting 'the best' music. Through the labour movement somebody like H. G. Sear had the resources and the access to printed media to be able to attempt to establish a full amateur symphony orchestra. Through this work being 'for the cause' (even though its connection to any benefits to Labour, or return on their investment, was at best insubstantial), members could be chastised and made to feel guilty when they fell short of 'the best'. And yet Sear, like many of his colleagues around the country, failed to make the most of this opportunity to realize his dream by making the goal too difficult and by limiting his 'catchment area' for players too greatly. Some of these combinations might have done better service for the movement and been more successful if they had employed the Clarion tactic of 'making socialists'. It is surprising that the Clarion choirs from those 'pioneering' days should have had a more practical outlook than Labour Party combinations in the mid-1920s. While the former looked to 'make socialists', along with other aims in the more familiar territory of utopian whimsy, the latter's functions were grounded on a vague notion of 'the arts' being 'a vivifying force in a movement devoted to the humanising and sweetening of life in all its aspects'.[110]

While it was these choirs and orchestras, with their musically utopian vision, that grabbed the headlines in the labour press, many other musical combinations performed to the best of their ability, raised money for the movement, provided good (if sometimes rather 'light') entertainment at 'socials' and, from time to time, assisted with propaganda activity. In the following chapter we shall consider the contribution of labour musicians to political struggle.

4

Song and Struggle

> Where you find humanity under strain, under stress in any part of the
> globe, you will find them putting it forward in song, because song is
> feeling.[1]

The inter-war years included periods of social unrest, confrontational industrial relations, struggle and the rise of fascism. A constant theme
throughout the period was unemployment; the image of hunger marchers
is strongly associated with the inter-war labour movement, as is the General Strike and the subsequent miners' lockout as well as British socialists
going to Spain to fight fascists in the Spanish Civil War. Hywel Francis,
writing specifically about Wales, referred to the 'grim and desperate
inter-war period when orthodox political activities were often seen as inadequate and ineffective'.[2]

Of course, the British working class did not experience a period of
struggle as a homogeneous group; we have already touched on the fact
that many workers experienced considerable gains in leisure time and disposable income during these decades. However, the 'grim and desperate'
characterization of the inter-war years was an accurate one for people in
certain geographical areas and working in particular industries.[3] Furthermore, some of the most enduring images of workers in struggle come
from this time; there was an aesthetic of struggle and hardship that has
been impressed upon subsequent generations. Within the socialist
analysis of many labour activists, all of the problems and crises they
were fighting against were intrinsically connected. As a writer in the
Socialist Leaguer put it in 1934, 'War, Unemployment, Poverty' – and
they would no doubt later have added Fascism – 'are the children of
Capitalism; let us plan to end the parents' rule.'[4]

Music and communities of struggle

The struggle against poverty and unemployment was a serious business,
often hard, unpleasant and dangerous; why should such activity have had

an accompaniment of music and song? While by no means questioning the seriousness of struggle or the sincerity of those struggling, such activity was often rather enjoyable in its own way. It was clearly no fun being hungry, or being locked out of work, but it *could be* engaging and enjoyable to protest against such things amongst large gatherings of comrades. The struggle made the long hours in committee meetings (or listening to bad choirs!) worth it. Struggle was what it was all about. For some of the more optimistic revolutionaries, each struggle sounded the opening bars of the revolution. The image of ascetic, earnest, cloth-capped marchers making their voices heard by sheer force of numbers and grim resolution is only part of the picture. Comedy jazz bands, humorous marching songs, fund-raising concert parties and dances were just as important aspects of the business of struggle for many in the inter-war labour movement.

The comrades did not just sing and play at the proverbial barricades because they were enjoying themselves. Long-established theories about the effects of music on crowds, and particularly on marching, had come to the movement through a variety of traditions. There was a pervasive view in pre-First World War British society that music could 'assist in building emotional bonds between individuals, bonds which would induce social harmony'.[5] A view was growing (the 'modern' view) that art should be for art's sake and this took a strong hold in the labour movement. However, the tradition of considering music as 'an object of social utility and balm for society's many evils'[6] had led to its use in many aspects of British life. Middle-class promoters of 'music for the people' from the 1840s onwards felt that 'the sacred art' could reduce drunkenness and act as 'social cement'.[7] In other words, it was felt that music could alleviate class antagonisms. Similarly, some employers used music making to help build 'corporate identity' and worker loyalty to the firm through works bands and choirs[8] as well as through sports and other pastimes that worked on the emotions.

It is not difficult to see how these views and uses of music in the nineteenth century could be re-appropriated for protest. Music could have a different 'social utility', to act as 'social cement' *within* working-class communities and to help build an identity as a union, a party or a class, and, indeed, inspire a degree of worker loyalty to such an identity. The following quotation, apparently from the Soviet composer Dmitri Shostakovich, shows that this was not a development confined to Britain: 'We, as revolutionaries, have a different concept of music. Lenin himself said: "Music is a means of unifying broad masses of people." For music has the power of stirring specific emotions. It is not a leader of masses, perhaps, but certainly an organising force . . .'[9]

There have been various studies of the use of song in political struggle, from Ian Watson's study of *Song and Democratic Culture in Britain* (1980) to Laura Mason's *Singing the French Revolution* (1996). These studies have tended to concentrate on lyrics as representations of political opinion: the public sphere for working people.[10] However, many songs that were sung or written at times of struggle were particularly (and deliberately) vague when it came to political specifics. Much of the lyrical content of the musical ephemera of struggle is close to doggerel. Music had to play a different role at such moments from a purely communicative one: it was both a planned and sometimes a spontaneous expression of solidarity. Furthermore, it was a method by which communities could be defined and delineated.

The role of music in shaping identity, including and excluding people from a defined community – developing class consciousness through 'stirring specific emotions' – is central to its role in these events. In each of the 'struggles' that we shall examine in this chapter, this central function for music is apparent. These small, localized, delineated communities, which we might call 'communities of struggle', were musically creative. While it might be argued that the most creative aspect of the community songs we shall look at was a literary creativity – new words put to old tunes was the normal practice – nevertheless it was music, not lyric, that performed this fundamental community-building role.

Having said that, it is very difficult to look at individual pieces of music that emerged in these 'communities of struggle' in terms of musical form rather than lyric. The first reason for this is the most obvious   we cannot hear what people at the time heard. Occasionally we know the familiar tunes, either because of famous recorded versions or because they are 'traditional', and so can make some comment. But even then we know little or nothing about the style or performance. Lyrics are sometimes accessible. And that very accessibility at least suggests that somebody at some point in time felt they had some value as a piece of writing to be read as well as to be sung.[11] Nevertheless, I would emphasize the point that 'songs of struggle' were significant as musical rather than literary phenomena. The most important thing was that the activists sang – *what* they sang was often secondary.

One important question that we will be examining in this chapter is: did these political and industrial struggles and the communities who fought in them develop what we might call 'cultures of struggle'? If so, what does that mean and how does it fit into existing concepts of 'culture from below', 'alternative cultures', sub-cultures, 'Second Culture' or counter-culture?

Besides struggle, one thing that united many of the people considered here was poverty. Whether it was the families of the long-term unemployed or those of workers on strike or locked out for long periods of time, what was required were 'defence mechanisms without which the poor could hardly carry on'.[12] When Oscar Lewis wrote in 1961 about a 'culture of poverty' – looking specifically at a poor family in Mexico – he stated: 'To those who think that the poor have no culture, the concept of a culture of poverty may seem like a contradiction in terms. It would also seem to give to poverty a certain dignity and status. This is not my intention.'[13] Ideas of 'cultures of poverty' have since become less contentious. Some of these ideas have been considered in relation to the poorest people in Britain (particularly with regard to 'defence mechanisms' and coping strategies) by writers such as David Vincent in *Poor Citizens* (1991) and in much of the work of the Birmingham Centre for Contemporary Cultural Studies.[14]

The 'collective' nature of day-to-day living in the South Wales coalfields during 1926 could be viewed as a 'defence mechanism' rather than as the fierce definition of a community in struggle. There is, however, an important distinction to be drawn between a 'culture of poverty' and 'cultures of struggle'. For Lewis, a 'culture of poverty' was 'a way of life, remarkably stable and persistent, passed down from generation to generation along family lines'. The 'cultures of struggle' identified here are ephemeral and localized. Furthermore, while it might not have been Oscar Lewis' intention to 'give to poverty a certain dignity and status', it is perhaps my intention to give that to 'struggle'. The most defining difference, however, is this: a 'culture of poverty' is one that looks to cope with, to live with, a crippling status quo. A 'culture of struggle', on the other hand, looks to support and bolster a sustained fight against the same. While these two 'cultures' might co-exist in a community engaged in struggle, what we are considering in this chapter is something distinct from the cultures that survive with stubborn longevity amongst the very poorest in society.

Ian Watson looked at what we might call 'protest' song as the product of a 'Second Culture' – an agitational, perhaps revolutionary, 'democratic' culture that might develop in opposition to the dominant, bourgeois culture. This concept is problematic for a variety of reasons. Firstly, it assumes that there is a homogeneous, national culture, which instils and encourages bourgeois values that most people share. Secondly it argues that a second culture, defined by its opposition to the national culture, exists for those who have developed a dissident consciousness. In fact, a study of British popular culture between the wars – even concentrating on one aspect of popular culture, music – reveals a fragmented reality with different cultural experiences resulting from geographical, social, economic and educational factors as well as simple questions of personal taste. Various scholars[15] have pointed to the inter-war years as a period of cultural homogenization where a national culture is in the process of formation. However, while there is much to be said for this thesis, British culture was still too fragmented for talk of 'two cultures' to be applicable.

As we shall see in the following chapters, aspects of popular culture such as folk and jazz music could be appropriated by a variety of political positions besides existing as mere diversion or entertainment. Agitational or propagandist art did not exist in a vacuum, isolated from other art forms; nor were political and industrial struggles free from commercial or 'bourgeois' art and music. We *can* talk of a multifaceted popular culture and a multifaceted working-class culture, and clearly any 'cultures of struggle' we find could best be seen as aspects of these cultures. But it would appear that something rather different occurred in 'communities of struggle' during 'moments of struggle' that were not permanent aspects of working-class or popular culture.

Unemployment

We shall hear more and more the music of marching feet. And when that music is heard in the land men know that great events are afoot. For it is to the tune of that music that all the great changes of the world have occurred. It is not sweet music. It does not soothe us to sleep. On the contrary it troubles the mind and stirs the pulse, and makes the heart of the weak faint.

To those who suffer, to the poor and the lonely, to those without influence, who have not the ear of the great ones of the earth, the music of the marching feet of their own people brings hope and courage and a surge of boundless strength.

In the Hunger March of 1936 we hear the opening chords of the music. It will not die away until the workers win the victory.[16]

While Nye Bevan employed the imagery of music to describe the hunger marchers of the later 1930s, his intention was to emphasize the earnest resolution of the marchers, the lack of pomp and noisy bands. While that was the aesthetic of the 1936 hunger march, it came on the back of a much more musical inter-war tradition.

Recreation for the unemployed

Unemployment was a serious problem throughout the inter-war years. In 1929 there were 1.1 million unemployed in the UK (just under 10 per cent). By 1932 this had risen to just under 3 million (20 per cent). As an illustration of this problem's bearing on the labour movement, in 1930 a third of the members of the Communist Party were out of work.[17] It posed a particularly thorny dilemma for the labour movement, especially the trade unions. Unemployment brought down wages and swung the industrial balance of power in the direction of the employers. Moreover, many potential schemes for relieving unemployment veered in the dangerous direction of non-unionized, underpaid work. Trade union practicalities, humanitarian concerns and socialist theories found themselves in potential (and occasionally actual) conflict over this issue. Compromises had to be found: the unemployed had to do something, life as an unemployed person had to become more bearable, economic policies capable of reducing unemployment had to be introduced, but this all had to be attained at little or no expense to employed workers. The best options, therefore, were deemed to be leisure activities and protests.

Most of the attempts to organize the unemployed into clubs – whether of a recreational or an occupational nature – were not carried out by trade unionists or other sections of the labour movement. Instead the task had 'fallen almost entirely into the hands of middle class people quite ignorant of, if not hostile to, the labour movement and trade union tradition'.[18] The Trades Union Congress (TUC) estimated that 50,000 men were passing through such clubs in the early 1930s, and it was determined to take a more central role. Having said that, the organizing success of the communists in the National Unemployed Workers Movement (NUWM) may have been as much of a spurring influence as the concern over middle-class clubs. There was a considerable degree of conflict between the 'official' labour movement's efforts to alleviate the unemployment problem (characterized by Labour Party and TUC co-ordinated schemes) and the 'unofficial' movement's activities, characterized by the communist-led NUWM. The official labour movement did, rather belatedly, become more involved in the unemployment 'problem', especially through the 1930s, but it still had to rectify the primary contradiction that existed between finding work for the unemployed and protecting the jobs and wages of employed workers.

Consequently, many of the activities and camps provided for the unemployed, particularly the huge numbers of unemployed in the 1930s, were centred on leisure. The Oxford University and Trade Union holiday camp that was held in July and August of 1935 promised the unemployed a 'complete holiday' with plays, social events and sports.[19] Where occupations were found for the unemployed, they were always of a kind that would interfere as little as possible with the local unionized labour force. The Bradford Unemployment Advisory Committee (under the auspices of the TUC) noted in its annual report for 1933–4 that work schemes had largely been 'land cultivation' (working allotments) and jam making.[20] They preferred to concentrate on the successful run of concerts that had been provided for the unemployed, including a performance by the internationally famous vocal and piano duo Layton and Johnstone. These 'successful American stars', who performed with one seated at the piano and the other standing with a hand on it, were in Bradford performing at the Alhambra Theatre at the time.[21]

The TUC's Voluntary Schemes for the Unemployed became quite an important part of its activities in the 1930s. The schemes included 'singly or in combination' recreational camps, educational courses, musical, dramatic and other artistic activities, sports and physical exercise. Various societies and organizations donated money and resources to the schemes, including the English Folk Dance and Song Society, and oddly, the Eugenics Society.[22] Once the local Unemployment Associations had been established, the TUC was not always able to give much central assistance. The Lowestoft Unemployment Association wanted to set up a brass band in 1933, which it felt would 'prove a great asset'.[23] It wrote to the TUC Organization Department asking for assistance in acquiring free brass instruments. It was instructed to purchase a very small number of second-hand instruments with its own funds, and hope for expansion.[24] Setting up choirs and orchestras was regularly considered to be a useful activity for unemployment schemes and associations. Sometimes local Trades Council schemes, in order to gain as much local support as possible, would make much of being 'non-political'.[25]

Unemployment protests

The TUC and the Labour Party also organized mass protests against unemployment and these were never regarded as 'non-political'. Such events often took place in London and were organized along the same lines as the metropolitan May Day demonstrations. These jointly organized occasions were repeated in major provincial capitals such as Glasgow and Leeds, but the 'national' protests were held at Hyde Park. On 5 February 1933, a large demonstration was expected in London and the Commissioner of Police made various stipulations about the nature of banners and distribution of literature at the event, insisting that banners should be 'of such a nature that they cannot be used as weapons'.[26] There was a considerable degree of preparation for the event, including advertisements in cinemas 'from Ramsgate to Glasgow', promotional stamps, and daily articles and advertisements in the *Daily Herald* for a month beforehand. Each marching contingent of the protest, coming from various parts of London and converging on Hyde Park, was to be led by a band.[27]

The various reports in the following morning's newspapers agreed that there were approximately 250,000 protestors present, although there was disagreement as to how many were taking part and how many were 'onlookers'.[28] While many concentrated on the large number of policemen present (15,000 according to the *Daily Express*),[29] who were in such large numbers owing to fears of 'undesirable visitors from Ireland',[30] the Tory and Liberal press were left with having to make rather petty criticisms of the event. These included criticisms of the musical aspect of the proceedings. The *Express* ridiculed George Lansbury as 'cheer-leader, community singing conductor, soloist and chief speaker all in one'. The 'soloist' jibe referred to how: 'He sang verse after verse of the "Red Flag" with no support outside the small circle of supporters grouped around him on a horse-drawn cart. His attempt to start community singing of the "Internationale" was an equally dismal failure.'[31] However, there are certain problems with this picture. Firstly, the 'small circle of supporters' does not ring true, whether there were 250,000 or 30,000 demonstrators; secondly, the suggestion was that the crowd did not know the words, yet the official programme of the event included the words for 'England, Arise!', 'The Red Flag' and 'The March of the Workers'.[32] Finally, although the *Daily Herald* referred to the demonstrators' 'resolute quiet', it is likely that any problems stemmed more from the limitations of the available amplification equipment in cutting through such a large crowd than from any lack of enthusiasm on their part.

There was, though, a good deal of self-criticism about the musical aspect of the demonstration. After the bands arrived in Hyde Park at the head of the marching contingents, they dispersed and the anthems had to be sung unaccompanied. Furthermore, there was a lengthy period between the first marchers arriving in the park and the start of the meeting. It was felt that it would be more sensible for the bands to stay and play in future, although the same concerns had been expressed about May Day celebrations throughout the country for some years without the problem being rectified. There were also unspecific criticisms of the quality of marching tunes and songs.[33] The point to stress is that the musical aspect of the event was taken very seriously. The bands and the anthems could make an event a roaring success that raised the spirits of the demonstrators and united them in their cause, or else it could be a demoralizing influence that sapped much of their enthusiasm.

The activities of the National Unemployed Workers Movement dwarfed the efforts of the official labour movement in protesting against unemployment, although there was a degree of local interdependence between the official and unofficial parts of the movement. The NUWM was founded in 1920 and the first major march of the unemployed took place in that year.[34] All such marches, throughout the 1920s, were characterized by cheering and singing, rather than the grimness of some later hunger marches. As with the demonstrations of the 'official' movement, bands and banners headed contingents of marchers, but these were often more improvised than their equivalents in the well-funded Labour Party and TUC events. The TUC severed links with the NUWM in 1927,[35] and the Labour Party and the TUC also declared it a proscribed organization.[36]

Earlier in the 1920s, the NUWM (or the National Unemployed Workers Committee, as it was then known) worked together with the TUC and local Trades Councils to organize demonstrations, such as a rally at the Bull Ring in Birmingham on 'Unemployment Sunday', 21 June 1925, with the local Irish Pipers' Band providing the musical entertainment.[37] However, fears that the NUWM could act as a 'front' for Communist Party recruitment and activity within the Labour Party led to their estrangement. It had no discernible effect on the success of the movement, however, which went from strength to strength and received plenty of Labour Party and trade union support on an unofficial basis.

One regular NUWM activity was the 'raiding' of workhouses. As a result of an organized raid, the targeted workhouse would become grossly over-subscribed, it would be cleared out of food and the insufficiency of its provisions would be highlighted. The primary tool for politicizing the workhouse experience for the inmates was the singing of socialist anthems ('The Red Flag' and 'The Internationale' were frequent favourites).[38] The same anthems were put to similar use when the NUWM raided factories that paid low wages yet offered overtime.[39] Wal Hannington's memoirs of the period are regularly punctuated with the mass singing of 'The Internationale' and 'The Red Flag' despite the many songs that were specifically written for unemployment protests. When he, Harry Pollitt and others were in prison in 1926, he recalled regular demonstrations in Wandsworth where they could hear the singing of 'The Red Flag' and 'The Internationale' from their cells.[40] One of the 1934 marchers, Thomas Gregory, recalled, 'I'd never sung "The International" before, before I went on the Hunger March', despite having been active in the Labour Party League of Youth before that time.[41] The use of general labour anthems at unemployment demonstrations was an important aspect of the NUWM's approach to the problem.

The essential principle of the NUWM, which looked to unite large numbers behind the cause of the unemployed, was that workers were workers whether they were in work or not. Unemployment was a social evil that affected the working class as a class and not just those sections of it who were currently out of work. The cultural aspects of the movement looked to reflect and cement this proletarianization of the unemployment problem. The NUWM was very active during strikes and lockouts, eager to assist employed comrades as part of its overall aim to 'proletarianize' the unemployed movement.[42] The same aim also led the NUWM to exclude the middle class from participation in unemployment protests. When the NUWM marched down Oxford Street, 'well-to-do shoppers . . . looked in vain for collecting boxes in which to drop small contributions for charity. They heard instead the singing of workers' battle-songs, particularly the "International" and the "Red Flag", and they saw . . . militant slogans.'[43] This image is in sharp contrast with Robert Tressell's depiction of an unemployed protest march from earlier in the century, in *The Ragged Trousered Philanthropists* (first published in 1914), where the humiliated and degraded unemployed marchers beg for charitable contributions.

> Haggard and pale, shabbily or raggedly dressed, their boots broken and down at heel, they slouched past. Some of them stared about with a dazed or half-wild expression, but most of them walked with downcast eyes or staring blankly straight in front of them. They appeared utterly broken-spirited, hopeless and ashamed . . .[44]

The new self-confidence was clearly part of the process of creating an independent, alternative culture, but singing performed an inclusive role as well as the aforementioned exclusive one. The use of the anthems of the labour movement helped the NUWM forge links, even if only for a short time, with non-communist parts of the movement – indeed, with the 'establishment', if one can describe any section of the labour movement in the early 1920s as such. When 150 unemployed protestors came to lobby their MPs and vocally protested in the Commons' lobby, they 'commenced lustily singing the "Red Flag"' and 'several Labour Members who were in the lobby at the time joined in the singing'.[45]

A large number of songs were composed during the hunger marches and unemployment demonstrations. Many of them were designed to aid marching, and they were not always written to a high lyrical standard. At the less musical and lyrical end were the ephemeral marching chants:

> One, two, three four. Who are we for?
> We are for the working class. DOWN with the ruling class.
> Mary had a little lamb whose fleece was white as snow,
> Shouting the battle-cry of TREASON.[46]

At the other end of the scale were some quite complex songs with several verses, and sometimes with newly composed tunes. These brand new songs were 'not only sung on the road, but in the big halls, at the demonstrations and at impromptu concerts. They always received an enthusiastic response from the workers and many times the local workers learned the words and sang the songs with the marchers.'[47] The idea that these songs should appeal to employed workers was very important to the NUWM project, and it was clearly important to Hannington in his recollections of the marches. Sometimes the songs were quite specifically intended for such an audience. At other times, the lyrics were merely playful nonsense. A student at an NUWM camp in 1935 wrote a song about Harry Pollitt entitled 'Harry Was a Bolshie'. In the song, Pollitt is murdered by 'reactionary cads'. After this unfortunate incident, he plays 'The Internationale' on his harp and 'brings the angels out on strike since he does not like the hymns'. In the end he becomes the 'people's commissar' in Hell!

> The moral of this story is very plain to tell:
> If you want to be a Communist you'll have to go to hell!

There were other songs that became popular during these events. 'Hallelujah, I'm a Bum' was an International Workers of the World song from 1908, but it became popular in the British unemployment movement in the 1930s.[48] While some songs were ephemera – composed for a specific march and then discarded – others were collected in song books and became part of the movement's treasury of verse. Similarly, while the marchers wrote some of the songs themselves, others were provided by professional composers such as Alan Bush (some included in his *Left Song Book* and discussed in Chapter 5). Thomas Gregory recalled singing 'Red Army songs, translated into English to Soviet music' on the 1934 and 1936 hunger marches. When asked to give an example of what they sang on the marches, he broke into an Irish republican song, Connolly's 'Rebel Song',[49] which was a favourite marching song in the Spanish Civil War amongst the International Brigade.[50] He described the hunger marches as 'a wonderful taste of what I'd got to come later on, in Spain'.[51] It is interesting that two such different activities – participating in a protest march and fighting in a war – should be so firmly entwined in the memory. What rendered those experiences similar was the hardship and the marching, yes; but more particularly it was the music.

Strikes and lockouts

The inter-war period, particularly the 1920s, was characterized not only by unemployment, but also by confrontational industrial relations.[52] Strikes provided the movement's song-writers with much inspiration, and music also played an important part in raising funds and building morale. There was already a British tradition of music during strike action: songs 'often quite spontaneously composed and ephemeral' emerged from the railway strikes of 1879–80 and 1886–7 and the Great Dock Strike of 1889.[53] However, music played a much more central role during some industrial action between the wars. Ian Watson used the example of the Rego strike of 1928, where 600 women clothing workers in London won their battle after a twelve-week unofficial stoppage. Song was not only a 'powerful agitational weapon' for them, but played 'a central role in the whole affair'. They became known as the 'singing strikers' and eventually collaborated on a book of 'strike songs' with 700 striking workers at the Polikoff clothing factory in 1929.[54] The author of the book remarked that 'it might be said that, combined with their militant leadership, the strikers sang themselves to victory'.[55]

Songs composed by workers on strike would regularly use heroic language to relate the story, often in ballad form. The striking clerical workers in Lurgan, Ulster, in 1920 sang the following lyrics to the tune of 'The Mountains of Mourne':

> Oh Mary this Lurgan's a wonderful sight,
> With the pickets by day and the meetings by night;
> For the Clerks are on strike and I've heard people say
> That they're fighting for principles rather than pay . . .[56]

Similarly, the story of the 1920 railway workers' strike began:

> When the call came up from London
> 'Ev'ry man must leave his post',
> We responded to the signal,
> Irrespective of the cost . . .[57]

One role of these songs was strongly to delineate the community of strikers and underline their identity. As one would expect, this involved fierce condemnations of strike-breakers. The *Clerk* (the monthly organ of the Clerical and Administrative Workers' Union) decided to omit the name of the strike-breaker's family from the published version of 'The Mountains of Mourne', but one can be sure that the singing strikers would have been less squeamish:

> You remember the _____ who made ginger beer,
> Well there's one of the family disgracing them here.
> Sure he used to be foremost in every debate,
> And his motto was: 'forward, or else you'll be late'.
> But he altered his sermon when offered a bribe
> And with five or six more of as shady a tribe,
> He has sold himself cheap, and he'll never be free
> While the Mountains of Mourne sweep down to the sea.

The railway strikers' song was even stronger in its condemnation:

> ... One or two notorious atoms
> Played the scurvy, grovelling game,
> They are welcome to the glory
> Likewise welcome to the shame,
> All their lives they will encounter
> Cold disdain on every turn;
> To the dust they'll pass unhonoured,
> Their demise, not one shall mourn.

The song from Lurgan sparked off some debate within the pages of the *Clerk* about song writing in the union. The editor asked, 'who writes songs for the National Union of Clerks and Administrative Workers? . . . apart from the Strike war-cries, such as the Lurgan efforts and the variant of "Fight the Good Fight" which the Scunthorpe lads produced, I have heard of not even an attempt to do this great thing.' His plea fell on deaf ears. The cultural production that these songs represent grew out of the existence of a nascent alternative culture. This, in its turn, would appear to have required struggle in order for it to begin to be formed, and to be sustained. The songs originated during a time when life was extraordinary, and it was the abnormality of periods of struggle that would appear to have made them so rich in counter-culture. In 1926, some areas of Britain were to experience this abnormality for longer than at any other time during the period.

1926

During the strikes and lockouts of that distressed year, the mining communities (and particularly their local labour movements) dispatched choirs and concert parties to various cities to raise funds. Nye Bevan and the Tredegar Miners' Relief Committee, for instance, sent two choirs around the country to raise money for strike pay during the lockout of 1926 as well as running free concerts in the Workmen's Institute and arranging a jazz band and sports contests.[58] In the South Wales pit communities, an 'alternative' culture grew up during this period of distress and struggle which presented itself in numerous ways, but none so new and bizarre as the comic jazz bands and their carnivals that were ever-present that summer.[59] This embryonic 'second culture' was fiercely co-operative, involving communal kitchens, co-operatives to repair boots and shoes, and these 'gazooka' bands.[60] Some of this alternative culture had its roots both in earlier struggles, such as the 1921 lockout, and in the important influence of the Miners' Federation, the various socialist political parties and the Chapel. At the same time, there was conflict between aspects of this new culture and aspects of the long-established South Wales culture: specifically, between the Chapel and the bands. Hywel Francis and David Smith refer to this conflict in *The Fed* (1980), quoting an Aberdare Methodist who described the bands as 'vulgar', 'immoral' and 'blasphemous'.[61]

These bands of locked-out miners were essentially escapist and comic in their repertoires, relying heavily on the 'kazoo'[62] for instrumentation; their role in the struggle was primarily one of building morale and raising funds. They provide perhaps the starkest contrast with the grimness of protest in the later 1930s: ten years on, struggle was beginning to lose some of its excitement and novelty, and was simply becoming a way of life for many. The hopefulness that fuelled the humour of the bands of 1926[63] subsided as the enemies grew: unemployment, the means test, fascists at home and abroad all combined to exorcise the spirit of frivolity from the business of struggle.

The city of Birmingham's labour movement played host to a succession of touring choirs in 1926 and gave a longer home to one Welsh choir, the Apollo Concert Party. Although it was unusual for a fund-raising choir to stay in one place, the Apollo Choir declared that it would stay 'in Birmingham for as long as this struggle lasts if the people still desire to listen to us, and are able to contribute to the cause which we represent'. The choir was sent to Birmingham by its local Distress Fund Committee in Monmouth, South Wales, in order to raise funds 'for the miners and their children'. Even before the crisis, the choir had been performing without fee to raise money for disabled miners and other causes. It included members who had won 'many Eisteddfod prizes' and its musical director was an Associate of the London College of Music. Although the Apollo Concert Party was much smaller than the traditional Welsh Male. Voice Choir (a photograph in the *Town Crier* showed ten men of varying ages),[64] parts of its repertoire were quite traditional ('Comrades in Arms', 'Soldiers' Chorus',[65] 'Land of My Fathers',[66] etc.)

Much was made in the local labour paper (the *Town Crier*) of the high musical quality of the Apollo Choir's singers as well as their authenticity as 'singing miners'. It was described how, before the strike, they would change from their pit clothes to go to the rehearsal rooms 'after toiling in the mines for seven hours'.[67] When reporting on one of the choir's concerts, at the Birmingham Central Hall, the reviewer remarked that a 'sceptical individual surveying the row of immaculately dressed artistes' had queried, 'are they really miners?'[68] The editor of the *Town Crier* remarked that 'while they are singing one feels that they are putting their very souls into their songs because of the ever-present picture of the women and kiddies whose sustenance depends on their efforts'.[69]

The *Town Crier* regularly published the amount of money that the Apollo Choir had raised during its stay. By October 1926 it had raised £1,000,[70] an impressive effort by ten men since the end of May.[71] On raising £1,000, the choir returned home only to be sent back to Birmingham by the South Wales Miners' Federation as 'the need for funds was as urgent as ever'.[72] Even when the choir was planning to leave, its leader 'Chandos' (the 'manager and elocutionist of the Apollo Concert Party') was advertising in the *Town Crier* as a tutor of 'voice production, elocution and public speaking' as well as offering himself for concert and 'At Home' engagements on 'moderate' terms.[73] Despite the circumstances under which he arrived in Birmingham, 'Chandos' was to become a regular feature of Labour Party and Labour Church concerts and social events long after the rest of the choir had eventually returned to home and work – or sadly for many, no doubt, home and unemployment.

This was just one way in which these imported musical influences changed the musical culture of the local labour movement: the Smethwick Choir discussed in Chapter 3 was undoubtedly influenced in its repertoire by the long association with the Apollo Concert Party. As in Birmingham, Bradford received a popular visit from a Welsh miners' choir that raised lots of money for the distress committees at home. It moved on from Bradford to Scarborough after a much shorter stay than that of the Apollo in Birmingham, clearly recognizing the fund-raising potential of the resort's holiday-makers.[74]

Some of the touring musical combinations from mining districts went overseas in 1926. The Blaina Cymru Concert Party toured the Soviet Union, often with a more political repertoire than was employed by groups touring Britain. It concluded its evening with the Leningrad Trade Unions with a rendition of 'The Internationale'.[75]

During the General Strike, the *Official Strike Bulletin* in Bradford urged people – especially various women's and youth groups – to organize concerts, games and lectures, amongst other activities, so that 'time need not hang heavily'.[76] During the lockout, outside the mining communities, the labour movement held fund-raising social events, such as dances and concerts, to raise money for the miners' distress fund.[77]

The hope that 'time need not hang heavily' during stoppages was clearly an important factor in the singing and musicianship of strikers. Furthermore, the keen need for funds was the foremost goal in the work of choirs and bands at these times. But neither the pursuit of entertainment nor the need for funds tells the whole story. As we saw with the struggles of the unemployed, the fight required the solidarity-building, community-delineating powers of music, and it also produced the extraordinary conditions where people looked to build their own cultures.

The fight against fascism

British fascism was a small and relatively unimportant part of British political life before the bizarre career of Sir Oswald Mosley found itself taking that direction. Mosley formed the British Union of Fascists (BUF) in 1932,[78] and received considerable support in some sections of the press. Despite this popular championing and the support they received, particularly from the middle class, but also in some working-class areas, they remained very much a minority force in British politics, albeit a decidedly vocal and violent minority. On 9 September 1934 the BUF held a demonstration in Hyde Park, the story of which illustrates their lack of support. Anti-fascists, led by the Communist Party and the ILP, held a counter-demonstration in the park that according to the *Manchester Guardian* outnumbered the BUF by 20 to 1. When one adds to this that the counter-demonstration was not supported by the Labour Party or the TUC, the BUF's lack of mass support – even in London, where it was probably at its strongest – is quite apparent. The fascists had their own songs, often with a certain mocking similarity to the style of labour anthems, but – in Britain, at least – they did not have enough voices to drown out the songs of labour. Much of the anti-fascist activity of the British labour movement was in the direction of international politics as the serious threat of fascism grew in Europe.

The Spanish Civil War

An important opportunity to fight fascism was to go to fight in the Spanish Civil War. This crisis began in July 1936 when there was a right-wing military revolt against Spain's Popular Front government.[79] Large numbers of socialists from various countries including Britain signed up as volunteers to defend the Spanish workers, and the Spanish Republic, from fascism. Over the following years socialists, anarchists and others from a variety of cultural backgrounds were thrown together (and at times against each other), and the 'international language' of music became an important communicative tool. Veterans recalled how people from different countries taught each other their own songs. Sergeant Bernard McKenna of the International Brigade spoke of the universality of song: 'Even if we didn't, perhaps, understand the words, we'd make our own version . . . [we'd] share the same feelings, the same emotion and get the same impact, the same comfort from it, maybe.'[80]

This experience was not that of all British Spanish Civil War veterans. Laurie Lee wrote in his autobiographical *A Moment of War* (1991):

> In this special army I'd imagined a shoulder-to-shoulder brotherhood, a brave camaraderie joined in one purpose, not this fragmentation of national groups scattered across the courtyard talking wanly only to each other. Indeed, they seemed to share a mutual air of unease and watchfulness, of distrust and even dislike.[81]

His recollections of people from different countries sharing literary and musical items betrays a certain kind of camaraderie, but one less idealistic than is more usually portrayed: 'As we drank the hot sour wine Sasha recited some poems of Mayakovsky, and Ben said they sounded better in Yiddish. While they quarrelled, Danny sang some old music-hall songs in a cheerless adenoidal whine, till Doug covered his head with a blanket.'[82]

That people occasionally retreated into national groups (and national songs) was not always presented in a negative light. While this war and these soldiers were extraordinary in their very political nature and motivation, they were still groups of mostly young men, far from home and loved ones, in circumstances of extreme difficulty and deprivation. 'There was always a place for the songs we'd learned at home when we were young.' Groups of Irish soldiers were heard to sing 'I'll take you home again, Kathleen' and 'Tipperary'. 'Nelly Dean' could be rendered with feeling by homesick Brigaders. One veteran recalled seeing Italian Brigaders (known as 'the Garibaldis') 'singing excerpts from opera' as they were firing in one battle. Many of the familiar uplifting marching songs popularized during the First World War were employed on the march, such as 'The Quartermaster Stores'.[83] At other times, political songs were used for marching. A recording made at the front of one marching song (an old trade union anthem, 'Hold the Fort for We Are Coming', accompanied by a recorder and some spoons) shows that there were some strong singers in the ranks, improvising harmonies with apparent ease.[84]

The role of political marching music has passed into International Brigade legend. One commanding officer recalled how a particular group of soldiers were beginning to flag and an Irish Republican, Private Ryan, got them back into step by singing 'The Internationale' and in turn stopped Madrid from falling at that point in the war. He asserted, 'that song, in my opinion, played a really crucial part'. Even Laurie Lee, who was hardly sentimental about the war, recalled the marching songs with some sentiment, and even idealism in interview: 'We, being rather isolated in our various fronts, in Spain, were the last to sing. But we didn't sing the glories of war, we sang to keep our spirits up.'[85]

As with strikes and protests, these events engendered numerous songs. Together with other areas that we have been examining, the dominant mode of song writing was putting new words to familiar tunes. There were a number of reasons why this should be the case in this context. Firstly, lyrics in various languages could be written to the same tunes so that large numbers of people of different nationalities could sing together – one of the benefits of a song like 'The Internationale'. Furthermore, although there were occasions where people could sing solos to their comrades, perhaps of their own composition, music was much more likely to be used as a communal activity, making the familiarity of tunes a necessity with or without the language barrier. Some of the songs that originated from the war were quite 'folkloric' in genre[86] and later entered the repertoires of some political, post-war folk singers.

While in Spain, members of the International Brigade and other bodies, including international volunteers, would hold concerts from time to time. The international aspect of such concerts was obvious. On May Day 1938, an International Brigade series of concerts in a prison camp included a choir made up of 36 nationalities and, in a competition, a small Welsh male voice choir won the second prize (singing songs like 'Men of Harlech') against twelve other national choirs. The prize was a pack of twenty cigarettes.[87] The choirs continued to perform at the prison camps in Spain, right into 1939. Morien Morgan was one of the last English-speaking prisoners left in the San Pedro prisoner-of-war camp, and on 8 January he wrote to his brother, Glyn:

> On Christmas Day we had a big concert. Also on New Year's Day and last night. The curtains and decorations were both striking and bizarre. Today's concert was by far the best we have had in this series. The International Choir reigns supreme . . . The room resounded to the cheering after each song.[88]

The experience of British volunteers in the Spanish Civil War had a profound effect on various aspects of the labour movement, including its musical side. The Clarion Singers, formed in Birmingham in 1939, were directly influenced by the experiences of some of the choir's founders in Spain.[89] They had been impressed by 'the way in which the Spanish people had used music as a weapon in every aspect of the struggle. The soldiers, the workers, the peasants and the children had fought with a song on their lips.'[90] Although a labour movement choir in Birmingham was nothing new, this represented a considerable change from earlier forms.

A choir that looked to use music as a 'weapon' in the 'struggle', in the place of the 'musical philanthropy' of the old Birmingham Musical and Dramatic Union, was characteristic of changes in socialist attitudes to music more generally, as we shall see in later chapters. It would appear that the experience of struggle was an important factor in these changes.

Conclusions

Two extraordinary features of life in certain communities for short periods of time in the inter-war period – struggle and poverty – combined to form localized, sometimes extraordinary working-class cultures. That these cultures could sometimes be jolly, comic and carnivalesque raises questions of culture, class and even psychology that can only begin to be considered here. The socially, economically and geographically determined nature of these short-lived cultures of struggle in the 1920s is what makes them so interesting, and similar cultural change can be identified in other lengthy strikes both in this period and at other times. They share certain characteristics with Ian Watson's concept of a Second Culture.

We have already looked at how inter-war popular culture was too fragmented and heterogeneous for the language of 'two cultures' really to be appropriate. However, one important aspect of this complex, fragmented cultural scene was the ephemeral, community-based culture of struggle that we have considered in this chapter. If neither 'second culture' nor 'alternative culture' seems like quite the right description of this phenomenon, neither does 'sub-culture'. In lieu of more appropriate terminology, 'cultures of struggle' may have to suffice.

One aspect of these independent, isolated, 'alternative' cultures of struggle that we have identified, which represents their cohesion and delineation, is the way in which ceremonies – particularly the burial and memorial of the dead – were carried out. A huge crowd of mourning hunger marchers from disparate parts of the country, united by their struggle against unemployment, sang labour anthems as a dead comrade was transported away from them by train, and others performed a similar ceremony at this same marcher's burial, in 1922.[91] In 1939, Birmingham mourned its five dead International Brigade volunteers at a meeting in the town hall with Señorita Isabelita Alonzi singing Spanish songs.[92]

Although there was always a 'labour' aspect to the funerals and memorials of long-standing activists in this period, there was not the extraordinarily fierce communal definition of otherness that was displayed at these times of struggle. A long-standing activist dying of natural causes under conditions of normality would be mourned as a labour activist, yes, but also perhaps as a local worthy, a member of a family, a church parishioner and a member of a local community. But during these short, extraordinary times, people were first and foremost hunger marchers, strikers, locked-out miners or International Brigaders – not only in death (which was, after all, the supreme sacrifice),[93] but in all aspects of life. This is particularly interesting when one considers the strong but largely vain efforts of Labour Churches and Socialist Sunday Schools to replace Church and State in the lives of socialists. The Socialist Sunday School hymn books included songs for funerals, weddings and 'naming services'. At times of struggle, agitational, counter-hegemonic cultures were quite easily built – they could often build themselves without the need for shaping by morally anxious intellectuals. But they required abnormality to prosper: what was strong and fundamentally important to a worker who first and foremost defined him or herself by struggle could once again appear odd and sectarian when political activism had returned to equal or lesser status amongst a myriad of identities and pursuits.

But what of song as a communicative tool: lyric as a literary representation of political opinion? Hannington referred to marchers who sang 'The Red Flag' 'meaning every word', and while songs seldom attempted analysis or explanation, lyrics often expressed a stark, clear message. While this consideration of the place of music in protest and struggle between the wars shows that it is too limited a task to consider songs of struggle as simply *text*, it would be wrong to underplay the importance of the lyrical content of the songs to the singers. While music played an extraordinarily important role in building a community of struggle and strengthening the bonds within that community, songs were also meant for those outside as items of propaganda.

Another influence on music making during these events was the business of myth making, legend telling and hero worship: these were great deeds that deserved to be set down in song. Such a function of song writing had a long tradition in the Irish Nationalist/Republican movement and it is clear that there was a direct influence from Ireland when one considers British labour's adoption of many Irish rebel songs amongst its repertoire. It is interesting that labour anthems were often referred to as 'Rebel Songs', as George Lansbury did in his foreword to the *Lansbury's Labour Weekly* song book.

It was sometimes said that 'English socialists sing in chorus as raggedly as they march in procession',[94] and there is often a suggestion of raggedness and disorganization in the reports and recollections of inter-war struggle. Whether it be that image of George Lansbury singing a faltering solo of most of 'The Red Flag', or the damp squib endings of many large protest meetings as crowds dispersed, the labour movement in protest would not always appear to have been a well-oiled, professional campaigning machine. Having said that, there were many occasions where the labour movement really did display its strength in mass assembly, and the bands and the raucous singing were no doubt important aspects of that.

What remains to be considered is the ideological justification for the selected genres and nature of the music used both in the everyday life of the labour movement and at these moments of crisis. In the remaining chapters we must bring our focus back to those essential questions about the music itself: what was 'the best', who did it belong to and how could socialists cope with or adapt to popular tastes?

5

The Best Music Available

We have noted a wide range of music used in the everyday life of labour associations, performed by labour musical combinations, at rallies and open-air demonstrations and during strikes and campaigns. However, when socialists wrote about music in this period, they frequently restricted their considerations to 'serious' 'art' music. We must attempt to consider this preoccupation in the light of some of the main tensions or debates that we have identified in the musical life of the movement. One such tension was 'the best music available' versus 'a music of their own'. In other words, should the working class (and particularly those who were socialist) listen to and appreciate 'great' 'art' music, or should they create or enjoy specifically working-class or socialist music, or that which was deemed to be so? Within both of these camps a further debate existed between those who were interested in establishing some kind of labour or socialist aesthetic theory and those for whom music was primarily a *pleasurable* activity.

The labour movement and classical/'art' music

There is no ideal description for what we now tend to give the rather limited title of 'classical music'. Throughout this chapter I shall use words that prefaced contemporary references to this music, all of them problematic: 'serious', 'great', 'art' and 'high-brow'. Between the wars, people essentially talked about *music* and it was the 'jazz', 'popular' or 'comic' 'musics' that were labelled. Probably the most useful academic description of the music we are dealing with in this chapter is 'Western art music', although even this has problematic implications for popular forms of music.

Many of those who particularly promoted Western art music in the labour movement certainly enjoyed it and wished to encourage the enjoyment of it. However, they also wished to encourage discrimination amongst socialists, so that they would cease to enjoy so much 'bad' music – whether that be music-hall songs, 'jazz', dance hits or whatever. In other words, there was an element within those who pushed for 'the best music available' who were essentially philanthropists looking to alleviate what they considered to be cultural poverty.

Musical philanthropy

There is no doubt that material poverty limited the opportunities for many members of society to enjoy the same accessibility to high culture and great art as the wealthy and leisured. Not only the financial cost of attending operas, professional concerts and plays accounted for this, but also the amount of time that one could devote to the pursuance of art. One needed both the free time to attend events (or read books, or play music at home) and also the time to devote necessary study to develop one's critical faculties or talents. Clearly the limited access to education beyond the elementary level for working-class people in this period was a huge factor in this inequality as well. Although the preoccupation of socialists with high culture and disdain for some popular cultural forms can easily be portrayed as elitist or conservative, there was, at least, an egalitarian logic behind some of the positions taken. In so far as one could say that this constituted a 'project', its flavour was philanthropic rather than socialist or labourist because it was essentially the work of members of an educated elite – the culturally wealthy – volunteering something of their wealth to the deserving poor.

The first aspect of musical philanthropy that we shall consider was the teaching of appreciation and discrimination, carried out primarily through newspaper columns and lectures. The presence of music columns in labour newspapers was highlighted as a particular selling point. The *Daily Herald*'s advertisements in 1925 made particular mention of 'Music Notes by Rutland Boughton' and 'Gramophone Notes'. However, it also pointed out the presence of a sports page and the purpose might have been as much to do with reassuring potential readers that the paper was not exclusively political (containing general interest features, one by a famous composer) than necessarily demonstrating enthusiasm for a musical philanthropic agenda. As Chris Waters describes in *British Socialists and the Politics of Popular Culture, 1884–1914*, pre-war socialist publications had music columns, and lectures on music were common at various labour movement events. Waters gives the example of Georgia Pearce in the *Clarion*, who often mystified readers with technicalities and sometimes received letters from readers who imagined that they should like the music she wrote about, if only they had heard it. The tone of such discourse appeared to change in the inter-war period towards one that was more open and populist and looked to encourage participation. This was assisted by technological advances and the increased opportunities for readers and audiences to hear 'classical' music.

The music columns of local and national labour publications were dominated by the lives and works of the 'great composers'. One popular music columnist was Harold George Sear. As 'H. G. Sear' he wrote the music column for the *Town Crier* in Birmingham, and had the same column included in other local labour publications such as the *Bradford Pioneer*. As 'H.G.S.' he also wrote a column for the *Daily Herald*. As we saw in Chapter 3, one of Sear's main contributions to the life of his local labour movement (in Birmingham) was as the conductor of the Birmingham Labour Symphony Orchestra. Although he was not a professional musician or journalist (the 1927 *Labour's Who's Who* lists his occupation as 'chemist'), he was no musical novice. He was the secretary of the Birmingham New Philharmonic Society from 1916 to 1920, secretary of the Birmingham Centre section of the British Music Society and a lecturer on all matters musical on radio and in various forums, both labour and non-labour, including schools.[1] He was clearly part of the local musical elite. This connection was, no doubt, of some benefit to the labour movement, such as when he was able to secure scores and other facilities for the Labour Orchestra. While his musical *curriculum vitae* gave him authority to speak and write at length on his subject, it also adds to the suspicion that his tone was occasionally somewhat condescending.

When the Birmingham *Town Crier* was first issued, its music writer (J.S.) wrote only for the already converted, appraising concerts that the majority of readers would not have heard, and comparing them with other performances of which readers were even less likely to be aware. He made statements about composers and their works that could only be of interest to the most musical of readers. As a brief example of his style, there follows an extract from a review of a piano concert in Birmingham: 'In playing the item of Chopin's Bursoni shows nearly the same lack as Mark Hambourg when the latter attempts to play Chopin, but without his elfish caprice. One felt the treatment was too noble and regular to be in keeping with the uneasy spirit of the composer.'[2]

When H. G. Sear began his series of articles, 'The men behind the music' in the *Town Crier* in 1925, a very different approach was taken. Rather than assuming considerable musical knowledge, Sear assumed none, although he made it clear that he possessed the knowledge himself. He started his lesson with the quotation I cited in Chapter 1:

Let me try to tell you about [the men behind the music] and their work, without cant and without display. I will promise not to be technical. I will not tire you with the rules of music. I will seldom mention key or time. You shall not be bothered with augmented sevenths or enharmonic minors. If I cannot make you realise the personality of that man behind the music I will have failed utterly and will withdraw. But I think I can.[3]

Sear rarely attempted to consider the life or music of any of the composers he studied through any kind of socialist analysis, other than the occasional reference to social origins.[4] His task, as he saw it, was to break down barriers and to persuade people that they could enjoy 'art' music as much as, or more than, they enjoyed the music they currently listened to: 'Because I mention Bach and Beethoven do not think that I don't like tunes. I do! I can undertake to find more tunes in three pages of either than in three pages of any ragtime piece you like to put before me.'[5]

Sear set out to try and teach this skill to his readers almost immediately. The second article in the 'The men behind the music' series was 'On discrimination'. He firstly explained why he considered musical discrimination to be important for socialists, or even a fundamental aspect of socialism: 'Music is not merely a drug to soothe the senses. We must listen with our brains. Socialist philosophy is giving us the intellectual use of our senses – it is teaching us discrimination.'[6] It is interesting that he includes himself amongst those who are being taught. Later on in the same article he remarks that 'we are entitled to the best'. Although the logic of his task points to him already having the discriminatory talent he speaks of (and that he intends to do the teaching), Sear uses collective language to escape from sounding too condescending, and to make his project seem more socialistic.

He was a talented writer and, to be fair, was willing to exercise his brain when listening to popular music too. When he later wrote gramophone record reviews for the *Town Crier* and the *Bradford Pioneer*, he did not just dismiss popular records out of hand. While, as we shall see in Chapter 6, some condemned the popular music of the day for a variety of reasons (its commercialism, its American – and possibly its African – origins, etc.), Sear made quite a simple test of such music based on melodies, rhythms and lyrics. Whether it is fair that discrimination based on the musicology of European 'art' music should be brought to bear on music from a different tradition is a separate question, but it would be wrong to consider Sear entirely as a musical 'elitist'. Indeed, the very nature of his project would have been abhorrent to some of the more elitist musicologists. To bring 'art' music to the attention of as much of the public as possible was anathema even to some Marxist students of music, such as Adorno, because of the risk it ran of changing the nature of the music itself. Popular audiences needed 'hummable' themes and memorable motifs, the very aspects of serious music that Sear would emphasize and champion, and that Adorno would despair of as commodification.

'The men behind the music' series ran through a large number of the 'great composers' and talked about their lives, music, inspiration and how people might 'study' their music now, normally assuming that the reader had either a piano or a gramophone or both.[7] When writing about Mozart he remarked, 'you can make a study in ecstasy by listening close up to your gramophone to "The Magic Flute" overture. I recommend it . . .'[8] Discussing Schubert, he insisted (perhaps a little optimistically) that 'almost anyone can play the tiny waltzes of Schubert. The accompaniments seldom get beyond a "vamp" . . .'[9]

Sear's interest in the 'home consumption' of classical music is rather important. He considered songs to be ideal for such study and insisted that 'we can examine them at our leisure'. Not only does this assume a gramophone or a piano, it also assumes that the reader had *time* for such an examination. Although, as we have considered elsewhere, leisure time was growing for many workers in this period (for some, far too much 'leisure' time as they joined the ranks of the unemployed) and access to a piano and/or gramophone was available for many working people, Sear appears to have been recommending quite a time-consuming pastime here. Could an average worker squeeze both the home consumption and examination of music *and* activism in one or more of the various political and industrial associations available, into his or her precious leisure time? Sometimes Sear would champion the superiority of actually playing music over just listening to the gramophone or wireless: 'chamber music is room music – *your* room music. Wireless has familiarised thousands with chamber music but, of course, that is not the real way to enjoy it. Wireless performances lack the necessary intimacy . . . it is better to play room music than merely to listen.'[10]

In encouraging his readers, Sear would quickly try and point out the accessibility of the music of any of the composers he was studying. With Haydn, for instance, he began by reassuring the reader that 'in his art there is nothing obscure, nothing aloof. You and I can handle it and smile.'[11] After referring to 'modulations from one key to another' in a piece by Mozart, he added, 'and let me whisper this, the words "modulation" and "key" are technical I know, but they do not make any real difference to the music. Try it.'[12] It is at moments like this that one is suspicious of some condescension. He had just written about musicians waiting 'with bated breath' for these modulations. Clearly they *did* make a difference to the music, however technical the words might be. Condescending or not, he wished to break down the contemporary fear of the 'high-brow'. 'It is a word used to frighten us from great things,' he wrote, 'knock it down and pass along this leafy way where lies an intimate perfection.'[13]

In the 1930s Sear reworked his gramophone reviews into 'An open letter to plain people': a fictional couple, William and Mary. He signed off his first letter:

> you know what I am, always sighing for symphonies. I often feel a snob about my preferences, but I'm not really, am I?
> Yours faithfully,
> H. G. Sear[14]

This form of article was by no means original. Robert Blatchford's famous 'Merrie England' was structured in a very similar way. Sending the letter to a 'plain' woman as well as Blatchford's 'practical working man' perhaps shows a change in attitudes over the thirty-year period, but essentially the same technique is being used. It is therefore perhaps better to view these articles as primarily an imitation of Blatchford rather than as a condescending characterization of Sear's working-class readers. The use of Blatchford's style gives the articles an air of evangelism that their content rarely matches.

While trying to appeal to the lovers of popular music, Sear was not reticent in his criticisms of some popular opportunities for hearing music, especially where classical music was performed: 'These "orchestras" that heighten the agonies of our film heroines by churning out Tchaikowski's Pathetic Symphony are not orchestras to serious musicians; while the fiddler-conductors who gyrate madly to amuse their audience not only tend to ruin their band but even insult the intelligence of the listeners.'[15] He only supported a popularization of the music he loved on his own terms. Musical arrangements for small combinations playing in cinemas, cafés or ice-cream parlours were far greater sins, for Sear, than a bit of jazzy syncopation. He was fundamentally opposed to any arrangements. After a description of some of Rachmaninov's pieces for the orchestra, he added as an aside:

> now, since I have shown that Rachmaninoff [*sic*] can and really does write for orchestra, don't you think if he had wanted his famous prelude orchestrating, he would have done it himself? So, when you next have a chance of asking a band to play a certain piece, don't let it be that one.[16]

He also could not disguise his dislike of 'musical comedy', 'from which', he wrote, 'both music and comedy are conspicuously absent'.[17] Similarly, when trying to say something positive about a gramophone record of 'Sidney Custard playing the Trocadero Cinema Organ in Liverpool', he could not quite disguise his scorn: 'In the "Cuckoo Waltz" you can actually hear the cuckoo. Isn't that nice?'

One unusual aspect of Sear's musical opinions (and 'The men behind the music' was an illustration of this) was his surprising lack of interest in performers. For Sear, composition was everything and performance very little. In a consideration of Italian opera, he referred to 'the tyranny of the singers'[18] who believed it was their right to meddle with the score as written, with improvised ornaments. In a special article in the Town Crier specifically dedicated to the subject of songs and singers, Sear remarked that 'the works of composers undoubtedly inspired are ignored for the sakes of pleasant noises made by individuals whom providence has endowed with a voice'.[19] This lack of appreciation for the talents of singers and musicians is rather singular. The primacy of music and composer is cemented further by his utter dismissal of the notion that lyrics might hold any relevance. For Sear, the success or failure of a piece of music has nothing to do with its lyrics: 'And, if you are tempted to say that these songs that are the latest rage die quickly because of their silly words, let me say at once that those of "Land of Hope and Glory" are pompous nonsense.'[20]

Sear, then, had little interest in the workers involved in the art of music, other than that great worker, 'the man behind the music', the composer. This allowed him to think and write about music in a manner quite detached from the industrial and political realities of the day, championing amateurism and voluntarism, and expressing unease at the idea of art for financial reward. He complained, for instance, that Tchaikovsky wrote the 1812 Overture 'for money, and not at the immovable dictates of his genius'.[21]

Sear went into greater detail on his subject at many lectures around the Birmingham labour movement, such as at the Labour Churches, and on the wireless, where he could illustrate his points with gramophone records. As mentioned in Chapter 2, he was one of many such lecturers throughout the country who illustrated musical lectures either with gramophone selections or with live singers and musicians. At Sear's lectures, the same non-technical approach was taken. Music was 'treated as a kind of delicate literature' and the object of the lectures was 'to stimulate enquiry and research'.[22] Although the value of much popular music was ignored or not recognized, the new technology and new opportunities for working people and their families to hear music were fully utilized. While there appeared to be a luddite attitude to new popular music (to be explored in greater detail in Chapter 6), philanthropists like Sear made extensive use of the gramophone and wireless.

In some ways, Sear might be equally well described as a popular musicologist and pedagogue than as a musical philanthropist, but one can never quite lose the suspicion that he strays beyond the positivistic boundaries of musicology into the troubled area of the effects of music on the individual. While inter-war musical socialists were not as concerned with the *civilizing* powers of music as those before the war are said to have been, they had not entirely dispensed with the influence of Hugh Haweis and the nineteenth-century musical moralists. The theory that just hearing great music could raise the individual was consigned to history (except perhaps when it came to the education of children). To learn to *appreciate* great music, however, could free the individual from the stultifying or demoralizing effects of 'bad' music. The next step in this process – the bridge from here to socialism – was rather outside the scope of music columnists, but was, essentially, that once the workers raised themselves from an intellectual torpor fed by dope culture, they would develop the necessary consciousness to bring down capitalist society. As such, the short-term philanthropic aim was often coupled with a long-term utopianism, both of which required a transformation of the individual.

Another aspect of what we have been calling 'musical philanthropy' in the inter-war labour movement was the provision of affordable opportunities to hear 'serious' music. Although many of the labour movement concerts mentioned in Chapter 2 were of a 'variety' nature, perhaps including some 'serious' selections but rarely complete pieces played 'as they were written', more formal classical concerts were sometimes staged. As well as the performances of the choirs, bands and orchestras of the movement (which, apart from the Birmingham Musical and Dramatic Union, rarely reserved their repertoires exclusively for 'art' music), labour associations sometimes staged concerts by non-labour performers. The Jowett Hall in Bradford (the home of the ILP) organized many 'classical' concerts, particularly in the late 1920s. In the first three months of 1929 there were performances by the Bradford Lyric Quartette with the cello of 'Master Coghlan',[23] a trio comprising a baritone, a pianist and a violinist who played arrangements by Grieg, Schubert and Vaughan Williams,[24] and a crowded chamber music concert, declared by the *Bradford Pioneer* to have been 'one of the finest concerts ever given in Bradford'.[25] The poor attendance at the second of these concerts (on the back of dwindling audiences for some time) was greeted with similar indignation in the pages of the *Bradford Pioneer* as was shown at poor turnouts for choir and orchestra rehearsals, referred to in Chapter 3. The *Pioneer* writer asked crossly, 'is it that music is not appreciated by Bradford folk?'[26] While it is unlikely to have been the result of this indignant chastening, the next Jowett Hall concert was apparently 'crowded'.[27]

There were also concerts such as those given by 'Casey' where 'art' music made up the bulk of the programme, along with some pieces of a folkloric nature. As we saw in Chapters 2 and 3, musical events would be put on for the 'poor children' by local labour movement musical combinations. Again these would sometimes be performances of variety music or dance/jazz music, but other groups would be more 'serious', such as the Edgbaston Labour Party Harmonic Society.[28] Furthermore, the labour newspapers would champion other opportunities to hear 'good music at popular prices', such as a sonata recital at the Midland Institute in Birmingham in 1925, which received a lengthy preview. The violinist and pianist were much lauded in the preview and emphasis was placed on admission prices (1s 6d and 2s 4d). The anonymous writer in the *Town Crier* insisted that the recital 'should not be missed by any lover of good music'.[29] Unfortunately, even the local ranks of musical philanthropists were not sufficiently organized for the beneficiaries always to receive coherent messages from their benefactors. H. G. Sear was quite exceptionally scathing about the recital, insisting that 'if I had been asked to write a critique, for the life of me I could not have uttered a word of praise'.[30] Opera seasons at local theatres and the performances by municipal orchestras would receive similarly enthusiastic previews in the labour press, and subsequent mixed reviews.

The last aspect of this philanthropic project was the provision of opportunities to learn, play and progress in the study and performance of Western art music. Lucky branches that included a music teacher could witness groups of young students reaching high standards and receiving laudatory remarks in their local labour newspaper. At the end of 1925, the *Town Crier* reported on the results of National Academy of Music pianoforte examinations, revealing 'the existence of musical talent amongst the members of Sparkbrook Labour Party'. George Bath, a fellow of the National Academy, trained the students for the exams. The youngest, aged seven, received a first-class honours in Class C (equivalent to a distinction in one of the early, beginning grades today); older students reached very high levels in the academy. Miss Dora Hunt had been made an Associate of the Academy for singing in 1923 and was now made an Associate for pianoforte; Mr Reuben Eastwood became a Licentiate of the Academy. Both Miss Hunt and Mr Eastwood had their own students who had 'successes in other examinations'. The correspondent to the *Town Crier* put particular emphasis on the successful students' 'deep interest in the work of the Sparkbrook Labour Party', 'frequently render[ing] service with their talent in the social work of the Party'.[31] The following year, in June 1926, Dora Hunt became a Licentiate of singing with the National Academy.[32]

It would be easy to condemn much of this activity as patronizing, patriarchal and elitist philanthropy, decidedly non-socialist and ignorant of the complexities and appeal of popular forms of music. Such an analysis would, however, ignore the value of such activity derived by some socialists who developed a deep love for classical music (or talent for performance) and might otherwise never have done so. We might estimate that such 'converts' were few, and the arguably more 'labourist' activity of forming musical associations did more to nurture such potential than this philanthropy. But if nothing more, these activities backed up the choirs, orchestras and solo instrumentalists who operated in the labour movement with a deeper understanding of the music they played. And in some cases it would appear to have achieved more than that. Some musically enthusiastic working-class socialists did more than pick up the crumbs from a self-satisfied, elitist feast – some received a high level of musical education.

A labour/socialist aesthetic

For some, the importance of the appreciation of 'serious' or 'art' music was not that it was *better* so much as that it was *more beautiful*. In such an analysis, the simplicity of a traditional air may be deemed 'better' than the technical, intellectual yet 'ugly' music of some 'great composers', particularly some modern ones. One function of socialism, it was felt, was to make the world – and life – less ugly and to introduce as much beauty as possible. Clearly this was the view of ILPer, Arthur Bourchier, actor-manager of the Strand Theatre, London,[33] and it was the founding principle of the ILP Guild of Arts. Music had to be 'fit for the workers' ear'. 'Classical' music, here, was just one aspect of a general view of the arts that could be characterized as essentially escapist: a diversion from the ugliness of life in a capitalist society. This idea was firmly based on the nineteenth-century aestheticism of John Ruskin. Bourchier expressed many of these opinions in an ILP pamphlet in 1926, most of which was reworked from his many lectures at ILP, Labour Party and Labour Church meetings across the country. For Bourchier, modern society was ugly. Cheap seats at the theatre or concert hall were irrelevant as long as society was organized in such a way that life was a 'chaotic' 'frantic scramble'.[34] 'It is painful to see that, as things are today, people live and die surrounded by ugliness; that the purer and more lasting joys never come to enliven and enlighten their sordid, toilsome and monotonous lives.'[35]

In this view, one of the primary reasons for the establishment of socialism is to make art and culture 'common property': to make life more beautiful. It was a reasonably common view and one that had a long heritage. Similar sentiments can be identified in the Clarion tradition, the 'golden age' utopianism of Edward Carpenter and others, and the maverick communism of the composer Rutland Boughton. Certainly Bourchier and the ILP Guild of Arts themselves considered their ideas to be very much in the tradition of William Morris. Even H. G. Sear, whom we have placed in a different 'project' or tradition, would occasionally remark on this aesthetic view of socialism, normally to bolster up the necessity for musical discrimination. When criticizing a concert party he had seen whilst on holiday, he insisted:

> As Socialists, whether we know it or not, our aim is towards perfectly ordered beauty. Only by putting our brains into our likes and dislikes are we going to compass that ordered beauty. We must not, even in holiday mood, tolerate such unloveliness. True Socialists cannot. Do not think that because I am pious there are to be no more cakes and ale. I see beauty in comedy as well as in tragedy.[36]

It would be easy to attribute a rather different form of 'golden age' yearning to Bourchier, and one that had a rather less egalitarian outlook. With his MA from Oxford, membership of the MCC and other establishment clubs, and a successful job as an actor-manager of a London theatre, one could easily parody his sentiments as a longing to be the squire rather than the jolly peasant. While this is probably unfair,[37] it is interesting to note that the England of village greens, cricket and 'old maids' on bicycles is not so far removed from that of harvest homes and may-poles.

In the early stages of the Guild of Arts, the Dramatic Section grew much faster than the musical, but the Guild did have Rutland Boughton on the committee and he held a weekend school for choral conductors under the Guild's auspices in 1926.[38] Locally, sections were set up that were not deemed to be in the true spirit of the Guild, such as the Operatic Section in Bradford. Light opera (generally Gilbert and Sullivan productions) was not considered to be 'pure' or 'beautiful' enough to perform the important role that Bourchier attached to the Arts.

In this tradition, the aesthetic of labour (or socialism) was *pure* beauty: the absolute opposite of all that could be seen in the industrial society in which they lived. Where possible, great art should pre-date industrialization. Where it did not, it had to ignore it and provide an escape. It was an aesthetic of labour that excluded any representation of or allusion to work: struggle and exploitation were ugly and therefore had no place in art. Art was not to represent or reflect real life – the role of art was to be beautiful.[39]

One question that arises from this discussion is: could art be employed in the service of socialism? This brings us back to a question first raised in

Chapter 1: can propaganda be art? There certainly appears to be some contradiction in the suggestion that great art is 'pure' and *just* beautiful on the one hand, and the suggestion that there can be some element of social control in art on the other. Whether that social control is to conserve the status quo, or to be wielded as a political weapon on the part of the workers, art must surely have some features beyond purity and beauty. There will be a discussion of the concepts of 'bourgeois' and 'proletarian' art in Chapter 6, when considering the importance of folksong. However, there were occasions where 'serious'/'art'/'classical' music (whichever description we wish to employ) was used as a tool of propaganda in the labour movement, and we must look at what the attitudes to such activities were.

These questions were considered in the pages of the labour press. It was often concluded that music, and art more generally, should not be propagandist, or at least not didactically so, but could be used to aid propaganda. Articles on this topic were deemed important enough to be reprinted around the labour press. C. Salway-Wallis's article on the 'power of music' to attract people was first printed in the *Socialist Review* but found its way into the *Town Crier*. Its essential point was important yet simple. Music in the churches, the music hall and the military acted as a magnet to many people, and socialist meetings could attain the same magnetism if they were to incorporate music in the same way. For Salway-Wallis there was nothing about military music, church music or music-hall song that leant it this 'power', other than the popular love of merriment. He believed that music could help socialist propaganda because it would 'make meetings merrier', not because people could write propagandist music.

The aesthetician Rutland Boughton rarely wrote propagandist pieces, but he was happy for his work to be used to add to the appeal of a propagandist meeting; Alan Bush and, for a while, Michael Tippett were not nearly so shy of the idea. The professional musicians, particularly Bush, introduced some quite different ideas about music and its possible function in the labour movement. It is to their contribution that we shall now turn our attention.

Rutland Boughton, Alan Bush and composers of the labour movement

Rutland Boughton and Alan Bush were the two best-known and popular composers associated with the labour movement between the wars. Other composers, like Michael Tippett and Dame Ethel Smyth, had passing associations, and Benjamin Britten was a vice-president of the

Workers' Music Association. There were other, amateur composers whose work made it into song books, newspapers and Socialist Sunday School revues, but Boughton was one of the most popular and highly regarded British composers of the period, while Bush was a well-respected academic musician and composer who was beginning to make a name for himself.

Rutland Boughton

Largely musically self-taught,[40] Boughton, who was born in 1878,[41] was already a well-known name by 1918 because of some successful compositions – particularly *The Immortal Hour*, which was to receive even more popular acclaim in the 1920s – and his music-drama festivals in Glastonbury. The two ideological forces that drove his composition from his earliest efforts were 'Socialism, of the William Morris variety' and 'the principles of Wagnerian music drama'.[42] After early ·'Wagnerian grandeur', 'folksong' was a 'purifying influence', leading to his music becoming much 'simpler, practical and individual'.[43] The Wagnerism conflicted to a degree with 'golden age' utopianism, and the grandeur with folksong simplicity. Boughton's music was described as a marriage of

> a strong vein of simple melody, much influenced by folksong, to a quasi-symphonic orchestral style and a bold use of the chorus, derived partly from oratorio and partly from the operas of Gluck . . . those works that are simpler in style (*Bethlehem*, for example) are most successful. Nevertheless, his capacity to develop his ideas grew and in *The Queen of Cornwall* came near to mastery. Boughton's harmonic vocabulary, like his melodic style remained conservative.[44]

Boughton was very strongly of the opinion that music required melodies and comprehensible rhythms, and that those modernist composers fond of atonality and dissonance were merely 'pretentious' and represented bourgeois 'decadence'. This was because there was a 'natural musical law'[45] that 'bad' music or 'antimusic' diverted from, or even inverted.

The Glastonbury Festivals, which Boughton organized from before the First World War, were modelled on the Bayreuth events of Wagner and were 'for the performance of musical and dramatic works based on legend'.[46] There was no specific political motivation behind the festivals and many of those involved did not share Boughton's convictions. While the festival did become something of a centre for the artistic left, involving Boughton, Bernard Shaw and others during its inter-war existence, Boughton's desire to 'found a colony of artists who preferred a country life, and felt . . . that the means of livelihood should be gained by other means than those of art, probably by farming'[47] never received wider support. Boughton's view was clearly based upon his political conviction that art should neither be driven by market necessities nor be aloof from human realities.

His Wagnerism was not restricted to his interest in music-drama; like Wagner, he wrote many words about his musical opinions in books (four), booklets (six) and a large number of articles. Not including his regular columns, these were in *Music* (three), *Music Opinion and Trade Review* (fourteen), *Musical Times* (twelve), *Music Student* (nine), *Sackbut* (thirty-one), *Clarion* (twelve), *Daily Citizen* (ten), *Daily Herald* (fourteen), *Musical News and Herald* (eight), *Musical Standard* (thirty-four), *Railway Review* (thirty-seven), *Sunday Worker* (twenty-three) and then one or two articles in the *Central Somerset Gazette and County Adviser, Workers' Weekly, Scallop Shell, World's Work, TPs Weekly, Musical Quarterly, Musician, Theatre Craft, Music Bulletin, Labour Magazine, Labour Monthly, Communist Review, Aria, Millgate, Author, New Britain, Fanfare, Philharmonic Post, Modern Quality, Our Time* and *Radio Times*.[48] Articles ranged from topics such as 'How not to praise God', through 'Music as fertilizer and dope' to 'D. H. Lawrence: fascist or communist?'

Boughton produced more than 250 pieces of published writing and some of these were series of articles rather than single ones. Therefore, more than with the majority of composers, it is not difficult to recover Boughton's guiding philosophy and musical likes and dislikes. He expanded on this further in numerous lectures. The Birmingham Bach Festival in 1926 received considerably more interest in labour movement circles than it might otherwise have done because of the 'special visit' of Boughton. He was to lecture on Bach (with illustrations). The *Town Crier* pointed out Boughton's well-known 'triple enthusiasm' for 'Labour, Music and Bach' and claimed that he was 'a fine lecturer' owing to his 'ruddy outlook' and 'vivid personality'.[49]

Rutland Boughton's artistic ambitions were often held back by controversy, both sexual[50] and political. His maverick politics led to difficulties in finding a political home. He had succeeded Montague Blatchford at the helm of the Clarion Vocal Unions and then, in the 1920s, performed a similar role alongside Herbert Morrison for the London Labour Choral Union and the plans for a national body, which he believed to have been 'sabotaged' by Labour Party officials.[51] He joined the Communist Party in 1926 but left it in 1929, the same year he departed the London Labour Choral Union. His decision to pass the Choral Union on to Alan Bush was based on both his political dissatisfaction with the Labour Party (that it was 'pledged to the conditions of a Capitalist constitution') and the impracticality of his changed geographical location after he had moved to a farm in Gloucestershire.

When first deciding to join the Communist Party in 1926, Boughton expounded on his reasons in a lengthy article in the *Weekly Worker*. The article was prefaced by some words from the editor 'disclaiming complete agreement' with Boughton's 'characteristically unorthodox opinions'.[52] This disclaimer was understandable: Boughton's confession of faith included a list of 'the real leaders of Communism', which included Plato, Jesus, Ruskin, Morris and Bernard Shaw alongside Marx and Lenin. He became a communist, he insisted, because state socialism was 'careless of individuals', thus placing himself in a very different, anarchist-leaning communist tradition, again perhaps of the William Morris school.[53]

Boughton's disillusionment with the Communist Party began early: during the General Strike he was put in charge of 'amusements', making brass band arrangements of 'The Red Flag' and 'The Internationale' (whether these versions were ever performed we do not know) and taking part in fund-raising concerts. Boughton was terribly depressed that the Revolution did not happen at this time.[54] However, he continued to champion the party over the next few years and never ceased to consider himself a communist, rejoining the party in 1945. He left it again, with so many others, in 1956.

Rutland Boughton's musical likes and dislikes were deeply infused with his political faith. His analysis of Wagner included the rather peculiar view that Wagner (particularly in the *Ring* Cycle) was essentially a Marxist,[55] telling the story of the class struggle via mythology and legend: 'Though not a realistic drama of Mr Norman the banker and Mr Trotsky the organiser of the Red Army, [the *Ring* Cycle] is a drama of the same human interests which have moved these men in their work.'[56] Boughton was not alone in presenting Wagner as a great revolutionary, although his attempts to portray him as a *socialist* are still quite unusual. Wagner's revolutionary past was highlighted in Sear's 'Men behind the music' and, in a preview of the National Opera Company's visit to Bradford in 1925, 'F.B.' (possibly F. W. Boddy, conductor of the Pioneer Choir) wrote: 'Wagner, the tempestuous Wagner, had a giant message of democracy and revolution and deliverance; it was wordy nonsense when he put it into a book, but a splendid storm and triumph in his music.'[57] Boughton did suspect, however, that George Bernard Shaw had a greater understanding of Wagner's socialism than Wagner himself![58]

The Immortal Hour was the music-drama that made Rutland Boughton a famous composer and a name that both the Labour Party and the Communist Party were proud to boast as one of their members. In the 1920s this opera, much to Boughton's embarrassment, was to become a society favourite. The columns of national papers that devoted their space to the lifestyles of the well known and wealthy kept the score of the number of times such people had seen it. There was no explicit politics in *The Immortal Hour*. It was an evocative production 'steeped in Celtic myth and legend',[59] and as such it could be enjoyed by people of any political persuasion as a piece of escapist music-drama. However, Boughton was not somebody who conveniently forgot his politics when composing – *The Immortal Hour* was, to those who looked carefully, utopian as well as escapist, evocative of a 'golden age' and striving to be beautiful. Indeed, the composition was *so* utopian that in many ways it could not actually be realised on stage or by orchestra. 'With a production such as "The Immortal Hour", one does not expect the difficulties to be completely overcome, for the music is continually striving towards a wider freedom, and defies rigid criticism.'[60]

This was a common problem for Boughton's pieces. While he sometimes tried to keep things simple and write for smaller musical combinations, he would often write for huge orchestras to which he had little or no access. He only ever heard his Symphony No. 2 in B minor once at a special performance. Some of his pieces he never heard performed as they were written. At the Glastonbury Festivals he would often attempt to sketch or give suggestions of the depth of his full orchestra score played on a single piano. Furthermore, he was often held back by the limitations of the amateur musicians and singers who were most often to perform his creations, 'to the despair of an artist's ideas of truth and beauty'.[61]

When *The Immortal Hour* was brought to the provinces – especially repeated runs at the Repertory Theatre in Birmingham – some socialist reviewers were able to recognize something of the composer's intent. An anonymous reviewer in Birmingham's *Town Crier* identified the utopian motivation, remarking that 'today, as always, we have to pass by way of dreams to the Land of Heart's Desire'. The reviewer also recognized a propaganda function for beauty which Arthur Bourchier and others did not. While remarking that *The Immortal Hour* was 'a beautiful work' he continued: 'It is not the beauty that pleases or satisfies: it is the beauty that is allied with pain. Greater even than beauty is the desire for beauty, and from such a feast we rise hungrier than we sat down.'[62] In other words, beauty is not simply desirable or a promise of what is to come under socialism. Small amounts of beauty and the promise of more could, according to this theory, provoke desire and, therefore, the will to destroy the society that robs the masses of beauty and creates such ugliness.

Regarded retrospectively as one of Boughton's finest pieces, *The Queen of Cornwall* (composed 1923–4) was greeted warmly, but with some trepidation, by labour's musical elite. H. G. Sear described the setting of an opera to the same story as Wagner's *Tristan and Isolde* as 'peculiarly dangerous' because it 'provokes comparison'. Sear was 'sure Boughton would never claim to be as good a composer as Wagner'. In that assumption, Sear was undoubtedly correct. Boughton's aim had not been to rewrite Wagner, but to set Thomas Hardy's poem as an opera.

Sear, in his review, concentrated primarily on the music and made hardly any comment about Boughton's politics. He mentioned that the 'music has much of his own violence, tempered by his own poetic feeling', and rather surprisingly said that 'it is his violence that betrays him into ugliness'. Boughton's conservative, symphonic music, occasionally striving for a beauty beyond his 'canvass' and occasionally stripped down to simple and aesthetically pleasing chamber-music, is very difficult to think of as 'ugly'. However, Boughton did sometimes criticize himself for succumbing to 'vulgarity' because of the temptation to overdo the big orchestral arrangements. Sear wrote his review on having only read the piano score, which is extremely impressive in many ways, but also renders his comments about the orchestration rather speculative: 'A reading of Boughton's work finds me very interested. I think it is a Boughton more mature than the Boughton of "The Immortal Hour", and I hope that my impressions may soon be confirmed by a hearing in its proper home, the theatre.'[63]

The piece gained impressive reviews outside the movement as well, the *Manchester Guardian* remarking that 'Mr Boughton's music almost glitters with psychological insight' and that 'the beautiful moments of dreamy passion are woven with wonderful art into the texture of the tragedy'.[64] The reviewer in the *Guardian* had not heard an orchestra play the piece either, seeing it at a Glastonbury Festival with Boughton on the piano as the only accompanist. The opera was not performed with an orchestra until April 1925 in Bournemouth. This is another example of the difficulties that Boughton had in having his creations realized in full on the stage. Boughton recognized the greater difficulty for others in staging performances at all, and he put on works at Glastonbury by composers who were unable to stage their creations elsewhere, including those by the socialist Edgar Baignton.[65]

Although it seems most appropriate to place Boughton in the tradition that we have mentioned, including William Morris, Edward Carpenter and Arthur Bourchier, there were times when he placed the importance of practical political change and the material conditions of the working class above his art. In 1926 the *Daily Express* asked him to join the organizing committee of a 'National Community Singing Movement'. Even though community singing had been an important aspect of the musical life of the labour movement, and began to be couched in those terms after this date, Boughton responded to the suggestion contemptuously: 'How can the Workers of Britain sing on empty stomachs? And how can the slackers of Britain sing with the knowledge that there is so much suffering among those who do the work for them?'[66] Despite Boughton's keen interest in the national music of Britain, it was the concept of a national movement in a *class* society that seemed to enrage him so particularly on this occasion, probably combined with the political position of the *Daily Express*.

In a speech in Moscow during the tenth anniversary celebrations of the Russian Revolution, Boughton paid great attention to the social and material well-being of musicians. He looked into the discrepancy in strength of organization between singers and musicians, and how female singers were only just kept out of prostitution by an agreed minimum wage. He argued in favour of a British Union for all artists, based on 'the Russian model'.[67] When he made this proposal in his column in the *Daily Herald*, the editor 'refused publication'. Boughton put this down to Hamilton Fyfe being 'MacDonald's man'.[68] Fyfe himself insisted that his objection was because there was 'quite enough Trade Unionism in other parts of the paper', and page 4 was 'a general reading page'. His letter to Boughton began: 'will you *please* write about music?'[69] On this occasion his comments on the *type* of music that people sang or should sing was limited to a comment that 'Welsh miners are given to singing bad hymn tunes' and that 'all [workers'] choirs suffer from a lack of suitable music'.[70]

I suggested earlier that, for this aesthetic tradition, art could not represent or reflect contemporary reality at all. However, Boughton did deviate from this pattern. As we shall see in Chapter 6, Boughton was not a believer in the view that folk music was a spontaneous, primitive expression of the masses but rather believed that there was as an 'interchange of material product and musical expression' between 'the masses of the people and professional musicians' which 'was necessary for both'. Music needed 'the cross-fertilisation of real life to keep it vigorous'.[71] It was an awareness of the 'music of the people' that prevented the great composers falling foul of 'decadence' and inverting 'natural musical law'.

Alan Bush

Alan Bush, born in 1900, had a considerably more academic musical education than Boughton. He studied at the Royal Academy of Music between 1918 and 1922, and studied philosophy and musicology at the University of Berlin from 1929 to 1931, somehow juggling his studies with conducting the London Labour Choral Union. Unlike most of the musical activists of the labour movement, he was quite aware of the twelve-tone serialist compositional methods of Schoenberg, and the philosophies behind the modern music that Boughton considered largely pretentious.[72] He might well have been aware of the ideas and compositions of the young Adorno. He spent time in Berlin discussing art with Bertolt Brecht and Hans Eisler.[73] Bush was an intellectual. From 1925 onwards he was a professor of composition at the Royal Academy of Music, and he became a 'fellow' in 1938.

In some ways you could not imagine two more different composers than Boughton and Bush, but they held a mutual respect. Bush was Boughton's deputy at the London Labour Choral Union before filling his shoes in 1929. Furthermore, Bush described Boughton's opera *The Lily Maid* as 'one of the most beautiful and one of the most truly original operas of recent times'.[74] Bush joined the Communist Party in 1935, but continued at the helm of the London Labour Choral Union as a communist for five years. However, he and Boughton were not both Communist Party members at the same time until 1945.

Bush's compositions varied to extremes, even before he simplified the style of his composition on the advice of the Comintern later in his career. He shared similar musical theories to Schoenberg, essentially a belief that every note should be 'thematically significant': there should be no incidentals, no notes included for the sake of prettiness. However, Bush wrote music and arrangements for socialist song books, co-editing *Twelve Labour Choruses* with Leonard Pearce for the ILP in 1930, and *The Left Song Book* in 1938 with Randall Swingler for the Workers' Music Association (WMA) and the Left Book Club Musicians Group. The former collection included two original songs and two arrangements by Boughton and the music was, for the most part, the 'turgid four-part setting in the manner of *Hymns Ancient and Modern*'[75] traditionally used for labour anthems. The second book was more unusual, although it did include many of the old favourites, such as 'The International(e)', 'The Red Flag', 'England, Arise!', 'Bandiera Rossa' and 'March of the Workers', which are to be found in many of these collections. This collection also included new songs with words by Swingler and music by Bush, such as the 'Song of the Hunger Marchers', which was a more sparse arrangement: a single voice over a steady, march-time, minimalist piano accompaniment.[76]

It is interesting to consider why there appears to be this inconsistency in Bush's theories. Ralph Vaughan Williams remarked, in a WMA tribute to Bush on the occasion of his fiftieth birthday, that 'Alan Bush has rather fantastic notions of the nature and purpose of the Fine Arts. Luckily for us when the inspiration comes over him he forgets all about this.'[77] Although this was meant as praise, Bush may well have found the suggestion that he had 'fantastic notions' and that he forgot them rather an insulting tribute.

Some have identified Bush's period in Berlin as the time when his 'fantastic notions' about composition really came of age. Most of his English contemporaries were devotees of 'conservative tonal romanticism', revering the 'the sensuous moment' as something truly English, whatever its relevance to the overall form.[78] Many of the famous English composers of the time may be considered guilty of such conservatism. Certainly Boughton was one such composer, although the explicitly political purpose of his romantic escapism rather blurs the boundary between 'content' and 'form'. For Bush, however, the 'impact of the moment' was secondary to the 'architecture'. All the elements of a Bush piece should be considered against the background of an 'expressive and cumulative architecture' because they 'have comparatively little interest as isolated phenomena'.[79]

Although his studies in Berlin appear to have cemented his compositional style as a more conscious, systematized method, the pieces that Bush wrote between leaving the Royal Academy and attending the University of Berlin (1922–9) were already characteristic. 'The first inkling of a new voice in British music'[80] was, for many, his 1929 string quartet sonata, intriguingly entitled *Dialectic*. 'Nearly every element in the composition is derived from the opening unaccompanied theme.' This was Bush's method, where 'every element of a work, down to the most insignificant detail, is thematically derived'.[81] The 'exhilarating' piece was a 'beautifully constructed exercise in pure thought', where the initial *motif* (or thematic premise) is 'led through discussion to the cogent conclusion'.[82]

Bush's music had a 'vivid sense of melody'[83] – indeed, rather 'a basic simplicity in harmony and melody'[84] – but he was clearly not primarily driven by a quest for purity or beauty. He attempted to academically transfer Marxist analysis into a compositional method, drawing on contemporary German ideas. Where he diverted from that orderly constructive process was not at the whim of artistic genius or the quest for beauty, but in the service of propaganda. Aside from what might be considered his less serious work in song books, one of Bush's key pieces, his 1937 piano concerto, saw him collaborating with Randall Swingler to propagandist effect. The piece was performed on BBC radio in 1938 with Bush playing the solo piano part. The first three movements were instrumental, but the fourth part introduced a chorus to sing Swingler's words. To demand that the attention of the audience should, for a while, be diverted from the piano, the chorus actually spoke the line: 'Friends, we would speak a little of this performance.'[85] There was a left-wing audience at the BBC performance and it reacted ecstatically. The conductor, Adrian Boult, was so surprised that he cut short the applause and moved into an unscheduled 'God Save the King'.[86] Bush was by no means a follower of the Bourchier aesthetic school. In the foreword to the 1938 song book he insisted that as socialists 'we must sing what we mean and sing it like we mean it or else our singing is but a pleasant way to pass the time'.[87] Bush's serious musical education and daunting authority led to early problems when he started conducting labour choirs. The secretary of the Finchley Labour Choir, which Bush conducted in the mid-1920s, severely chastised the young composer for his thorough methods, which were initially to shock the amateur singers. Labour choirs would become used to his approach over the period, and he did modify it somewhat, despite his assertion that his was 'the only method of learning the notes'.[88]

Despite his rather 'high-brow' (to use the contemporary parlance), academic theories of music, Bush, in founding the WMA, would be a key player in the development and sophistication of theories of 'music of their own'. The WMA was founded in 1936, out of the music section of the Workers' Theatre Movement and the London Labour Choral Union, 'in order to extend the influence of a progressive musical culture which would consciously draw its sustenance from the struggle of the masses to free themselves from economic exploitation, a culture which it would be their purpose to unfold for themselves'.[89] This is how Will Sanhow, General Secretary of the WMA in 1950, saw the Association at its founding.

In the early years of the Association, this musical culture unfolded by the masses and sustained by struggle was still often 'classical' in nature. However, the WMA did recognize the possibilities of being an 'Association for the music of the workers' from the beginning. Its motto was never 'only the best is good enough for the workers',[90] and it therefore represented a shift away from the labour aesthetic of Arthur Bourchier and friends. Instead it provides a link between the labour movement's inter-war musical life and the efforts of Ewan MacColl, A. L. Lloyd and others after the Second World War. Bush himself adopted a more folk-like idiom as he strove for a broader and more popular appeal,[91] and as he became increasingly involved with the concept of 'People's Music'.[92] The folk idiom was 'consciously fostered as a result of his political convictions' but only really began to make a noticeable impact on his composition after 1945.[93]

Retrospectively, Bush claimed that even the London Labour Choral Union was exclusively political, never performing music for entertainment and with no interest in 'awakening the interest of the working class in the traditional classical heritage of music' or raising musical standards. In an interview with Ian Watson in 1978, Bush had no recollection of what we have referred to as musical philanthropy, or a pedagogical aspect to the labour musical movement, or even music for pleasure. Bush recalled that 'politically progressive musicians' 'concentrated on getting the workers to use music as a political and agitational weapon'.[94] One reason for this selective recollection might have been Bush's metropolitan focus ('it was only important in London') and also that the 78-year-old was concentrating on his own specific interests, rather than the whole range of socialist music making and music ideas. Even so, this extremely delimited and specific task which Bush said was before 'politically progressive musicians' in the 1930s is extremely interesting both to this chapter, as a contrast to the dominant musical views of the 'official' movement, and more especially to the next chapter, when we come to consider 'music of their own'.

Michael Tippett

Although later in his career Michael Tippett moved away from the political left and wrote some specifically anti-Marxist pieces,[95] in the 1930s he found himself attracted to the ideas of Trotskyism. His rather short association with the labour movement began with his musical roles in two schemes for the unemployed, one in Cleveland, North Yorkshire, the other in London. At the Cleveland work-camp, attended by unemployed miners and steel-workers from the north-east, he staged two operas. The first was a production of *The Beggar's Opera* in 1933 with locals taking many of the major roles, and with some music students being brought in as well. The following year he wrote an opera especially for the camp. It was called *Robin Hood* and was written in the folksong idiom. He did not shirk from including quite a political libretto:

> And every man and every maid
> Shall freely live in peace.
> None shall be rich nor any poor,
> The curse of hunger cease![96]

As part of the London County Council's unemployment schemes, Tippett also set up the South London Orchestra, which grew to be one of the most successful schemes. The orchestra did not pursue Tippett's quite modern and original musical interests, instead performing popular orchestral pieces such as *Pomp and Circumstance*. At this time, two of Tippett's friends in London were Francesca Allinson and Alan Bush, both involved in the London Labour Choral Union. Allinson conducted the Clarion Glee Club, which had been Boughton's choir, and Bush had succeeded Boughton as the conductor of the Union. Tippett followed their lead by becoming the conductor of the choirs of the Royal Arsenal Co-operative Society, which was affiliated to the Labour Party.[97]

However, unlike Boughton and Bush, Tippett did not spend long organisationally associated with the labour movement, either 'official' or 'unofficial'. He had some connection – he certainly bought the paper, the *Red Flag* – with the Trotskyist Communist League, until it was disbanded in 1935 owing to disagreements with the International Left Opposition and Fourth International policies. He then joined the Communist Party as a Trotskyist entryist, hoping to stir up anti-Stalin feeling in his cell and follow the example of the Balham Group, pioneers of British Trotskyism. He only stayed in the party for a few months.[98] He was then associated with an entryist group in the Labour Party: the 'Militant' Group.[99] But it was not long before he began to drift away from the political left altogether, adopting a humanist viewpoint in later life that some have characterized as extremely anti-Marxist. His reaction to the USSR's views and action in the arena of music theory (the famous issues surrounding the compositions of Shostakovich) was very different from that of Alan Bush. While Bush responded to the ideas entirely in terms of music theory, and was able to adopt the realist approach into his modernist serialism, Tippett considered the issue in terms of freedom of artistic expression.

Amateur composers

Amateur composition in the movement was widespread, and coupled with the efforts of amateur poets, the results were printed in the labour press in large numbers, as well as sometimes making it into song books. Because the lyrics that appeared in newspapers are not always accompanied by a suggested tune to which they might be sung, it is sometimes unclear whether they are socialist *songs* or examples of socialist poetry. The latter were not always graciously welcomed by newspaper editors. In 1922, under the headline 'Politics and "poets" – alarming outbreak', the *Town Crier* remarked: 'In spite of a much enlarged waste-paper basket we find it difficult to cope with the devastating flood of "poems" that pours into the office.'[100] On other occasions the music was included or the words were to be set to a well-known tune – only rarely of a particularly 'serious' or 'artistic' nature, such as the Gounod setting referred to in Chapter 2. Some of the songs were specifically referred to as 'folk songs' and will be considered in the next chapter. There were some serious attempts at writing hymn-like choral arrangements for new socialist songs that demonstrated amateur efforts at serious composition.

Sometimes amateur efforts would stretch to operettas. The Socialist Sunday Schools were particularly fond of staging socialist light opera, such as *The Youth Called Ideal* composed by Arthur Scott, with words by

May Westoby, in 1930. The idea was that this production would be staged at many of the schools, and it was certainly taken up in Manchester[101] and Bradford.[102] The piece was published by the National Council of Socialist Sunday Schools and sold at 2d a copy. Although occasionally obscure, the story is never subtle and the *Pioneer* sold it as 'useful to those who desire matter containing a message'.[103] The various adventures of King Ease, Queen Custom, Lord and Lady Makewar, Lord Progress, Princess Reala and the Youth Called Ideal himself certainly did not limit themselves to the quest for beauty. Unfortunately, the script did not contain the musical score, and it even recommended reciting the songs as poetry for schools lacking 'competent musicians'.[104]

The bulk of socialist composition was made up of those ephemeral creations considered in Chapter 4: short songs usually written to very familiar tunes, which either poked fun at some contemporary political issue or were used on marches and protests as the comrades kept step. Although most of these were very localized and many were never written down, some were published and used more widely. Alan Bush and Randall Swingler's *Left Song Book* (1938) even included some marching songs to be sung as 'rounds' to tunes such as 'Three Blind Mice', 'Frère Jacques' and 'London's Burning'. Many songs sung by socialists, then, were perhaps collectively written and orally transmitted and might be considered as folksong. I shall look at these in more detail in the next chapter.

Conclusions

Very little concern was shown by the champions of classical music in the labour movement that theirs had been the music of the aristocracy and the bourgeoisie. While the idea that music could express values or morals was an essential part of their theories – from the dislike of the 'Tannenbaum' setting of 'The Red Flag' to everything that was wrong with commercial music – it seemed that, for many, *great* art could only ever be beautiful. In the next chapter we shall consider both socialist perceptions of the music of the working class and the actual music performed and appreciated. Although, as we shall see, some socialists were keen to search for a working-class or socialist musical culture – a 'music of their own' – the quest was not really set up *in opposition* to the view that there was a wealth of great art that was simply beautiful. Even H. G. Sear, who went into such detail about the lives of the great composers and whom they composed for, never really thought about the motivations or purposes of classical music beyond 'genius' and 'beauty'.

If one were to emphasize musical ideas above political ones, the different debates and traditions considered in this chapter could be reconsidered as the various academic traditions of music study. We could see Sear as primarily a popular musicologist, and his primary distinction from earlier columnists as the distinction that existed outside the labour movement between musicologists and critics. Musicology had an entry in the *Oxford English Dictionary* for the first time in 1919.[105] Similarly, Bourchier (and perhaps Boughton) could be seen as primarily aestheticians, and Bush was a music theorist of the modernist school. Through the Workers' Music Association, Bush could be seen as having introduced ethnomusicology (called comparative musicology until the post-war period) into this academic forum as well. Although a fairly new term, popular musicology was a well-practised study by this period, on concert programmes and gramophone sleeves as well as in papers and journals. It is the introduction of modernist music theory and comparative musicology via Bush, and some of his less successful contemporaries,[106] which is particularly interesting. Here we can see sophisticated academic theories – new and exciting ideas in the academies of Germany and the USA – being introduced into Britain, not into the academy but into workers' movements, and particularly the cultural side of the Communist Party in the late 1930s. The introduction of comparative musicology will be considered in the next chapter.

For Boughton to condemn modernist, avant-garde music as 'bourgeois decadence' while seeing all that went before as *just* beautiful would appear to be a rather selective use of class analysis, although he did attempt to take his theories beyond this, as we shall see in the next chapter. For Bourchier to have condemned the 'crude, savage, cacophonous jazz that we hear on every hand today' as 'the musical expression' of modern capitalist society, without questioning whether the beautiful music he praised might have been 'the musical expression' of equally non-socialist societies, seems similarly flawed. Of course, part of this can be put down to the naivety of 'golden age' utopianism's analysis of pre-capitalist society. The championing of the simple 'beauty' of early music should not be surprising, but much 'beautiful' music was not pre-capitalist. Boughton could justify his admiration for Wagner by characterizing him as a revolutionary and even as a socialist, and for other composers because of the folk influences and references in their work, but essentially, half-formed theories that were easy to apply to popular music (and folk music and modernist music) fell down in the face of genius. The only excuse that could be given for this was that 'the great composers' stood outside their society and class in a way that peasants, jazz musicians and decadent bourgeois German academics could not.

6

A Music of Their Own

As we considered in Chapter 1, socialist thought about 'music of their own' – working-class or socialist music – has quite a long tradition. Although the American academic field of comparative musicology and ideas about new, agitational, counter-cultural musical forms only really found their way into the inter-war labour movement via the Communist Party in the 1930s, the problem of whom music belonged to' was much older. On founding the Clarion Vocal Unions in Halifax in the 1890s, Montague Blatchford talked about workers not wanting 'high art they didn't understand', but needing 'art of their own that is built upon their lives'.[1] Although we might be puzzled by his logic in thinking that Tudor madrigals fitted that bill, his essential question was the same as that asked by those musical socialists conscious (on any level) of arguments about bourgeois and proletarian culture. Should workers inherit the musical and artistic heritage of the bourgeois society they were to overthrow or instead develop their own art? Did that art, that culture, already exist, or was it to be constructed and designed by an artistically conscious, organized labour movement? Should the musical tastes of working people be taken more seriously, despite their perceived vulgarity and banality?

These were the questions that musical socialists had to address when confronted with the reality of inter-war popular music. Rutland Boughton, for one, was acutely concerned by these questions, for all that we have tended to paint him as a middle- to high-brow aesthete. His answers were primarily arrived at through his thoughts about folk music, and it is to this that we must first turn our attention. Following that we shall look at popular music, and finally we will consider ideas about a specifically socialist music; those considerations will conclude this chapter.

The labour movement and folksong

'The first phase of the Folksong Revival had petered out into amiable ir-relevance in the 1920s and 1930s', according to Dave Harker.[2] Although there is certainly some truth in this assertion, it seems as though the inter-war Folk Revival suffers the condescension of posterity for its lack of dramatic upheaval. Steady progress is hardly the stuff of exciting his-tory, but in many of the revival's original aims, it is the best way to describe the work of the English Folk Dance and Song Society (EFDSS) between the wars.[3] It is not so much that the Society itself prospered, but its general social influence in the fields of popular and professional music, and especially in education, was far from 'irrelevant'. A glance at the music syllabus for infants produced by the City of Bradford Education Committee in 1933, for instance, would reveal a section on 'Folk Dancing' and recommendations for schools to have books such as *English Folk Songs for Schools*.[4] At all times the task of teaching children 'the love of good folk music' was central to the syllabus.

The 'authenticity' of British folksong has become a highly contentious issue in recent decades. Many of the current debates surrounding folksong critically undermine the basis of the labour movement's em-brace of the revival.[5] Most socialist folk enthusiasts bought into the musical and antiquarian theories of collectors like Cecil Sharp. There were exceptions: Boughton's singular views on folksong differed from Sharp's in a number of ways. Generally speaking, however, the labour movement did not just adopt the treasury of traditional song and dance; it opted into the *ideology* of the revival as well, and helped to shape that ideology.

The labour movement's recurring interest in 'folksong' provides a con-structive focus for examining the varying socialist and labourist ideas about culture and the arts, and particularly music. The folk music revival of the late Victorian period, typified by Cecil Sharp, was by no means a socialist project, although Sharp himself adhered to a peculiar form of conservative socialism.[6] It did, however, engender a considerable amount of socialist in-terest, particularly in the idea of a national treasury of song that had somehow sprung from the workers. Furthermore, it was music that pre-dated the twin evils of industrialism and commercialism, and so demonstrated how capitalism blunted the creativity of the workers. The music represented a glimpse of that imagined 'golden age' and therefore perhaps hinted at what could be produced in an imagined future. It was a perfect addition to the popular nationalist tradition of labour thought (the Clarion school of *Britain for the British*), asserting that Britain's 'national'

culture was not that of a privileged few, but was instead the work of 'ordinary' working people.

Unfortunately, the myth had very little to do with the reality. On the
one hand, the word 'folk', far from celebrating workers' cultural production, denied the primacy of class when considering this music, putting the
nation in its place.[7] On the other hand, this 'pure', 'unsullied' workers'
music all passed through the hands of educated musicians – enthusiastic
and well-off amateurs, or professionals in the field of 'serious' music –
before the selected or published 'national treasury' was 'given back' to
the nation. In these respects, the criticisms of the 'folksong myth' expressed by Dave Harker in *Fakesong* have some validity. However, the
essential argument of his book – that working people are absent from the
history of folksong – can be challenged here, at least to a certain extent.
As we have already hinted elsewhere, 'Merrie England' was disputed territory claimed by conservatives, socialists and fascists alike. Having said
that, labour 'folklorists' often gained the upper hand in the political struggles of the Revival, the story of which is told by Georgina Boyes in *The
Imagined Village: Culture, Ideology and the English Folk Revival*
(1993). The whole concept of a 'revival' is at once revolutionary and conservative, which is one reason why the folk movement lent itself to such a
wide variety of political positions.

Champions of English folk culture

It would be wrong to attempt to place the labour movement close to the heart
of the Folk Revival in its early years, but it certainly produced some of the
most vociferous champions of folk culture in the inter-war period. Furthermore, labour publications would sometimes call attention to folk events,
such as displays of Old English Dances at the Birmingham Repertory Theatre, given by the English Folk Dance Society in 1920.[8] *Labour Magazine*, a
popular monthly amongst Labour Party members and trade unionists in the
1920s, included two evangelizing articles for folk arts in 1923.

Alec Hunter, who wrote the first of these articles, acted as a pure
mouthpiece for the Revival, hardly bothering to give it a labourist slant.
'Back to Merrie England' was essentially a consideration of folk musical
arts – particularly morris dancing and other traditional English dances.
Hunter came from that ethical, religious socialist tradition and announced
it almost immediately: non-socialists were described as people who
thought that only a minority of men were 'Sons of God'. It was for that
reason, he asserted, that such people could not understand why anyone
would take any interest in the arts or creations of the majority. 'They
consider such things as folk dances and songs as mere crude and rustic

expressions of *joie de vivre* – pretty perhaps, but because of their origin unworthy of serious consideration.'[9] Hunter attempted to give such pursuits serious consideration in this article, illustrated with action photographs of morris dancers. As testament to the quality of folk tunes, he pointed to the fact that 'the greatest composers' openly used their melodies. Of course, where such open borrowing was used there was often an agenda other than the 'pure' aesthetic at work. This might have been to give the music a 'national' flavour, since many patriotic pieces from Europe leant on folk tunes, or to lend them a certain simplicity (later Alan Bush, for example) or a pastoral feel (Vaughan Williams).

This 'open use' has recently been characterized, by Dave Harker and others, as expropriation. This position is not entirely unreasonable; the Cecil Sharp Trust and Novello Publishers made considerable profits from these 'songs of the people'. In 1936 Novello joined the Performing Rights Society to cash in on the burgeoning community singing movement and its use of folksong.[10] That Cecil Sharp was able to sustain a movement entirely devoted to the popularization of music, from which he received healthy royalties, might be a testament more to his business sense than to any other qualities. Aside from this explicit expropriation, the worker-artists were afforded no rights of ownership over their cultural products, either as individuals or as a class. Their product was 'clearly a heritage of the nation as a whole'.[11]

When Alec Hunter wrote of these 'melodies of the people', his passion clearly went beyond personal taste. He saw 'their extraordinary beauty and perfection' not merely from the position of the aesthete: he planted himself firmly in the shaky territory for which the Revivalists have been much criticized. His view, widely held by folk dance and song enthusiasts of the time, was that 'folk art is not produced by any one "conscious" artist. It is the unconscious product of a group of people – each person and each generation adding and altering so that a very great perfection is attained.' Here Hunter, along with many of his fellow Labour-supporting folk enthusiasts, fell foul of the 'ungodly' prejudices that he had begun by noting. The key word, and he was far from being alone in using this, was 'unconscious'. To suggest that folk art was an unconscious product insists upon total passivity on the part of the worker-artist. This view stemmed from an elitist perspective, which was entirely cemented by collectors like Sharp, that the poor and uneducated could not *consciously* write music of quality.

There is little doubt that different people and different generations greatly changed older pieces of music via 'the oral tradition' – various regional and even national variations of traditional songs demonstrate this to have been the case. But there is no reason to read from that that such alterations were unconsciously made. There was a peculiar and contradict-ory element in the Revivalists' ideology: they wanted their folk art to be 'artless': songs and dances that showed signs of recent creativity were passed over. It was not until after the Second World War that leading proponents of folk music began to question the 'unconscious' argument, portraying the folk singers as local autodidacts with active, interpretative and creative intellects.[12] This position had some of its intellectual roots in Gramsci's ideas about organic intellectuals – that 'all men are philosophers'.[13]

Hunter's repeated references to nationalism and 'Englishness' are almost inevitable results of the championing of folk culture. He did try and give it all an internationalist slant, but it was rather obscure. 'This is the true nationalism,' he wrote, 'the recognition and love of the good things of your own country and the development of them as a contribution towards the true internationalism.' This was fine as far as it went, but that 'recognition and love' did not restrict itself to the rational or demonstra-ble. When talking about folk cultures internationally, he quickly staked a claim for the English as world leaders: 'The English are particularly for-tunate. There are no finer songs or dances in the world.'

This is clearly more than a question of personal taste. It is not just that Hunter really liked this music, but rather that there was ideology at work that necessitated this conclusion. The late-nineteenth-century rediscov-ery of 'English music' came at a time of prolific invention of tradition, as has been considered by Eric Hobsbawm and others. Those labourites who bought into the nationalism of the Revival would presumably not have seen their actions as part of the same process as the increase in national and monarchical pageantry, but it is certainly an arguable case. The Re-vival fed off a perceived crisis in national identity that pervaded much more than Britain's musical life.[14] 'The folk' predated the classes; folk culture had the potential to be the culture of a one-nation Britain.

Finally, Alec Hunter further undermined his case by insisting that 'all that is best in the English culture' is contained in the 'rhythms and ca-dences' of morris dances. The northern sword dances that he briefly commented upon required some intricacy in execution, but morris dances are generally rather simple. Yet Hunter talked up morris dancing with all the zeal of a fanatic: 'The morris, which requires great skill in the perfor-mance, is a splendid example of pure masculine beauty, very strong and yet always restrained.'[15] The homo-erotic aspect of this statement echoes the depiction of the healthy, heroic 'worker' in some pieces of labour art-work, although the appended images of handkerchief-wafting Cotswold morris-men provide a rather comic juxtaposition.

It is interesting that in the article Hunter never really made the point that inspired much labour writing on the folk arts: that this art was of 'genuine proletarian' origin. This certainly was a fundamental aspect of Rutland Boughton's thoughts on the subject. For Boughton, vocal music was the art 'most easily come by when people are poor, for they have been endowed by nature with a most beautiful instrument – the singing voice.' He explored the role of folksong as proletarian music in a *Labour Magazine* article, also in 1923. It is because of the ready availability of a singing voice, he concluded, that 'it is in the direction of vocal music . . . that proletarian art is likely to find itself first'.[16]

Boughton therefore celebrated unaccompanied folksong as genuine proletarian music. He made particular reference to work songs, although primarily to agricultural work, as we shall see later.

> The workers have produced beautiful songs without any sort of conscious musical training, and so proved that aesthetic emotion is a common gift of humanity, and not a special attribute of a small professional or cultured class. And in unaccompanied singing we possess the means of artistic expression without the need for any great capital expenditure.[17]

Although he wrote about the artists' 'consciousness' again here, the emphasis was on musical training rather than on the composition, allowing him to make rather a neat socialist point about folksong. Furthermore, Boughton was able to avoid the nationalist tendencies of folklorists by considering the regional and supranational traditions in folk music. Although his final rendering of mainland Britain into three large folk regions was rather contrived, the thinking behind it was sophisticated and ahead of its time.[18]

In other respects, Boughton's views on folksong were less progressive. His musicological 'grand narrative' was a peculiar form of Darwinism, where a musical evolution could be followed from the cry of a gibbon through folk music to art music, with some contemporary popular 'degeneracy'.[19] It was from the view that folk music was a formative evolutionary stage in the story of art music, which was by no means a premise peculiar to Boughton, that its role in musical education was bolstered. H. G. Sear, no great folk enthusiast, insisted that 'a judicious supply of folk music is excellent' for children: 'it smells of the soil; it is, for the most part, unsophisticated; its rhythm is grasped almost instantaneously'. Most importantly, 'from folk-song to great music is not so great a step as it seems', although 'only the very best is good enough for the children of Socialists'. 'Children play with rhythms', he insisted, 'and rhythm to tune is the tiniest step.'[20] This was very much in keeping with the contemporary ideas of musical education – both the benefits of eurhythmics, and the idea that the education of a child should follow the development of the race. However, it also shows how folk music was seen as a formative stage of 'great music'.

Industrial folksong

The nascent field of ethnomusicology in the USA in the 1930s was generally able to consider various world musics, including Western folk music, as having their own stories and contexts[21] rather than simply being phases in the one great evolution of art music. Indeed, Western art music had to begin to be considered as simply another musical idiom in its own social and cultural context. These ideas came to Britain in the 1930s via American and German left-wing musical academics, who found the most receptive ears in the Workers' Music Association. The ideas had consequences way beyond folk music, as will be considered later in this chapter. Following American and German interest in comparative musicology (the direct ancestor of ethnomusicology), exiled German musicians injected ideas into the London Labour Choral Union and Workers' Music Association, and those organizations began to propagate the contemporary wealth of American progressive song.[22] It is not surprising, therefore, that the WMA quickly began to work in the direction of folksong and to take some interesting new positions, forming the soil from which the work of MacColl and Lloyd was eventually to spring.

Later folksong collectors, closely connected with the labour movement (particularly with the Communist Party), uncovered another treasury of 'national' song that had – so it is generally considered – been previously ignored. A. L. Lloyd gave this music the name 'Industrial Folksong', and in the second half of the twentieth century where folk music and the labour movement were considered together it was in connection with this wealth of song. Many of the industrial songs collected in works such as *Come All Ye Bold Miners* (1951) were written in the nineteenth century; others originated from the inter-war years themselves. Were these songs entirely ignored by the labour movement, even on a local basis, and if so, why?

Some of them would appear to have been *products* of a local labour movement, such as those about particular strikes, lockouts (referred to in Chapter 4) and disasters. The Gresford pit disaster in 1934 became a major political issue in its day and acquired great significance in posterity as a symbol of the heroic status of the miner.[23] At least two pieces of music were inspired by the event. One was a serious, hymn-like piece that became the theme song of the Durham Miners' Gala; the other a 'folk song' with an uncertain lineage: 'The Ballad of the Gresford Disaster'. It was brought to light by Ewan MacColl and there have been suggestions that MacColl wrote it himself.

MacColl had included a scene about the Gresford disaster in his 1940 Manchester Theatre Union production, *Last Edition*, which did not include 'The Ballad'. However, Roger Laidlaw suspected that it originated from a similar milieu: a piece of satirical socialist drama. This is quite possible, but the suspicion persists that rather than MacColl learning the song 'from the singing of a young miner'[24] as he claimed, he wrote it himself. There are certainly reasons to question such a conclusion. MacColl wrote numerous songs and was always happy to accept the credit; several of them were written in the industrial folksong idiom, particularly in the post-war period. There were also some errors of fact in the song, surprisingly understating the number of deaths, which suggests that it was probably written near the time. If MacColl were writing a song on a pit disaster some time after the event, he might have chosen to research the number of fatalities and would have had no motivation to come up with a lower figure. Of course, if the song were hastily written and motivated primarily by a desire to have a polemic effect rather than provide a historical account, then that would not necessarily be the case. MacColl, though, might have been further tempted to make a song that fitted more neatly into the tradition of nineteenth-century pit disaster songs – 'The Ballad' was fiercely secular by comparison and involved some humour. Furthermore, the meter of the lyrics strongly echoes the style of the music-hall monologue (of the Stanley Holloway variety), and it is at least a reasonably educated guess to suggest that the lyrics began their life that way and were given a tune later.

> Now a fortnight before the explosion,
> To the shotfirer Tomlinson cried,
> 'If you fire that shot we'll be all blown to hell'
> And no-one can say that he lied.[25]

The monologue style is quite apparent in the build-up to the punch-line at the end of each stanza. The humour is all of a dry, cynical kind; the writer comes down firmly on the side of the miners in the matter of the subsequent inquiry and uses various socialistic words, such as 'comrades'. The strange, incongruous waltz-time melody to the bitter words is a very interesting aspect of the song, however. This song is interesting, then, whoever wrote it, as it would appear to have originated from the labour movement in one way or another, and unarguably entered the national folk heritage. Having said all that, we have no evidence to suggest that the song pervaded the consciousness of the labour movement – even in a local area – before MacColl and Lloyd popularized it.

Numerous so-called industrial folksongs were the products of the northern musical hall, which was often a lower-key, less commercialized[26] affair than its southern equivalent. The edges between the music hall and the workers' club were always blurred. In inter-war Bradford, the regular variety concerts staged at a wide range of clubs across the city were listed in the *Pioneer*, and labour and trade union clubs became part of that particular 'circuit'. Doubtless songs of the sort collected by Lloyd and MacColl were sung and enjoyed in labour clubs, particularly in the north of England, but they were never adopted as the music of the movement: they were harmless frivolities. Some no doubt raised a few knowing smiles amongst the politically aware; the semi-professional singers of the northern club scene were often workers who, for various reasons (mainly health-related, but they might have been black-listed for strike activity) had had to find new ways to earn a living. For that reason, dialect songs about strikes or black-legs were not unusual inclusions amongst the usual bawdy and frivolous fare. Other 'industrial folksongs' of inter-war origins may well have never been performed outside family groups before their post-war collection. The famous Eliot family of Birtley, with songs such as 'Pit Lie Idle', had some political motivations but would not appear to have considered using their compositions for the good of the movement in the inter-war years.

The ideology of the Revival, before it was adapted by the post-war industrial folklorists, meant that the rural was always prioritized over the industrial. The invented history insisted that agricultural workers did not keep up their traditions when they became industrial workers. For this reason, the Yorkshire sword dances collected by Cecil Sharp in 1913 were never properly credited to the Sheffield miners and steelworkers who demonstrated them to him.[27] The interesting fact that these dances were more ingenious and intricate than the morris dances of rural England was given little or no attention. Even MacColl and Lloyd were generally apologetic about their industrial folksong thesis, and about the 'roughness' of the songs. It is perhaps not surprising, therefore, that the labour movement did not fly in the face of the perceived wisdom of folklorists and declare the existence of folk culture amongst the industrial proletariat. Indeed, the rendering of industrial workers into being just parts of a capitalist machine, no longer capable of artistic expression, was deemed a central aspect of their critique of capitalism. Capitalism had stolen art and aesthetics from the workers. Where local working-class songwriters became part of the labour movement, their songs became labour or socialist songs, and the various newspapers published a huge wealth of these, of varying quality. Ideas about the potential value of a culture of struggle were talked about in the 1930s, particularly amongst communists, but it was some years before the existence of a 'treasury of song' belonging to the industrial proletariat was made nationally available.

Folk songs were regularly included in the concert programmes that we have discussed through this book. Choral programmes and community singing programmes would generally include some traditional songs, such as 'The Ash Grove'. Variety bills would invariably include the singing of traditional ballads, often Irish or Scottish ones, amongst the other well-known pieces. The national or regional character of some songs was used from time to time. While hardly a folk song by Sharp's definition, 'Ilkley Moor Baht 'At' would often compete with 'Will Ye Go Lassie Go' when Yorkshire and Scottish ILPers' throats were sufficiently lubricated to do battle at various conferences and summer schools. At the Bradford ILP's 'International Fancy Fair' in 1925, a large entertainment section under the title of 'International Dances, Playlets, etc.' was put on by a selection of nursery school children conducted by Miss Chignell. The programme included a variety of folk dances,[28] short plays of folk tales,[29] some traditional songs[30] and a maypole dance. The combined Socialist Sunday School groups of Bradford, who regularly appeared as 'Sunbeams', provided similar entertainment.[31]

May Day celebrations

There was some concern, expressed intermittently throughout the period, that May Day celebrations should particularly include folk arts. This is an interesting aspect of the different thoughts about May Day. May Day was, in the labour movement, particularly intended to be an *international* celebration, an international workers' tradition of late-nineteenth-century origin to rival many of the new national 'traditions' of the same period. It was instigated, initially as a one-off, in 1890 by the Second International as an 'international festival of the working-class movement'.[32] In England there were older 'folk' traditions associated with a May festival, and many felt that the international 'form' of May pageantry – marches, speeches, the passing of an international 'motion' and the singing of internationally known anthems – rather neglected the peculiarly English aspects of an earlier May Day. The traditional activity that made the strongest come-back was the inclusion of tableaux or floats in the procession. However, morris dancing, maypole dancing and folksong all managed to be included in May Day programmes during this period. The May celebrations in Smethwick in 1921 included morris dances, old English music and songs, and maypole dancing;[33] similar activities were seen at the Plymouth May Day celebrations in 1936, as well as Highland dancing! Variations from the customary international forms were often in the hands of local organizers, usually the local Labour Party and Trades Council.

The championing of a folk May Day was particularly evident in socialist writing for children. The Birmingham *Town Crier*'s 'Children's corner' insisted that 'May Day was one of the gayest times in Old England', lamenting that 'almost all of the old customs have died out'. 'Right away back down the ages, the country-folk danced round the maypole on May Day, but nowadays, with picture houses, concerts and wireless, no one seems to care any longer about the jolly old games.'[34] Socialist Sunday School May Day tableaux regularly featured maypoles in Birmingham, Bradford and elsewhere.[35]

The 'folking' of May Day was quite possibly part of a general and international attempt to diminish the socialist character of May Day. In 1920 the French parliament considered making May Day a national holiday, where 'all classes . . . of the nation should fraternise, inspired by the same idea and the same ideal'.[36] Of course, despite the international aspects of May Day, the various protests did have some differences of national character. The holiday never had quite the same atmosphere in the Southern Hemisphere; most north European countries had traditional flower festivals at that time of year that had some influence on the activities.[37] There would appear to have been attempts, however, to replace the labour tradition with a national one and those attempts did not all come from outside the movement. 'W.A.E.', the writer of the 'Smethwick Notes' in the *Town Crier*, praised a 'parson with vision' who led 'the only place in Smethwick where they try to keep May Day the way it ought to be': 'children . . . dancing round the Maypole'. While he did attempt to give it a touch of the William Morris, 'golden age' romanticism ('everyone who sees it is taken out of this drab, every-day world of ours for a short time'), he was more or less openly suggesting that May Day should have been a general civic event rather than a specific labour tradition. Also in the *Town Crier*, the editor William Chamberlain (as 'Watchman') wrote under the headline, 'In "Merrie England"':

> Time was when the ploughman and the lord, the milk-maid and the lady went out together on May Day with horn and tabor and merry garlands of May-blossom. Lads and lassies from cottage and castle danced around the Maypole and sang songs of welcome to Mother Nature. These were the days of morris-dancing and folk-songs and all kinds of healthy fun on the village greens . . . "Merrie England" knew nothing about sanitation or electricity or wireless or airships or medical science. But her people knew how to enjoy themselves.[38]

This was a classic exposition of the contradictions rife in 'golden age' utopianism: the idea of an agrarian past where all were happy in their places and enjoyed mutual respect regularly recurred in the late summer as well, when similar pieces would be written about the 'Harvest Home'. A correspondent to the *Town Crier* expressed similar concerns about the modern May Day, worried that previous demonstrations 'had been a little too solemn for the joyous Spring festival'. 'Could not some of the old folk-songs be revived and sung by the children?' he asked, 'and a shade less materialism introduced?'[39]

Generally speaking, however, in this period, May Day maintained a peculiar aesthetic form all of its own. The 1931 London May Day official programme included a drawing that invoked many of the traditional folk symbols of May: rural workers dancing around a tree. However, the central figure was an international symbol of May Day, a scantily clad female, half-May Queen, half-Liberty, and all the writing carried a strong, clear socialist message. The definitive aspect of the May Day celebrations was the inclusion of 'bands and banners' in the procession.

Other occasions where folk music was used or considered in the labour movement were lectures, 'gramophone recitals' and newspaper/magazine articles. In 1927 at the Erdington Labour Church, Birmingham, a gramophone recital was given on 'Ballads and Folk Songs'. It is difficult to glean how academic a discussion of folksong Mr J. L. Tedstone gave to the Erdington comrades, but his comments were described as 'most interesting'. He began by hoping that a selection of folk songs would manage to please a mixed audience, some who 'wanted all jazz and others all classical music'.[40] The idea that folk music had a universal appeal was one that was widely articulated.

As we have seen, although there were numerous folk evangelists amongst the ranks of labour, no coherent labour theory of folksong was developed separately from the ideology of the Revival. Consequently, folk music never became *the* music of the labour movement and though, of all genres, folksong was probably the one most readily thought of as 'a music of their own', it was seldom viewed as more than an important stage in a more general musical education.

The labour movement and popular music

From the Welsh male voice choirs, the Yorkshire and Lancashire brass bands and the workers' jazz bands of the North-East, to the new dance music and gramophone records of the Capitalist leisure industry, the popularity of music undoubtedly influenced the Labour movement...[41]

The idea of 'popular' music is problematic for all sorts of reasons. In this context I am essentially referring to that music which had demonstrable *popularity* rather than to the broader question of music 'of the people'. The popularity of different musical genres should not only be considered in terms of market share, although the various figures for sheet-music sales and gramophone-record sales are readily available. Amateur music making remained popular, and perhaps the most notable feature of popular music in the period – the dance-hall craze – is difficult to quantify: anecdotal evidence remains important even in this most commercial of areas. As we shall see, amateur and voluntary organizations were able to compete favourably, on a local scale, with the commercial *palais de danse*. Between the wars, the most popular music in Britain was heavily anglicized American dance music. Whatever popular nationalists, folksong enthusiasts or serious musical philanthropists might have thought about it, commercial music, written to be danced to, became extraordinarily dominant.

It is important to consider the wider popular music scene in Britain between the wars, so that we can attempt to understand the dominant attitudes in the labour movement. While some cultural ideas and arguments were peculiar to the labour movement, others were echoes of arguments that existed in the wider community. Outside these narrow considerations, how was the world of popular music transformed in this period from the voluntaristic and parochial Victorian picture painted by Dave Russell to the ocean-hopping popular jazz scene of the 1920s and 1930s?

The changing culture of popular music

As this was a period of considerable change in the field of music in Britain, it was also a period of struggle, reaction and radicalism. The world of music was at once unified and divided by the new influences exacted upon it. The biggest influence upon the art of music after the First World War – both on its production and on its consumption – was the birth of broadcasting. When the new BBC entered into this area of the entertainment business, it quickly found itself the most powerful operator in the field.[42] It was not a field dominated by powerful interests – indeed, it is stretching a point to call it a 'field' at all. Before 1922 there were a number of 'musics', each with its own social, economic and regional setting:

> the choral societies, brass bands and military bands with their competitions and festivals; the concert publics, elite and popular, in London

and the major provincial cities and resorts; the background music performed in cafés, restaurants and cinemas; music hall and the emerging
musical shows and revues; the vogue for opera and operetta, the beginnings of the dance music craze.[43]

Radio took these cultural forms from their context and rendered them
'popular' and 'national'. It was only really when broadcasting
co-ordinated this musical collision that terms like 'high-brow', 'middle-
brow' and 'low-brow' became meaningfully applicable to music and
broadly used.[44]

This fragmented musical culture did not universally welcome radio's
interference. There was the broad concern that the growth of broadcasting
would lead to a decline in various live music experiences (concert attendances, for instance), and the music publishers were concerned that
sheet-music sales would suffer. The conductor, Sir Thomas Beecham, felt
that the broadcasting of serious music was a 'stupid' sin against 'the unfortunate art of music'.[45] There were also suggestions that people who
listened to 'the wireless' would stop practising or playing the piano.[46] In
fact, there is some evidence that serious music concerts gained larger audiences because people wished to see what they had heard on the
wireless, and sheet-music sales increased sharply owing to the huge
demand for live dance music.[47]

An influence upon music to rival that of broadcasting was the rapidly
increasing demand for leisure brought about by rising purchasing power,
the reduction of working hours and the extension of paid holidays.[48] The
effect this had upon 'the unfortunate art' was manifold. While more
people could afford to make good any promise they showed for performance with the improved affordability of musical instruments and the
increased leisure time for practice, the more striking influence was the increase in leisure time and disposable money that could be spent in the
commercial leisure industry.

Dance music

Of all the various 'musics' we are referring to, it was dance music (which
included various forms of jazz and 'crooning') that really exploded in this
period. This constituted the roots of 'pop music', where particular numbers could be considered 'hits', although an actual 'hit parade' or chart
was a post-war phenomenon. There were different strata within the appreciation of dance music. The most popular dance or jazz music in Britain
was of a basic, anglicized kind, concentrating upon melody rather than
rhythm, such as that provided by the long-standing BBC dance-band

leader, Henry Hall. He was not interested in 'the extremes of hot jazz', but preferred tunes that could be whistled.[49] Enthusiasts or 'connoisseurs' of dance music, such as the writers and readers of *Melody Maker*, idolized American musicians like Duke Ellington and Louis Armstrong. However, when those two did a studio performance for the BBC, the general dance music appreciating public did not appreciate it at all. They much preferred Henry Hall. *Melody Maker*, which was initially a musicians' trade magazine, considered Henry Hall 'not interesting enough to be called bad'.[50]

Working-class dancers in the commercial *Palais* would dance to music not dissimilar to that danced to at middle- and upper-class society functions:[51] there was a degree of 'one-nationism' in dance music's listening public, although not much social integration in dancing itself. It was a music characterized by the youth of its audience rather than the *class* of its audience, and those who were appalled by the music were similarly united by age across the classes. With that in mind, Dave Harker's assertion that 'popular culture' is a euphemism for 'working-class culture' from the position of 'ruling-class culture' – an 'unhistorical falsification of class culture'[52] – is particularly interesting. While dance music was not a classless cultural phenomenon (while young people of all classes danced, they did not all dance together), its cross-class appeal rendered it popular rather than plebeian. The 'musically interesting forms of jazz',[53] to use the phrase of BBC policy-makers, were broadcast but remained a specialist interest. Some of the 'catchier' dance tunes and songs were broadcast purely as songs rather than as music to dance to: it was thought that such songs were replacing Victorian and Edwardian ballads in the public imagination.[54]

Popular music was regularly controversial. One example was the reaction to 'crooning'. Prior to the development of broadcasting and gramophone recording, vocal styles were based upon acoustic performances. A new generation of singers, such as Bing Crosby and Al Bowley, manipulated the microphone. This is an interesting example of some social attitudes to this revolutionary phase in the history of popular music. Crooning was banned by the BBC in 1936 because the style was considered to be in bad taste and morally dubious.[55] The ban did not remain in place long, however, as it was difficult to enforce. It was impossible to regulate all outside broadcasts (many dance programmes were broadcast from a live performance in a dance hall or club) and there was no strict definition of crooning. When we come to discuss labour attitudes to popular music we shall see that they often echoed the concerns of establishment figures such as BBC bosses, and the roots of some misgivings may well have been generational rather than ideological or musicological.

Similarly, concern about the commercialization and Americanization of culture through the dance craze was not reserved to socialists and labour movement thinkers. There were internal divisions amongst BBC policy-makers that ranged from believing that 'syncopated music is here to stay',[56] to considering that such music was a sign of 'moral degeneracy' and 'cultural barbarism', and linking this to the cultural form's racial origins.[57] Some jazz music innovations spread to the metropolis and to national broadcasts from the provinces: swing music was initially broadcast in Aberdeen. The Controller of Programmes, Cecil Graves, 'felt that Aberdeen would be better advised to encourage a local choral society rather than to put its money into a jazz combination'.[58] One can easily imagine a local Labour chairman making a similar recommendation. When a swing-music programme was broadcast under the heading of a 'jam session', Graves declared that central supervision should be introduced 'to prevent this sort of thing'.[59]

A strong strand in BBC policy making stemmed from the middle-class, philanthropic tradition of promoting social harmony amongst the working classes via music.[60] Many of the socialist ideas and concerns of the early part of the twentieth century were echoed here. This same tradition promoted chamber music (considered 'a negation of market values')[61] and was concerned that music should not be commercialized. Concerns about the commercial nature of the popular music business led to the BBC trying to prevent bands 'plugging' songs on the radio and thus making money for the publishers in sheet-music sales. They experimented with banning vocal numbers so that the song title could not be heard, and then, after complaints from listeners, attempted to prevent band members from announcing songs.[62] By the late 1920s commercial radio was beginning to lead the field in the broadcasting of popular music,[63] which rather forced the BBC into taking a less dim view of commercial music.

The growing concern that culture and the arts were being commercialized was grounded on a number of basic facts. The gramophone industry expanded greatly during the 1920s, especially after the introduction of electric recording in 1925, and held its own during the depression. Although forty gramophone companies were formed between 1927 and 1929, EMI completely dominated the market by 1932.[64] The 'talkies' made big business of musical film stars like Shirley Temple, Fred Astaire and Ginger Rodgers in Hollywood, or Gracie Fields and George Formby in the UK.[65] As this commercialization was seen as the intrusion of capitalism into the lives of the workers, it was a matter of great concern to socialists. However, this element of capitalism did, arguably, bring benefits to the workers: 'more cinemas, more dance halls, and more radios'.[66] The benefits of such advances were not universally felt, though, and the working class by no means experienced greater leisure as a homogeneous group. For many there was little enough money for the basics of subsistence: commercial and popular leisure was still a luxury for many on the poverty line.[67] The popular music boom also helped other areas of the music industry: the musical instrument trade was nearly twice as big in 1937 as in 1907, and various instruments were given a boost by popular trends: piano by ragtime, the ukulele by George Formby and wind instruments by jazz.[68]

Another revolutionary aspect of the dance music 'craze' was that it opened the way for working-class musicians to become professionals, and make a living from their talent.[69] Most of this work was in dance halls or cinemas, although the latter source declined with the advent of 'the talkies' from the late 1920s.[70] Some dance musicians, especially in Scotland, had originally played music for more traditional sequence dancing and country dancing, and had to develop their style towards jazz by emulating popular bands.[71] This was not just done musically; they would also strike 'jazzy poses' to maintain popularity,[72] showing that despite the popularity of dance music on the radio, the enjoyment of such bands was not just an aural experience.

Musical combinations at the beginning of the period, playing country-dance and tea-dance music, were often just piano and violin duets; but as the American influence worked on the popular music scene through the 1920s, so combinations had to expand and have drummers and brass players.[73] It was the experience of one dance band (Scottish pianist Arthur Allen's band in the late 1920s) that they would be told that some performances were being broadcast by the BBC, but never see any fee.[74] There were blurred edges between professional, semi-professional and amateur musicians; often the same musicians would play at dance halls, ice-cream parlours, restaurants and cinemas and would sometimes even play 'light classical things' and 'opera'.[75]

Despite the transformation of a large number of amateur working-class musicians into a new class of worker, and (though sometimes well paid) a brand of worker particularly vulnerable to exploitation, the labour movement was always rather ambivalent about the status of musicians and their union. While Boughton, for instance, used his platform to campaign for the creation of a union for all artists, some trade unionists felt that musicians should choose which job they were doing and which union they were to join. Most musicians were of uncertain, semi-professional status, working in one job during the day and as a musician in the evening – this activity was not always viewed with favour by leading unionists. In 1921, however, the Birmingham *Town Crier* devoted some of its space to the Amalgamated Musicians' Union's demands for recognition by the Cinematograph Exhibitors' Association, with minimum rates for different 'classes' of cinema musician.[76]

While commercial music was the real growth area in this period, musical activity in the voluntary sector should not be ignored. Socialist music groups, of one kind or another, were always a minority interest in Britain, but other voluntary music groups achieved considerable local popularity. The trend of working-class, non-commercial musical activity had, for many years, been away from middle-class patronage and towards more identifiably working-class organizations, such as 'the village choirs of South Wales' and 'the brass bands of the Industrial North'.[77] As we have already discussed, these organizations enjoyed great popularity and their competitions, such as the Welsh choirs' eisteddfod,[78] engendered considerable enthusiasm. It has been suggested that participation in the brass band movement was in decline between the wars, perhaps due partly to the increased accessibility of other forms of musical entertainment and partly to the bands being located in areas badly affected by the depression. Despite this, however, there were thousands of amateur brass bands in action at that time.

This diverse and radically changing popular musical culture was what musical socialists had to come to terms with or satisfactorily challenge. A critique of popular culture is a dangerous undertaking for a popular party, and the Labour Party never made any official attempt to form one. It was left to a number of individuals to use their intellects and prejudices to undertake such a task.

The labour movement and dance music

Reaction to jazz from within the labour movement was no less violent and polarized than it had been in society more generally. When attempting to answer the question 'What is Socialism?' in a symposium of the same title, that roguish wandering minstrel, Walter "Casey" Hampson declared: 'In art it means that Bach, Beethoven, Mozart, Bantock and Boughton shall take the place of coon cacophony, cake walks, rag and bone time and jazz.'[79] However the historian might seek to half-excuse Casey's racism by historicizing comments and use of language, the statement is at best terribly reactionary and extraordinarily bizarre. It is not as if he were simply saying which music was *better*, in his view, but which music was *socialism*. One can accept his nod to his comrade and patron Rutland Boughton, but the way he set up the binary in this sentence (and the preceding ones)[80] suggests that popular music, the preferred music of thousands of working-class people in Britain and elsewhere, was the *antithesis of socialism*. Furthermore, he made no attempt to justify this with socialist analysis: it was not that such tunes were commodified in the capitalist entertainment industry, nor even that their lyrics were fatalistic opiates of the masses. It was just because the music was noisy and played by black Americans. So much for the 'delightful' person who had spent his life 'teaching the workers love of music and love of their fellow man'.[81]

Sir Arthur Bourchier used similar language in his dismissal of 'jazz' music. He described it as 'the crude, savage, cacophonous jazz that we hear on every hand today'. Not only does this echo Hampson's thoughts on 'cacophony', but also the word 'savage' hints at the playing of the race card again. Although there were strong internationalist and anti-colonialist aspects to the labour movement at this time, it was not a party free of racism or immune to popular social Darwinist theories about Aryan superiority. In 1920 the National Administrative Council of the ILP voted unanimously in favour of a policy demanding the withdrawal of all 'black troops' in Europe because such 'uncivilised' people would be a danger both to themselves and to European women. They claimed to put forward the policy in a spirit 'without race prejudice'.[82] Indeed the ideas of E. B. Tylor (1832–1917) about Darwinist social progress from savagery and barbarism to civilization (and the associated idea of residual primitive cultures) were used to 'empirically defend' imperialism and Aryan superiority as well as the 'scientific' explanation of folk arts[83] and the backbone of Boughton's *longue durée* musicology.

If, as has been repeatedly suggested,[84] musical socialists were influenced by the writings of the Reverend Hugh Haweis, then the connection between race and music would have been noted in his famous text. Indeed, by comparison, Hampson and Bourchier could be seen as having toned down the racism of Haweis, who wrote about 'the conquering nigger' proclaiming 'the glories of Niggerdom throughout the length and breadth of this benighted land'.[85] Certainly Haweis' references to race demonstrate the prevalence of such views in society, and how well established those concerns about the demoralizing effects of music of black origin were. Both detractors and evangelists for jazz made reference to its status as 'negro music', although more thoughtful criticisms of jazz, such as those made by Adorno, questioned its authenticity as 'black music' in much the same way that the authenticity of folk music has been questioned. Despite this preoccupation with jazz music's African origins, however, it was its American origins that made it the spirit of the age, the essence of modernity. 'Jazz bands came from the same country as Henry Ford'[86] and Hollywood movie stars.

Bourchier, as we have already considered, attempted a more thoughtful critique than Hampson; the problem with jazz was that it was 'the musical expression of capitalist society'.[87] That opinion was widely expressed in the movement, sometimes in sloganistic form. Printing its question with no headline or explanation, the *Bradford Pioneer* asked, 'what has Capitalism done for art except exploit it for £.s.d?'[88] Such concerns went way beyond music to other aspects of popular culture: a speaker at East Birmingham Labour Church, in 1921, 'wished the workers would take as much interest in things that matter as they did in football'.[89] It was often this disappointment with the attitudes of the working class – Blatchford's reluctant Messiah or Tressell's 'ragged-trousered philanthropists' – that fuelled the anti-popular perspective.

The strange thing about all the most serious debates about jazz is that they were really discussing something rather different from what British working-class youngsters were listening and dancing to. Eric Hobsbawm, a genuine jazz evangelist, remarked that people in the 1930s had to distinguish 'real stuff' from the 'surrounding sweet or syncopated dross'. Real jazz enthusiasts would have agreed with many of the criticisms levelled by musical socialists and other cultural critics against the most popular forms of dance music. Therefore, when considering popular music, the debate about 'hot' jazz's claim to being some kind of avant-garde art music is rather beside the point.

One 'hot' jazz trend that did become broadly popular was the 'swing' craze which, as we mentioned earlier, entered England via Aberdeen. Interestingly, swing music in the USA was promoted by an anti-racist broad left encompassing communists and New Dealers.[90] Some of the swing artists joined the Communist Party, such as Dizzy Gillespie, who later claimed that he had done so in order to get more gigs![91] Why was there no similar socialist embrace of such music in Britain? By the late 1930s there was some feeling that jazz, blues, folk and various 'roots' musics constituted a 'People's music',[92] especially in the WMA, but there prevailed an abiding interest in English music and in considering what sort of music was 'the best'.

To large numbers of musical (and not so musical) socialists, it was self-evident that modern popular music was not 'the best' and was quite possibly the worst music available. The editor of the *Town Crier*, while lamenting the passing of 'Merrie England', complained that 'now the village green has disappeared . . . we dance to jazz "music"' and that the new 'folksongs of the people' were 'Yes, sir, that's ma baby' and 'Chick, chick, chick, chick, chicken, lay a li'le egg for me'![93] For such people there was never any question that modern popular music might have had any merit as music: it was one of the many absurd and damaging features of industrial capitalist society.

All of this sheds new light on what we found in Chapter 2: that local labour movements were acutely aware of the propaganda, fund-raising, recruitment and entertainment possibilities of dance music and dancing. Whatever were the emotions and forces that filled the *Palais de Danse* each night filled the Co-op dances, ILP dances, Labour Party dances and Young Communist dances as well. Similarly, whenever groups of socialists and trade unionists got together to have a really good evening, their musical programme was not restricted to chamber music, folk songs or labour anthems: a good variety bill was the preferred choice.

Locally, labour activists recognized that 'everyone dances nowadays, and even if they despise this simple amusement they can enjoy looking on'.[94] Special mention was made of dancing at any social event advertised in labour newspapers from the beginning of the period, and dances became more and more frequent through the 1920s as the 'craze' swept the nation. As early as 1920 the Midland Clarion Club at Sheldon presented itself as 'The Keen Dancers' Paradise', and it held dances every Saturday.[95] Other labour institutions came to dwarf this paradise with their regular provision of readily affordable dancing with increasingly better 'floors', bands and dance tutors. The Birmingham Co-operative Society was such a case, hosting dancing most nights of the week. From 1921, members and friends of the Witton ILP branch became fanatical dancers with regular packed dance-floors on Saturday nights.[96] These events became easier to stage through the period as more and more local parties attained 'rooms' or a club.

Along with the 'perfect band' and 'tip-top programme', labour dances were sometimes advertised with the instruction to 'SUPPORT ONE OF YOUR OWN', recognizing the interest in dancing and trying to harness that interest for the movement. As we saw in Chapter 2, the same sort of picture can be painted in Bradford, Keighley and, by studying the notes in the *Labour Organiser*, right across the country. Furthermore, it would appear that – if the intention was to fill its own halls rather than empty the commercial ones – the labour movement's sally forth into the world of popular dance was rather successful. In the Socialist League in the 1930s, for instance, dancing was the primary social activity of the organization, often combined with discussion and deliberately aimed at 'ecumenical' Popular Frontist sociability.[97]

The movement even gave rise to some of its own jazz bands that would advertise for engagements. As well as some that were voluntary musical combinations organized along the same lines as the choirs and bands, such as the short-lived Birmingham Labour Party Dance Band, other new semi-professional bands advertised that they were made up of Labour Party members in the labour press.[98]

Ewan MacColl's account of a Young Communist League 'social and dance' in his autobiography, *Journeyman* (1990) gives an idea of what such events were like at the less well-funded end of the movement. The room had 'a plank floor varnished to make it look like a real dance floor; a small platform for the "band", inadequate lighting and usually a few paper decorations from three Christmases ago'. The 'band' was a trio of local amateurs with the peculiar combination of piano, saxophone and drums. In the middle of the dance, various local communists did 'turns' – usually the rendering of popular ballads.[99]

Clearly such events were never going to challenge the dominance of the commercial dance hall. However, they did perform one function that we did not consider when looking at the entertainment, fund-raising and propagandist functions of labour socials: they provided an opportunity for young socialists to meet like-minded comrades of the opposite sex in a more convivial atmosphere than the branch meeting. Sex was obviously a driving force behind the dancing craze and the Young Communist League dance was no exception. 'It was an occasion where unattached males were intent on capturing unattached young females,' MacColl wrote. The last hour and more especially the last half-hour of the dance would be an increasingly panic-ridden struggle to find somebody pre-pared to be walked home.[100] MacColl describes his and his comrades' sexual awakening, courtesy of the Young Communist League dances; better by far if the next generation of socialists were born into the move-ment rather than having to be converted.

The rights and wrongs of the type of music involved were rarely the subject of local debate. In the columns of labour papers, there would oc-casionally be an ironic swipe at one form of popular music or another. The existence of 'comic songs which don't deal with mothers-in-law or the love of beer' was thought 'marvellous but true' by one writer in the *Bradford Pioneer*.[101] One writer in the *Town Crier* hoped that a 'MUSI-CAL COMEDY WITH A PLOT' might start a new fashion.[102] The *Town Crier*'s Smethwick correspondent lamented the passing of the old dances, such as the waltz. Similarly, in a consideration of the English character and national pride in the ILP *New Leader*, in 1926, a joke was made about the volume of jazz music: 'in music we have lost all claim to progress since in a recent contest the American band was heard three and half miles further away than ours'.[103]

Other aspects of the dance-hall culture were sent up in the labour press. The 'flapper' was a particular figure of fun – and, occasionally, horror. In a cartoon representing falling wages and rising prices, a well-built working woman (representing the proletariat) stood beside a thin, short-skirted 'flapper' (representing the bourgeoisie). The skirts represented wages and prices, and the working woman was saying 'They've made me lower my skirt, I hope they're going to make her do the same.' The extreme end of the dance-hall craze that was characterized by the flapper dancing every night was considered the worst kind of bourgeois decadence, although such keen dancers were often young, working women. Presumably there were enough men at these events as well, but it was the girls who became the symbols of excess.

In the *Railway Review*, the journal of the National Union of Railwaymen, its comic writer 'Battersea Bowser' wrote a piece on 'a modern produck', 'a sample o' the risin' generation', who 'hinsisted on tryin' to teach the whole family to dance. To dance, mindjer!' This piece was rather light-hearted and self-deprecatory about the older generation's difficulties in coming to terms with the dance phenomenon. 'A grammyphone struck up a tinny sort o' tune, all jerks and spasms like a Communist orator, and I see Peggy tryin' to show Mrs Smithie ah to chuck 'er legs abaht in all sorts o' hangles.'[104]

Male fashions were sometimes commented upon, again with tongue-in-cheek admiration of the 'audacious' new styles. The latest trouser design – 'Oxford Bags' – received considerable column space in the *Town Crier*.

> At a dance held last Saturday, at Ruskin Hall, Aston, considerable excitement was caused by the appearance of a young man in Oxford Bags! At first everybody seemed amused. But towards the end of the evening it was noticed that the young ladies were keen to dance with the wearer of the bags. So keen was the competition, in fact, that at times certain of the ladies in question were seen to be 'having words', no doubt owing to one or other having 'rushed' the young sport![105]

Jazz and dance became particularly strong symbols of all that anyone wanted to damn or praise in the 1920s and 1930s – they were either symbolic of modernity and progress, or else the symbols of decadence and degeneracy. The reasons for the varied reactions to this popular music went way beyond technical or aesthetic considerations of music: they were the essence of the era.

Socialist music

For some, the counter-culture or 'music of their own' was not already in existence in working-class communities, waiting to be promoted; it had to be assembled and shaped by socialists for socialism. Folk music had its attractions, particularly the perceived communal composition, but the music was simplistic, rustic: a phase in musical development, but not powerful in itself. The popular musical forms of the day, jazz or variety songs, were fascinating because of their very popularity and power to attract an audience; but they were simply commodities produced by the capitalist leisure industry – opiates rather than clarion calls. Art music had the power to impress and elevate, and evoke sophisticated ideas; yet it was aloof, inaccessible and of the ruling classes. What was required, some began to feel, was some manner of synthesis: a *socialist* music. A *class-conscious* 'music of their own'.

The Workers' Theatre Movement

In the 1930s, one area where specifically socialist art was talked about, thought about and practised was the Workers' Theatre Movement, the cultural wing of the Communist Party. Some of its ideas about socialist drama began to be considered in its music sections too. In 1931 an editorial from the *Workers' Theatre Movement Monthly Bulletin* (later *Red Stage*) declared that it would be 'the height of folly' for its singing groups to 'entertain thoughts of competing with established choirs and choral societies in the Labour and Socialist movement'. Because of the 'untrained' nature of the 'comrades' and the movement's usual materials and methods, it was believed that its music groups should perform 'agit-prop' music.[106] At this stage there was no clear idea of what that might mean, and Alan Bush argued retrospectively that, at least in London, the established choirs of the labour movement were strictly agitational in their repertoires.[107]

One example of what sort of music the WTM might have been looking at was a song included in the same issue of the bulletin from the Red Megaphones[108] group in Manchester. This 'local group song', apparently written communally by the whole troupe, but certainly bearing hallmarks of its leading member Ewan MacColl,[109] was to be sung to a German tune: 'Red Rockers'. The song was filled with local references ('workers from Salford, from Cheetham and Hulme') and uncompromising communism:

> Forward, young workers, come surging ahead,
> Hacking the pathway that our class must tread.
> Smash the oppression and boss-class greed,
> Led by the fighting Young Communist League.[110]

Clearly there was no concern about the 'dangers' of art being used as propaganda in this composition, although it was not so very different, other than in its local character, from some earlier labour movement anthems.

Later that same year the *Red Stage* declared that 'Art is a weapon in the Revolution' and included a song entitled 'Comintern' with English text by T. Thomas put to a tune by Hans Eisler. Once again the lyrics served to press home a point with no aesthetic frills: 'our aim is united, our flag is unfurled, a Soviet Republic all over the world'.[111] T. Thomas continued to provide pro-Soviet English text to new communist music in the pages of *Red Stage* on subjects such as the Five-Year Plans.

In later issues of *Red Stage*, increasingly interesting syntheses of the various musics available were discussed and used. The traditional folk tune 'Billy Boy' was given new words:

> Shun the forces of reaction;
> Put your faith in mass class action;
> And get in the workers' party –
> Get class conscious, Billy Boy![112]

A Workers' Theatre Movement collective communally wrote 'The Soviet Airmen's Song', a simple tune praising the Soviet fighter planes 'defending the US-SR!'[113] At the same time, there were discussions about amending the words of jazz songs because 'jazz does definitely bring us closer to the workers as, for one thing, it is easier to sing and memorise . . . let us use those tunes, there is rhythm and life in their music'. It was the words not the music that was wrong with jazz, according to this correspondent from Castleford:

> The lyrics of most of them are rank piffle, and lead the worker into a sense of fatalism that everything will come right bye-and-bye . . . cut out the words and put in words expressing our class consciousness. Words that will inspire all right-thinking workers to help build the future state of society, the workers' state.[114]

This coincided with some communist interest in jazz in other countries: 'central European cultural bolsheviks . . . associated [jazz] with the proletariat and revolution. Britain escaped this phase.'[115]

Britain might have escaped a phase quite of that nature, but the idea of putting new communist words to popular jazz tunes was attempted. The popular song 'Breakaway' was amended to 'twelve-hour day' as part of a longer sketch on 'Love In Industry'.

> Boss: Let's do that twelve-hour day,
>   Of course you'll get less pay
>   And that you'll only get by and by . . .
> Workers: Oh boss how good we feel
>   Our love for you is real
> Boss: You're proving it every day in every way![116]

Another piece, written by the pro-jazz correspondent from Castleford, S. R. Gough, was 'Oh Workers!' to the tune of 'Oh Mona!'

> The boss cut your wages, you'll not deny
> (Oh, workers)
> Then he'll put you on the Means Test, by and by
> (Oh, workers)
> He'll put another penny on your pint and then
> (Oh, workers)
> Send you out to China[117] to kill working men
> (Oh, workers)
> Oh workers! When will you be free?
> Oh workers! You can be free!
> Organise for Liberty![118]

There was nothing new about the use of well-known tunes for the setting of socialist lyrics. Whether we consider the old favourite anthems of *Chants of Labour*, which included ironic settings to the National Anthem and 'Rule Britannia' as well as numerous familiar airs, or the Tannenbaum setting of 'The Red Flag', or numerous 'parodies' in labour newspapers,[119] familiar music was an important tool of the trade. What was different was the specific use of popular music, not because of its familiarity, but because of it popularity. It was not just that these tunes were known, rather it was that there was something powerful in them that made them a more effective weapon in the struggle than the old, hymn-like anthems. There were also interesting ideas about the infectious and propagandist properties of rhythm. The use of rhythm to propagate was a recurrent theme in the WTM: the agit-prop drama-style itself was often intensely rhythmical, in the manner of beat-poetry or 'rapping'.

However, the Workers' Theatre Movement continued to persist with some of the older labour musical forms. It published *The Workers' Song Book*, which included 'words and music of eight revolutionary songs' and then 'words-only' versions of nine more songs and 'parodies'. The WTM also looked, despite its earlier castigation of the idea, in the direction of choral music and forming small choirs. Choral music was considered 'another step forward', and the WTM planned to start issuing four-part arrangements of songs to theatre groups. This was with a view to 'enable those workers who appreciate the great value of good, disciplined singing to form small choirs of their own, which in time should add another weapon to the cultural armoury of the working class'.

The first ammunition came in the form of 'excellent choral versions' of 'The Internationale' and 'The Red Flag' by Rutland Boughton. However, the given reason for this experiment with choral music was not to carry on the labour tradition, but once again to fuse popular culture with socialist agitation: 'before long we will have enough choral music to keep the good comrades in South Wales and Yorkshire who want to sing good music and at the same time assist the workers' struggle fully occupied'.[120] Where choral singing was perceived to be a very popular musical pastime, the coupling of that activity with propaganda could be viewed in the same bracket as putting political lyrics to popular jazz tunes.

Some of the communist songs and 'parodies' of the 1930s entered the movement's own 'oral tradition'. 'When the Red Revolution Comes' was sung to the tune of 'John Brown's Body'. This song was largely playful, including such verses as 'We'll make Anthony Eden wear a fifty-shilling suit' and 'We'll stick a mast in Churchill and float him down the Thames'.[121] Other songs, like 'Jimmie Maxton and All of His Men', were included in large numbers of song books as well as *Red Stage* and other publications. Many of the National Unemployed Workers Movement songs mentioned in Chapter 4 gained similar notoriety.

Some of the songs of the labour movement that found their way into papers or became favourites at marches and protests might also be called industrial folksong. A. L. Lloyd strayed on to difficult territory when insisting, in *Folk Song in England*, that 'The Internationale' could not be considered 'folkloric'; nor could any of the 'non-folkloric labour anthems and "literary" political mass-songs with their agitational content, elated feeling and hymn-like style'.[122] His reasoning might not have extended to some of the songs of struggle referred to in Chapter 4, communally written and sustained by the crowds, and amended over years to engage with new struggles. The likes of Alan Bush began to take such music more seriously, including marching 'rounds' in song books, as I mentioned in the previous chapter. Similar songs were written to be sung at election times, such as 'Liberals Three' to the tune of 'Three Blind Mice':

> Liberals Three,
> Liberals Three,
> See how they vote,
> See how they vote,
> The first says 'Aye' and the next says 'No',
> The third isn't certain where to go;
> Was there ever so fine a variety show
> As the Liberals Three?[123]

Come All Ye Bold Miners included songs, such as John Eliot's 'Aa Wes Gannin' Inbye' – based on 'Moonlight Bay', a 1930s pop song – that were parodies of inter-war popular music.[124] Lloyd's definition of industrial folksong was more rigid in theory than in practice.

A political counter-culture

Underlying all of this was a burgeoning conception of counter-culture and ideas of hegemony. 'C.B.M.' – a regular contributor to *Red Stage* – wrote that

> every form of popular art and entertainment, public opinion and 'moral direction' is controlled by capitalist interests – or their agents, the Government and the Church . . . Even 'sport' is a commercialised affair that reflects the dirty mismanagements of its capitalist promoters . . . That is what we are up against. A capitalist state; capitalist control; capitalist propaganda making use of every form of thought to poison the thinker, or, better still, to keep him from thinking at all . . . We are not competing with capitalist entertainment, we are exposing it.[125]

While this analysis might lack the subtlety of Gramsci, it reveals that thought about the political role of culture, and something approaching a thesis of hegemonic control, existed in the cultural wing of the Communist Party.

That these questions were considered, albeit on no great level of sophistication, is further evidenced by the concerns of the Left Theatre Ltd in 1936. A letter was sent to the *Socialist* (the organ of the Socialist League) requesting shareholders. In the correspondent's argument about the importance of the Left Theatre, he mentioned the political power and role of 'capitalist' theatre by referring to songs like 'Tipperary' and 'Keep the Home Fires Burning'. The purpose of Left Theatre, it was argued, was to culturally challenge the conservative sentiments in the music and other aspects of the popular theatre.[126] Even at this stage, the writer was very unlikely to have heard of Gramsci, but Lenin's musings about the existence of 'two cultures' would appear to have had some influence. These ideas are central to Ian Watson's studies of 'democratic' music. For Watson, the inter-war labour movement represented a 'largely unrecorded "second culture" phenomenon'.[127] While I am not seeking to dismiss this, his assessment that this movement 'ran parallel to, but separate from the mainstream of bourgeois musical activity of the time' places insufficient importance on the increasingly self-aware cross-pollination between the activities in the labour movement and those in the wider musical world.

The Workers' Music Association (WMA) represented the crystallization of these burgeoning musical ideas into an organisation or movement. While, later in its history, the Association became an educational organization, in its early period, according to Alan Bush, the WMA concentrated on 'what was *singable* to them [the working class], what was *performable* to them and *appropriate* for their particular political requirements'.[128] Springing from the London Labour Choral Union and the WTM.'s music section, the WMA never managed to attract the provincial musical combinations such as the Clarion choirs (now stragglers, rather than pioneers).

Essentially, however, the WMA was a foundation upon which left-wing cultural politics of the 1940s and 1950s would be built. While it provided a fascinating coda to the inter-war period, the inter-war labour musical movement belonged to the likes of Boughton, Sear and Hampson, not to Bush and certainly not to MacColl or Lloyd. It is therefore strange that the views of those first three men should become so anachronistic and of novel antiquarian interest so very quickly. However, their work in making sections of the labour movement able and willing to embrace the radical cultural and aesthetic ideas that became important after the Second World War should not be underestimated.

Conclusions

On commencing the early notes for this book, I was in a position greatly to sympathize with H. G. Sear and his vain labours at the helm of the Birmingham Labour Symphony Orchestra. Like him, I found gaps in my orchestra. On deciding my area of study and composing some early research questions, I was far from certain that music had played an important role in the lives of inter-war labour activists at all. Equipped with the contingency plan of asking 'Why did the labour movement stop singing?', I began to search for what sources might be useful and which historical figures, from both the labour and musical worlds, warranted further investigation. My research was radically and mercifully to shatter my concerned preconceptions about inter-war labour music. Instead of finding the sad, dying chords of a late Victorian golden age of pioneering, religious labour culture, I found the crescendo of cultures old and new (sometimes in harmony, sometimes in discord) and an inexhaustible contemporary literature of musical comment in newspapers, magazines, pamphlets and books.

Clearly the work of certain individuals – H. G. Sear, Rutland Boughton and Alan Bush, in particular – was absolutely central to the role and importance of music in the inter-war labour movement. There would have been music without them – and plenty of it – but in terms of the organization of musical activities and the production of ideas about music, the importance of a small number of committed individuals cannot be overstated. Nevertheless, the interests and labours of committed individuals are not enough to account for the near constant musical accompaniment to labour movement activism between the wars. There was something specific about the nature of labour movement politics that drew it to music and to aesthetic theories. Similarly, there were properties of music that made it an invaluable weapon for any movement that looked to win over hearts and minds.

The politics of the inter-war labour movement, from the dry reformist to the fiery revolutionary, from the most secular materialist to the most zealous, spiritual evangelist, looked to alleviate or eradicate the drudgery of work, and of the life of workers, in a modern capitalist society. As such, they felt that they were in common cause with art and aesthetics – genuine art and aesthetics, that is. Art that failed in that key aesthetic task might have had other merits, but it was not the ally of socialism in that particular fight. Much of the apparent prejudice and intolerance shown by musical socialists stems from that assertion. 'Bad' music was often 'bad' because it duped (or doped) the workers, or because it simply reflected or replicated industrial or commercial drudgery instead of transcending it. That aesthetics and social progress had common cause had long been ruminated upon. The great nineteenth-century theorist of aesthetics, John Ruskin, in a lecture in 1858 'would invite Bradfordians to leave their selfish little kingdoms behind in favour of a broader "commonwealth" in which life and lives "will join and increase into one magnificent harmony"'.[1] William Morris had no doubt that his design, his poetry and his political activism were but different means to the same end.

Through the 1930s, the possibilities of agitational art were explored and with that the notion that there could be merit in the idea that works of art and pieces of music could represent the realities of industrial capitalism or working-class life. But for much of the period, the role of art was to be beautiful, and to be beautiful was to entirely negate the industrial capitalist reality (and yet somehow to arrive at a 'truth'). *Proletkult* or social realism this was not. Although some Soviet cultural ideas and debates made their way into Communist Party of Great Britain discussions, particularly in the 1930s, labour musical thought was largely conservative and did not attempt to challenge the nineteenth-century, bourgeois, romantic heritage. Instead, it recognized a radical potential therein.

It is clear that thought about music changed considerably through the inter-war period. These changes were partly inspired by intellectual developments, particularly imported ideas from the Soviet Union, Germany and the USA. While socialist – and particularly communist – interest in intellectual and artistic developments in the Soviet Union is unsurprising, it was the very successful embrace of the arts by the German Social Democrats that inspired British musical socialists to strive for greater things in the 1920s. As well as mass choral organizations and musical and dramatic pageants, the German labour movement had its own impressive collection of top artists. Like Boughton, Bush, Auden and Shaw in Britain, Hans Eisler, Kurt Weill and Bertolt Brecht were to employ their considerable talents in the service of the movement. Their influence extended beyond their own country when people like Kurt Weill fled Germany and spent time in exile in the UK. Weill's music was characterized by contemporary jazz influences, and this, in turn, appears to have influenced groups like the Workers' Theatre Movement.

The International Workers of the World in the USA had already been interested in song before this period, proud to have songwriter Joe Hill as a prominent member. In the 1920s and 1930s they became interested in American folksong, including industrial song – an interest that was to start to influence British socialists by the end of the period. This interest was taken up by the American left-wing musicologist, Charles Seeger, whose ideas were to have their greatest influence in Britain after the Second World War, both via the academy, through the invention of the discipline of ethnomusicology, and through the music of his children. Pete Seeger was a very successful folk singer after the Second World War and Peggy Seeger – Ewan MacColl's wife and musical partner – was to play an important part in the communist folk record label, Topic,[2] the Charles Parker Radio Ballads and the British Folk Revival.

Perhaps equally important, it would appear that experience – and particularly the experience of *struggle* – inspired people to look more closely at music as 'a weapon in the struggle' rather than simply as 'beauty'. This led to the labour movement developing quite distinct aesthetic and cultural theories after the Second World War, looking to express a working-class consciousness and to present working-class life. This found its musical expression primarily through the industrial folksong movement and later through protest song.

For this reason, the history of the musical culture of the British labour movement between the wars is in fact an important stepping stone in a fuller understanding of cultural change in twentieth-century Britain. While many national cultures experienced a period of avant-garde experimentalism in the early part of the twentieth century, the arts in Britain remained conservative. Avant-garde art, cubism and futurism, and general cultural 'leftism' did not entirely pass Britain by. They were represented in Alfred Orage's Leeds Arts Club between 1903 and 1923, for instance, which looked to nurture and promote the aesthetic and artistic left. But one only need look at the most successful and influential artists to have been involved in that club to see why the 'provincial avant-garde' whom it represented did not come greatly to challenge the romantic tradition. Its contributors included G. K. Chesterton, George Bernard Shaw and Edward Carpenter. Carpenter was considered a founding influence.[3] While it is interesting that these characters approved of an avant-garde Arts Club, they were exceptionally traditional themselves. While Chesterton's associations with the *political* 'left' are doubtful, and he later had rather more concrete associations with the political right, Shaw and Carpenter were part of the cultural vanguard of the socialist movement at the turn of the century. With regard to music, Shaw was 'the perfect Wagnerite'; both were the perfect radical romantics, following in the footsteps of Ruskin and Morris. The British cultural left had its own story of the romantic tradition and, as such, prolonged a certain type of artistic conservatism beyond its course elsewhere. In music, Alan Bush was virtually alone as an inter-war British avant-garde composer, and his attendance at the University of Berlin would appear to have been an important factor.

The longevity of the romantic tradition was not just because of the artistic predilections of some individuals; there was a long labour tradition of romantic art, exemplified best by Chartist poetry and lyric.[4] Carpenter quite particularly drew from that tradition, as is evidenced by the content of his song collection, *Chants of Labour* (1888). Socialist Romanticism (even Communist Romanticism) survived between the wars in the compositions of Rutland Boughton amongst others, and poetry by the likes of Carpenter and even W. H. Auden. What caused the transformation from radical romanticism in the 1920s to agit-prop and social realism in the 1930s? When did art cease to be simply about beauty and begin to lend an importance and significance to ugliness as well?

Agit-prop and *Proletkult* were not just British phenomena, and the overseas influences through the international labour movement – perhaps most especially through the international communist movement – helped disseminate new ideas, as did the migration of European radicals under the threat of fascism. But that is not the whole story: after all, Soviet futurism did not have much impact on the communist movement in the early 1920s. Experience was an important factor, as were 'cultures of struggle'. These cultures of struggle, explored in Chapter 4, were artistically creative, as we discussed. The art that emerged from cultures of struggle, and particularly the musical art, was often satirical and keen to put across a political message clearly and simply. The aim was for the audience to be in no doubt as to the convictions, and the hardships, of the performers; this undoubtedly helped shape the form of agit-prop drama and satirical song in the 1930s Workers' Theatre Movement at least as much as overseas intellectual influences. These cultural forms, in their turn, helped shape the whole 'working-class aesthetic' in post-war Britain from the *Radio Ballads* and the 'angry young men' to Billy Bragg and *Brassed Off*.

Clearly, for many, music *was* just 'a pleasant change from politics', but it was also deemed to have an important value as a 'weapon in the struggle', whether that was to bring beauty where there was ugliness, or to hammer home the socialist message with sharp satire.

Notes

Introduction

1. Ian Watson, 'Alan Bush and left music in the thirties', *Gulliver*, no. 4, 1978.

Chapter 1   Socialism and Music

1. There is a general survey of this debate in John Marriott, *The Culture of Labourism: The East End between the Wars* (Edinburgh, 1991), pp. 4–5.
2. Ross McKibbin, *The Evolution of the Labour Party, 1910–1924* (Oxford, 1974), p. 240.
3. Tom Nairn, 'The nature of the Labour Party', in New Left Review (ed.), *Towards Socialism* (London, 1965).
4. Stephen Yeo, 'A New Life: the religion of socialism in Britain, 1883–1896', *History Workshop Journal*, no. 4, 1977, pp. 5–56.
5. Chris Waters, *British Socialists and the Politics of Popular Culture, 1884–1914* (Manchester, 1990), pp. 100–1.
6. As well as Chris Waters' assertion that this text influenced socialist ideas about music, it is described as 'influential' by Dave Russell and something of its popularity or perceived importance can be assumed from its running to fifteen editions between 1871 and 1888.
7. Hugh Haweis, *Music and Morals* (London, 1871) was divided into four books. Book One is called 'Philosophical: Music, Emotions and Morals' and Book Four: 'Critical: Music in England'.
8. Ibid., pp. 42–3.
9. Ibid., p. 115.
10. Tony Brown (ed.), *Edward Carpenter and Late Victorian Radicalism* (London, 1990), p. 7.
11. Ibid.
12. Robert Blatchford, *Merrie England* (1908), p. 9.
13. Haweis, *Music and Morals*, pp. 21–4.
14. Ibid., p. 28.
15. Ibid., p. 98.
16. Ibid., p. 104.
17. Ibid., p. 117.
18. Ibid., p. 574.

19. Dave Russell, *Popular Music in England, 1840–1914: A Social History* (Manchester, 1987), p. 4.
20. Ibid., p. 17.
21. Ibid., p. 44.
22. By 1909 Messrs Murdoch and Company claimed to have provided violins for 400,000 pupils in over 500 schools. At the same time there were claims in the *School Music Review* that 10 per cent of English children were receiving violin tuition at school. More girls received lessons than boys. Ibid., p. 47.
23. Cyril Ehrlich, *The Piano: A History* (London, 1976), p. 159.
24. Waters, *British Socialists and Popular Culture*, p. 101.
25. Ibid., p. 105.
26. *Worker*, 19 April 1919.
27. Waters, *British Socialists and Popular Culture*, pp. 106–7.
28. Ibid., p. 107.
29. 'Up Ye People', words by J. Gregory, in Edward Carpenter, *Chants of Labour* (London, 1922), p. 52.
30. 'To Liberty', words by P. B. Shelley, in Carpenter, *Chants of Labour*, p. 55.
31. Waters, *British Socialists and Popular Culture*, p. 121.
32. Russell, *Popular Music*, p. 53.
33. Waters, *British Socialists and Popular Culture*, p. 124.
34. Gareth Williams, *Valleys of Song: Music and Society in Wales, 1840–1914* (Cardiff, 1998), pp. 2–3.
35. Ibid., pp. 174–5.
36. Ibid., p. 194.
37. Russell, *Popular Music*, pp. 40–1.
38. Waters, *British Socialists and Popular Culture*, pp. 126–7.
39. Brown (ed.), *Edward Carpenter*, p. 17.
40. Raymond Williams, *Keywords: A Vocabulary of Culture and Society* (London, 1988), p. 87.
41. Antonio Gramsci, 'Why we need a Cultural Association', in Antonio Gramsci, *Pre-prison Writings* (Cambridge, 1994), p. 35.
42. Robert Witkin, *Adorno on Music* (London, 1998), p. 181.
43. Rutland Boughton, *The Reality of Music* (London, 1934), p. x.
44. Ibid., p. 173.
45. Walter Benjamin in Maynard Solomon (ed.), *Marxism and Art* (Brighton, 1979), p. 552.
46. Boughton, *The Reality of Music*, pp. 144–6.
47. [EM/PS] *Red Stage*, June–July 1932.
48. 'The Left Theatre', *Socialist*, July–August 1936.
49. [EM/PS] Ailie Monro, 'Folk music, politics and the WMA', Workers' Music Association Occasional Paper, March 1988.
50. V. I. Lenin, 'L. N. Tolstoy', in Solomon, *Marxism and Art*, p. 176.
51. Leon Trotsky, 'Proletarian culture and proletarian art', in Berel Lang and Forrest Williams (eds), *Marxism and Art* (New York, 1972), p. 68.
52. Waters, *British Socialists and Popular Culture*, p. 181.

53. H. G. Sear, 'The men behind the music', *Town Crier*, 3 April 1925.
54. Waters, *British Socialists and Popular Culture*, p. 125.
55. Donald Brook, *Composer's Gallery* (London, 1946), p. 34.
56. 'The right to leisure', *Worker*, January 1919.
57. Rutland Boughton, 'The Arts as a part of the worker's life', *Labour Magazine*, vol. II, no. 7, November 1923, p. 303.
58. Edward Carpenter, *Towards Industrial Freedom* (London, 1917), p. 50.
59. Waters, *British Socialists and Popular Culture*, p. 6.
60. Russell, *Popular Music*, p. 52.
61. Brown (ed.), *Edward Carpenter*, p. 23.
62. William Morris, *News from Nowhere and Other Writings* (London, 1993), p. 53. This is a recent 'Penguin Classics' edition.
63. This tradition in lyric and poetry is documented in Anne Janowitz, *Lyric and Labour in the Romantic Tradition* (Cambridge, 1998).
64. Edward Carpenter, 'Engand, Arise!', in Carpenter, *Chants of Labour*, p. 18.
65. Labour Church hymn: 'Heaven on Earth', *Town Crier*, 8 October 1926.
66. Labour Church hymn: 'Break the Chains!', *Town Crier*, 1 October 1926.
67. Edward Carpenter, 'The Day of the Lord', in Carpenter, *Chants of Labour*, p. 94.
68. 'Opera at the Repertory Theatre: The Immortal Hour', *Town Crier*, 8 July 1921.
69. Keith Nield, 'Edward Carpenter: the uses of utopia', in Brown (ed.), *Edward Carpenter*, pp. 24–6.
70. Martin Wright, 'Robert Blatchford, the Clarion movement, and the crucial years of British socialism, 1891–1900', in Brown (ed.), *Edward Carpenter*, p. 75.
71. Ibid., p. 77.
72. 'Opera at the Repertory Theatre: The Immortal Hour', *Town Crier*, 8 July 1921.
73. Wright, 'Robert Blatchford', p. 74.
74. Marriott, *The Culture of Labourism*, pp. 7–8.
75. Sydney A. Court, 'Music and the people: a message to the labour movement', *Labour Magazine*, vol. II, no. 10, February 1924, p. 445.

Chapter 2 Pleasure, Pennies and Propaganda: Music in the Associational Life of the Labour Movement

1. Dave Russell, *Popular Music in England, 1840–1914: A Social History* (Manchester, 1987), p. 2.
2. Stanley Sadie (ed.), *The New Grove Dictionary of Music and Musicians*, Vol. 3 (London, 1980), 'Bradford', pp. 151–2.
3. Ibid., 'Birmingham', p. 126.
4. F. Reid, 'Socialist Sunday Schools in Britain, 1892–1939', *International Review of Social History*, 11 (1966), pp. 18–49.

5. 'John Trevor and the decline of the Labour Churches', in Joyce M. Bellamy and John Saville, *Dictionary of Labour Biography*, Vol. VI (1982), p. 251.
6. Ibid.
7. *The Labour Church Hymnbook* (1906).
8. Bellamy and Saville, *Dictionary of Labour Biography*, p. 251.
9. John Boughton, 'Working-class politics in Birmingham and Sheffield, 1918–1931', University of Warwick Ph.D. thesis (1985), p. 286.
10. Throughout the 1920s the Birmingham *Town Crier* had both a 'Labour Church Announcements' section amongst its advertisements and a section headed 'Labour Churches' amongst reports of meetings and events, which would primarily include reports on the last meeting and occasionally messages to the congregation, such as when the Church would be closing or if there had been a change to the programme.
11. Boughton, 'Working-class politics in Birmingham and Sheffield', p. 286.
12. *Town Crier*, 16 January 1925. Sparkbrook ILP Labour Church on the Stratford Road (Sparkbrook had two Labour Churches in 1925) announced: 'There is an opening for a regular pianist at this Church and offers will be greatly appreciated.'
13. *Town Crier*, 2 September 1921.
14. John Boughton referred to the 'utmost variation' in topics covered by Labour Church speakers in his description of a typical meeting. Boughton, 'Working-class politics in Birmingham and Sheffield', p. 286.
15. *Town Crier*, 4 December 1925.
16. *Town Crier*, 5 March 1926. H. G. Sear did his 'The Men Behind the Music' talk at the Handsworth Labour Church on 7 March 1926, for instance.
17. *Town Crier*, 24 July 1925.
18. *Town Crier*, 9 January 1925.
19. *Town Crier*, 31 March 1922.
20. *Town Crier*, 7 April 1922.
21. 'A grand musical programme by the Lozell's Co-operative Choir', *Town Crier*, 24 February 1922.
22. 'The AEU Male Voice Choir provided an excellent programme of chorus and song', *Town Crier*, 17 March 1922.
23. The 'friendly orchestra' who provided the 'excellent programme' were not named in the *Town Crier*, 31 March 1922.
24. *Town Crier*, 7 April 1922.
25. *Town Crier*, 13 February 1920.
26. Correspondence from William MacBeath on the subject of 'Labour Choirs', *Town Crier*, 4 March 1921.
27. For example, they conducted a 'musical service' at Sparkbrook Labour Church on 3 February 1924. *Town Crier*, 1 February 1924.
28. *Town Crier*, 2 October 1925.
29. The National Labour Choral Union is the subject of a section in Chapter 3.

30. The 'Selly Oak Labour Church Choir' provided 'an enjoyable musical evening' at the Selly Oak Labour Church on 14 February 1926.
31. *Town Crier*, 19 November 1926.
32. On 27 March 1927, Ladywood Labour Church had one of these 'lecture-recitals' for the Beethoven centenary celebrations given by Mr O. G. Willey. The advertisement in the *Town Crier* mentioned that the 'gramophone selections' would be played on the 'new HMV Instrument'. *Town Crier*, 25 March 1927.
33. On 3 April 1927, Ladywood Labour Church had 'Another Beethoven Night' with 'Wildred Whiteley and the Gramophone' including the following selections: 5th Symphony, *Egmont* Overture, *Coriolan* Overture and *Leonora* Overture No. 3. *Town Crier*, 1 April 1927.
34. *Town Crier*, 26 November 1926.
35. At the Ward End Labour Church on 27 March 1927, the report in the *Town Crier* recorded that 'after the meeting we had community singing'. *Town Crier*, 1 April 1927.
36. Also on 27 March 1927 there was community singing. The advert in the *Town Crier* announced that 'Mr H. G. Sear will conduct COMMUNITY SINGING.' *Town Crier*, 25 March 1927.
37. Boughton, 'Working-class politics in Birmingham and Sheffield', p. 286.
38. John Trevor, *The Labour Church Hymn-Book* (1891).
39. *Town Crier*, 13 August 1926.
40. Ibid.
41. *Town Crier*, 24 September 1926.
42. *Town Crier*, 1 October 1926.
43. 'Old English Tune 573 (Bristol) – Jesus Refuge'. Taken from the Bristol collection of Old English Tunes.
44. 'Tune 403 (Bristol)'.
45. *Town Crier*, 8 October 1926.
46. *Town Crier*, 26 November 1926.
47. *Town Crier*, 11 March 1927.
48. *Town Crier*, 18 March 1927.
49. Boughton, 'Working-class politics in Birmingham and Sheffield', p. 287.
50. Ibid., p. 286.
51. Ibid.
52. Ibid., p. 289.
53. *Town Crier*, 5 December 1924.
54. Boughton, 'Working-class politics in Birmingham and Sheffield', p. 287.
55. *Bradford Pioneer*, 27 February 1925.
56. [WYA-Kly] 2D80/A/7 Keighley ILP Minute Book, 1920–1 – various references to pianos.
57. Jim Ainsworth, *Accrington and District, 1927–1934: The Cotton Crisis and the Means Test* (Hyndburn and Rossendale TUC, 1997), p. 330.
58. Numerous examples, such as Great Horton Socialist Sunday School

'Open Sunday' with speaker (T. Blythe) and soloist (Mr. H. Brooke), reported in *Bradford Pioneer* on 28 February 1919.

59. Great Horton Socialist Sunday School 'Open Sunday' (advert), *Bradford Pioneer*, 25 October 1918.
60. *Bradford Pioneer*, 4 April 1919.
61. *Bradford Pioneer*, 3 January 1919.
62. *Bradford Pioneer*, 31 January 1919.
63. *Bradford Pioneer*, 2 April 1920.
64. Various references are made to this effort in labour publications in the early 1920s. He had raised £700 by the beginning of 1923. *Bradford Pioneer*, 23 February 1923.
65. [WYA-Kly] 2D80/A/8 Minute Book 1927–1930, 5 August 1930.
66. V.Eff, 'Casey and Dolly', *Bradford Pioneer*, 14 December 1928.
67. Labour Publishing Company, *Labour's Who's Who* (London, 1924), p. 74.
68. Keith Laybourne, *The Rise of Socialism in Britain c.1881–1951* (Stroud, 1997), p. 32.
69. *Bradford Pioneer*, 26 October 1923.
70. For example, in early 1930 there was a lecture on 'Music and the Proletariat', illustrated by gramophone records, given by the 'well-known wireless lecturer Mr M. Baritz', *Bradford Pioneer*, 10 January 1930.
71. *Bradford Pioneer*, 15 February 1929.
72. *Bradford Pioneer*, 22 February 1929.
73. *Bradford Pioneer*, 1 March 1929.
74. Reid, 'Socialist Sunday Schools in Britain', p. 20.
75. *Town Crier*, 19 December 1919.
76. [WYA-Kly] 2D80/F/1-2 Socialist Sunday School Song-book (1910).
77. [WYA-Kly] 2D80/F/1-2 Socialist Sunday School Song-book (1925).
78. [WYA-Kly] 2D80/F/1-2 Socialist Sunday School Song-book, Hymn No. 70 (1925).
79. No. 12 in 1910 and No. 10 in 1925.
80. Once again no apology is made for the gender specificity.
81. [WYA-Kly] 2D80/F/1-2 Socialist Sunday School Song-book, Hymn No. 12 (1910) and No. 10 (1925).
82. Reid, 'Socialist Sunday Schools in Britain', pp. 46–7.
83. The Woodcraft Folk was the Co-operative movement's alternative to the Scout movement. Set up in 1924, it was largely based around folksong and, like the Socialist Sunday Schools, attracted a lot of attention from the Communist Party.
84. A Manningham Socialist Sunday School meeting in 1930, for instance. *Bradford Pioneer*, 6 June 1930.
85. *Bradford Pioneer*, 30 March 1923.
86. *Bradford Pioneer*, 31 March 1922.
87. Reid, 'Socialist Sunday Schools in Britain', pp. 46–7.
88. *Bradford Pioneer*, 22 March 1929.
89. *Bradford Pioneer*, 23 June 1933.
90. *Bradford Pioneer*, 30 January 1931.
91. *Bradford Pioneer*, 20 February 1931.

92. *Town Crier*, 21 November 1919.
93. *Town Crier*, 7 January 1921.
94. [WYA-Kly] 2D80/C/1 ILP Social Committee Minutes. Numerous examples, such as 21 November 1921.
95. [WYA-Kly] 2D80/C/1 ILP Social Committee Minutes, February (? – no date) 1922.
96. [WYA-Kly] 2D80/B/1 Women's Labour League Minutes, 1914 and 1917.
97. [WYA-Kly] 2D80/B/1 Women's Labour League Minutes, 24 January 1922.
98. [WYA-Kly] 2D80/B/1 Women's Labour League Minutes, 7 February 1922.
99. [WYA-Kly] 2D80/B/1 Women's Labour League Minutes, 21 February 1922.
100. [WYA-Kly] 2D80/B/1 Women's Labour League Minutes, 21 March and 4 April 1922.
101. [WYA-Kly] 2D80/B/1 Women's Labour League Minutes, 30 January 1923.
102. [WYA-Kly] 2D80/C/1 ILP Social Committee Minutes, 22 January 1924.
103. Pamela Graves, *Labour Women* (Cambridge, 1994) enters this debate.
104. [WYA-Kly] 2D80/B/1 Women's Labour League Minutes, 25 March 1924.
105. Ibid.
106. [WYA-Kly] 2D80/C/1 ILP Social Committee Minutes, 11 August 1924.
107. Keith Withall, 'The Voluntary Organising Committee of the Musicians' Union, 1935–1939: a study in rank and file trade unionism', Ruskin College thesis (1976).
108. [WYA-Kly] 2D80/C/1 ILP Social Committee Minutes, 25 August 1924.
109. [WYA-Kly] 2D80/A/8 Keighley ILP Minute Book, 11 November 1929.
110. [WYA-Kly] 2D80/A/8 Keighley ILP Minute Book, 9 November 1931.
111. [WYA-Kly] 2D80/A/8 Keighley ILP Minute Book, 27 March 1934.
112. [WYA-Kly] 2D80/A/8 Keighley ILP Minute Book, 21 July 1921.
113. *Town Crier*, 17 October 1924.
114. *Town Crier*, 9 October 1925.
115. The most successful of these was Witton ILP, whose dances were regularly advertised and reported in the *Town Crier* through the 1920s: 'the weekly dances are meeting with great success', *Town Crier*, 24 September 1926; 'the usual weekly dance was very successful on Saturday last', *Town Crier*, 1 October 1926.
116. For example, there was 'vocal and instrumental music' advertised at the ILP Garden Party in Birmingham to be held on 17 July 1920. *Town Crier*, 9 July 1920.

117. *Bradford Pioneer*, 11–25 August 1922. An open-air meeting at Shipley Glen required 'choirs to be present to help the meeting with a good old hymn or two'; 'all branches which boast a choir are urged to bring it along to assist in discoursing sweet music before the speeches and leading the crowd in some good old Labour hymns'. The Huddersfield ILP Choir was especially engaged for the meeting 'and they know all about choirs in Huddersfield'.
118. *Town Crier*, 25 August 1922.
119. *Bradford Pioneer*, 29 June 1923.
120. *Bradford Pioneer*, 22 June 1923.
121. *Bradford Pioneer*, 6 July 1923.
122. *Town Crier*, 10 October 1919.
123. *Town Crier*, 16 April 1920.
124. *Town Crier*, April 1920.
125. *Socialist Leaguer*, June–July 1934.
126. Sidney A. Court, 'Music and the people: a message to the labour movement', *Labour Magazine*, vol. II, no. 10, February 1924.
127. *Town Crier*, 11 November 1921.
128. These took place at Saltley Ward (a 'victory tea and social' which was 'spent in games, music and dancing'), *Town Crier*, 2 December 1921; Washwood Heath Ward (with 'whist, dances, and splendid glees and solos by the Lozell's Co-operative Choir'), *Town Crier*, 9 December 1921; Sparkbrook Labour Party (who enjoyed a 'musical programme . . . of an exceptionally high standard', featuring female impersonations, songs, pianoforte solos, duets and 'humorous items'), *Town Crier*, 16 December 1921; and Victoria Ward in Smethwick (with a 'most successful social and the "Red Lion"', featuring 'real high class music'), *Town Crier*, 16 December 1921.
129. *Town Crier*, 15 December 1922.
130. *Town Crier*, 15 April 1921.
131. *Town Crier*, 22 April 1921.
132. *Town Crier*, 26 August 1921.
133. *Town Crier*, 9 September 1921.
134. *Town Crier*, 16 September 1921.
135. There were many events all around the country, including brass band competitions and labour hymn singing.
136. [WYA-Bfd] *Bradford Independent Labour Party International Fancy Fair: Souvenir Programme* (1925), p. 1.
137. [WYA-Bfd] *Souvenir Programme* (1925), p. 6.
138. [WYA-Bfd] E. Priestly (Superintendent of Music and Assistant Inspector of Schools), *City of Bradford Education Committee Syllabus of Music for Infants* (October 1933).
139. [WYA-Bfd] *Souvenir Programme* (1925), p. 12.
140. [WYA-Bfd] 5D87/1/1 Heaton ILP Group (Minutes), 4 December 1928.
141. [WYA-Bfd] 5D77/5/3 Miscellany 1933 ILP Socialist Bazaar material.

142. There are many references to concerts, dances and socials raising money for the NUR Orphans' Fund across the country in the *Railwayman* (the weekly, national NUR journal) throughout the period.
143. [WYA-Kly] 2D80/C/1 ILP Social Committee Minutes, 14 October 1918.
144. [WYA-Kly] 2D80/C/1 ILP Social Committee Minutes, 11 November 1918.
145. [WYA-Kly] 2D80/C/1 ILP Social Committee Minutes, 25 November 1918.
146. [WYA-Kly] 2D80/C/1 ILP Social Committee Minutes, various references to paying or tendering for bands.
147. *Town Crier*, 6 February 1920.
148. Ibid.
149. *Town Crier*, 12 March 1920.
150. *Town Crier*, 9 April 1920.
151. *Town Crier*, 24 February 1922.
152. *Town Crier*, 24 November 1922.
153. *Town Crier*, 8 December 1922.
154. For example, 'Ladywood Labour Party entertains 500 kiddies' including 'a charming piano and mandoline duet' and singing, reported in the *Town Crier*, 21 January 1920.
155. *Town Crier*, 6 January 1922.
156. *Town Crier*, 27 January 1922.
157. *Bradford Pioneer*, 11 May 1928.
158. *Town Crier*, 4 March 1921.
159. *Town Crier*, 28 May 1920.
160. *Town Crier*, 11 February 1921.
161. *Town Crier*, 14 May 1920.
162. *Town Crier*, 7 July 1922.
163. *Town Crier*, 13 February 1925.
164. 'Witton ILP: . . . the weekly dances are meeting with great success', *Town Crier*, 24 September 1926; 'the usual weekly dance was very successful on Saturday last', *Town Crier*, 1 October 1926.
165. *Town Crier*, 10 December 1926.
166. *Bradford Pioneer*, 27 November 1925.
167. *Bradford Pioneer*, 23 October 1925.
168. *Bradford Pioneer*, 14 November 1930.
169. Anonymous, 'The ILP Arts Guild', *Bradford Pioneer*, 4 September 1925.
170. Arthur Bourchier, *Art and Culture in Relation to Socialism* (London, 1926), p. 7.
171. Ibid., p. 15.
172. *Town Crier*, 5 March 1920.
173. *Town Crier*, 11 February 1921.
174. A 'first class programme' was promised for such a social event in the *Town Crier*, 1 April 1921.
175. *Town Crier*, 9 June 1922.
176. *Town Crier*, 19 May 1922.

177. The story of the *Town Crier* and its changing editors and editorial policies is told in Peter Drake, 'The Town Crier: Birmingham's Labour
Weekly, 1919–1951', in Anthony Wright and Richard Shackleton
(eds), *Worlds of Labour: Essays in Birmingham Labour History* (Birmingham, 1983), pp. 103–22.

Chapter 3 Choirs, Bands and Orchestras

1. Michael Hurd, *Rutland Boughton and the Glastonbury Festivals*
(Oxford, 1993), p. 171.
2. Chris Waters presents quite a detailed history of the CVUs before 1914
in *British Socialists and the Politics of Popular Culture, 1884–1914*
(Manchester, 1990).
3. H. G. Sear, 'Labour choirs and orchestras', *Town Crier*, 22 October
1926.
4. 'An "eisteddfod" for labour', *Town Crier*, 14 August 1925.
5. Sydney A. Court 'Music and the people: a message to the labour movement', *Labour Magazine*, vol. II, no. 10, February 1924, p. 445.
6. Hurd, *Rutland Boughton*, p. 171.
7. Ian Watson, 'Alan Bush and left music in the thirties', *Gulliver*, no. 4,
1978, pp. 85–6.
8. Court, 'Music and the people', pp. 445–6.
9. Ibid., p. 446.
10. Ibid.
11. Watson, 'Alan Bush and left music', p. 87.
12. Hurd, *Rutland Boughton*, pp. 171–6.
13. Watson, 'Alan Bush and left music', p. 87.
14. Hurd, *Rutland Boughton*, p. 176.
15. Watson, 'Alan Bush and left music', p. 85.
16. E. D. Mackerness, *Somewhere Further North* (London, 1974).
17. *Town Crier*, 21 January 1921.
18. *Town Crier*, 20 May 1921.
19. Advertised in the *Town Crier*, 21 January 1921.
20. *Town Crier*, 28 January 1921.
21. *Town Crier*, 22 April 1921.
22. *Town Crier*, 29 April 1921.
23. *Town Crier*, 25 August 1922.
24. *Town Crier*, 17 August 1923.
25. *Town Crier*, 24 August 1923.
26. *Town Crier*, 31 August 1923.
27. *Town Crier*, 21 January 1921.
28. *Town Crier*, 11 February 1921.
29. *Town Crier*, 4 March 1921.
30. *Town Crier*, 11 March 1921.
31. Ibid.
32. It was felt, rightly or wrongly, that they could rely on established combinations for any of their musical needs.
33. *Town Crier*, 16 May 1924.

34. The BLMS (later the BLMU) reported on its first rehearsals in the *Town Crier*, 25 April 1925.
35. *Town Crier*, 3 September 1926.
36. *Town Crier*, 10 September 1926.
37. *Town Crier*, 18 February 1927.
38. *Town Crier*, 15 April 1927.
39. *Town Crier*, 27 May 1927.
40. *Town Crier*, 20 May 1927.
41. In August 1927 the choir visited Rowley Labour Club and 'a local singer in the person of Mr Woodhouse gave "My Wild Irish Rose" in fine style'. He also promised to visit Smethwick the following Saturday. *Town Crier*, 24 June 1927.
42. *Town Crier*, 8 July 1927.
43. H. G. Sear, 'Labour choirs and orchestras', *Town Crier*, 22 October 1926.
44. C. Salway-Wallis, 'Socialism and song: a plea for music: make meetings merrier', *Town Crier*, 16 January 1925.
45. *Town Crier*, 30 January 1925.
46. *Town Crier*, 27 February 1925.
47. *Town Crier*, 24 April 1925.
48. *Town Crier*, 1 May 1925.
49. *Town Crier*, 19 June 1925.
50. *Town Crier*, 3 July 1925.
51. *Town Crier*, 14 August 1925.
52. *Town Crier*, 19 February 1926.
53. H. G. Sear, 'A plea for pure music', *Town Crier*, 2 October 1925.
54. *Town Crier*, 26 February 1926.
55. *Town Crier*, 5 March 1926.
56. 'An educated guess would be for a circulation of about 1500 in the early 1920s, rising steadily to possibly 3000 just after the 1929 General Election and then declining to 2000 throughout the 1930s.' Peter Drake, 'The Town Crier, Birmingham's labour weekly, 1919–1951', in Anthony Wright and Richard Shackleton (eds), *Worlds of Labour: Essays in Birmingham Labour History* (Birmingham, 1983), p. 109.
57. *Town Crier*, 23 March 1926.
58. *Town Crier*, 19 March 1926.
59. *Town Crier*, 16 April 1926.
60. *Town Crier*, 23 April 1926.
61. *Town Crier*, 4 June 1926.
62. *Town Crier*, 25 June 1926.
63. *Town Crier*, 2 July 1926.
64. *Town Crier*, 6 August 1926.
65. *Town Crier*, 10 September 1926.
66. *Town Crier*, 15 October 1926.
67. *Town Crier*, 22 October 1926.
68. Ibid.
69. Ibid.
70. *Town Crier*, 5 November 1926.

71. *Town Crier*, 10 December 1926.
72. *Town Crier*, 17 December 1926.
73. Ibid.
74. Labour Publishing Company, *Labour's Who's Who* (London, 1924), p. 143.
75. There was a brief biographical note about Jabez Hall when he was standing for the Council in the *Town Crier*, 30 October 1925.
76. *Town Crier*, 1 May 1925.
77. *Town Crier*, 24 December 1926.
78. *Town Crier*, 21 January 1927.
79. *Town Crier*, 28 January 1927.
80. *Town Crier*, 4 February 1927.
81. The article was written in the first person plural.
82. *Town Crier*, 4 February 1927.
83. *Town Crier*, 11 February 1927.
84. *Town Crier*, 15 April 1927.
85. *Town Crier*, 22 April 1927.
86. *Town Crier*, 8 July 1927.
87. *Town Crier*, 29 April 1927.
88. *Bradford Pioneer*, 1 November 1918.
89. *Bradford Pioneer*, 11 July 1919.
90. Martin Wright, 'Robert Blatchford and the Clarion movement', in Tony Brown (ed.), *Edward Carpenter and Late Victorian Radicalism* (London, 1990), p. 96.
91. *Bradford Pioneer*, 15 May 1919.
92. 'Pioneer Choir, musical evening at the Britton Hall on Saturday 3 May', *Bradford Pioneer*, 2 May 1919.
93. *Bradford Pioneer*, 5 September 1919.
94. [WYA-Bfd] *Souvenir Programme* (1925), p. 10.
95. Advertised regularly in the *Bradford Pioneer* from 10 February 1922.
96. *Bradford Pioneer*, 10 March 1922.
97. H. G. Sear, 'HMV C2106', *Bradford Pioneer*, 1 May 1931.
98. *Bradford Pioneer*, 26 March 1926.
99. 'Mus. Bac.', 'The Pioneer Choir concert', *Bradford Pioneer*, 27 March 1925.
100. Ibid.
101. Anonymous, 'A triumph for the other Pioneer', *Bradford Pioneer*, 20 November 1925.
102. 'As is usual the singing of the Massed Choirs was the finest feature.' Jack Ramsden, 'National CVU contest at Sheffield', *Clarion*, May 1928.
103. Anonymous, 'A triumph for the other Pioneer', *Bradford Pioneer*, 20 November 1925.
104. *Bradford Pioneer*, 6 July 1923.
105. *Bradford Pioneer*, 20 July 1923.
106. *Bradford Pioneer*, 27 July 1923.
107. *Bradford Pioneer*, 30 October 1925.
108. 'On Sunday last in the King's Hall, White Abbey Road, the orchestra

of the West Ward Labour Club gave two magnificent concerts, which were magnificently appreciated by the people of the neighbourhood.' *Bradford Pioneer*, 6 October 1922.
109. *Bradford Pioneer*, 16 March 1923.
110. Court, 'Music and the people', p. 444.

Chapter 4 Song and Struggle

1. [IWM, SCW, SA] 12942/1 Sgt Bernard McKenna (International Brigade) from: 'In our hearts were songs of hope' (BBC Radio broadcast, presented by Jim Lloyd and researched by Roy Palmer).
2. Hywel Francis, *Miners Against Fascism: Wales and the Spanish Civil War* (London, 1984), p. 23.
3. 'For the nation as a whole, poverty and ill health were less pronounced during the inter-war years than before 1914. Nevertheless, it is clear that in areas where there was high structural unemployment, and in all those districts which suffered high cyclical unemployment in the early 1930s, poverty and ill health were probably more rife than they were before 1914.' Keith Laybourn, *Britain on the Breadline: A Social and Political History of Britain, 1918–1939* (Stroud, 1990), p. 65. 'Britain was still one of the richest countries in the world in the 1930s, yet far too many were excluded from its benefits.' Tony Mason, 'Hunger . . . is a very good thing', in Nick Tiratsoo (ed.), *From Blitz to Blair* (London, 1997).
4. *Socialist Leaguer*, June–July 1934.
5. Chris Waters, *British Socialists and the Politics of Popular Culture* (Manchester, 1990), p. 99.
6. Dave Russell, *Popular Music in England, 1840–1914: A Social History* (Manchester, 1987), p. 17.
7. Ibid., pp. 18–19.
8. Ibid., pp. 21–2.
9. Dmitri Shostakovich in 1931, cited in Ian Watson, 'Alan Bush and left music in the thirties', *Gulliver*, no. 4, 1978. Watson does not give details of where Shostakovich wrote or said this. It is an interesting quotation in the light of debates about the extent to which Shostakovich might be considered a revolutionary.
10. This idea of music (or more especially song) as a point of access to civil society for the illiterate is pursued in both of those texts and also in Roy Palmer, *The Sound of History: Songs and Social Comment* (London, 1988).
11. Sometimes the words will have been printed with music for people to sing elsewhere. Sometimes, however, lyrics were printed without the music or the intended tune.
12. Oscar Lewis, *Children of Sanchez* (London, 1962), p. xxiv.
13. Ibid.
14. There is a detailed examination of changing approaches to these

questions in John Clarke, Chas Critcher and Richard Johnson, *Working-class Culture: Studies in History and Theory* (London, 1979).
15. Such as D. L. LeMahieu, *A Culture for Democracy* (Oxford, 1998).
16. Aneurin Bevan, 'Challenge of the Hunger March', *Socialist*, November 1936.
17. Noreen Branson, *The History of the Communist Party of Great Britain 1927–1941* (London, 1985), p. 74.
18. [MRC] MSS.135.7/1 TUC Memorandum on Unemployed Clubs (n.d. 1933?).
19. [MRC] MSS.135/7/1 Advertisement for the Oxford University and Trade Union Holiday Camp, July–August 1935.
20. [MRC] MSS.135/7/1 Bradford Unemployment Advisory Committee Annual Report, 1933–4.
21. *Bradford Pioneer*, 18 May 1934.
22. [MRC] MSS.135.7/1.
23. [MRC] MSS.135.7/1 Correspondence, 29 December 1933.
24. [MRC] MSS.135.7/1 Correspondence, 2 January 1934.
25. [MRC] MSS.135.7/1 Nottinghamshire Trades Council schemes, 6 November 1932.
26. [MRC] MSS.292.135.2/8-9 Report from police commissioner for National Demonstration (1933).
27. [MRC] MSS.292 135.2/8-9 TUC records on National Demonstration of Unemployment. The Committee allowed £117 in their budget for the hire of bands for this event.
28. '200,000 voices join in Labour's protest', *Daily Herald*, 6 February 1933. '250,000 massed in Hyde Park', *New Chronicle*, 6 February 1933. '250,000 in Hyde Park demo' (250,000 onlookers and 30,000 demonstrators), *Daily Mail*, 6 February 1933. 250,000 'took part', *Star*, 6 February 1933.
29. '15,000 police in Hyde Park comedy', *Daily Express*, 6 February 1933.
30. *Daily Mail*, 6 February 1933.
31. *Daily Express*, 6 February 1933.
32. [MRC] MSS.292.135.2/9 Official Programme of 'Great March', February 1933.
33. [MRC] MSS.292.135.2/8-9 Minutes of Area Secretaries and Marshall's Conference, 20 February 1933.
34. Wal Hannington, *Unemployed Struggle, 1919–1936: My Life and Struggles amongst the Unemployed* (London, 1977).
35. Branson, *History of the Communist Party of Great Britain*, pp. 14–15.
36. Ibid., p. 74.
37. *Town Crier*, 19 June 1925.
38. Hannington, *Unemployed Struggle*, pp. 31–2.
39. Ibid., pp. 45–7.
40. Ibid., pp. 137–8.
41. [IWM, SCW, SA] A:8851/9/1 Oral History interview with Thomas Walter Gregory (Spanish Civil War veteran).
42. Hannington, *Unemployed Struggle*, pp. 64–5.

43. Ibid., p. 50.
44. Robert Tressell, *The Ragged Trousered Philanthropists* (London, 1993), p. 288.
45. Hannington, *Unemployed Struggle*, p. 90.
46. Laybourn, *Britain on the Breadline*, p. 32.
47. Hannington, *Unemployed Struggle*, pp. 191–2.
48. Palmer, *The Sound of History*, pp. 117–18.
49. [IWM, SCW, SA] A:8851/9/1.
50. [IWM, SCW, SA] 12942/1.
51. [IWM, SCW, SA] A:8851/9/1.
52. 'A galvanised trade union movement facing the problems of high un-employment and constant wage reductions was bound to find itself in conflict with both employers and government in the inter-war years'. Laybourn, *Britain on the Breadline*, p. 110.
53. Watson, 'Alan Bush and left music', p. 81.
54. Ibid.
55. *Rego and Polikoff Strike Songs* (London, 1929), p. 3.
56. [MRC] MSS.192/CA/4/1/8 The *Clerk*, November 1920.
57. [MRC] MSS.127/NU/4/1/8 *Railway Review*, 8 October 1920.
58. Michael Foot, *Aneurin Bevan*, Vol. 1 (London, 1962), p. 71.
59. Although these bands represented an 'alternative' culture (they were something new and alien to the South Wales valleys), they shared characteristics with 'pierrot' bands and minstrel shows that performed in British holiday resorts.
60. Hwyel Francis and David Smith, *The Fed: A History of the South Wales Miners in the Twentieth Century* (London, 1980), pp. 56–8.
61. Ibid., p. 58.
62. The desired effect of this popular and inexpensive instrument, also known as a 'Tommy-Talker' and used as a child's toy, was to imitate the jazz trumpet.
63. Francis and Smith, *The Fed*, p. 274.
64. *Town Crier*, 18 June 1926.
65. 'South Wales Miners' Choir at the Central Hall', *Town Crier*, 4 June 1926.
66. W.A.E., 'Smethwick Notes: The Choir', *Town Crier*, 18 June 1926.
67. 'The South Wales Miners' Choir: why they have come to Birmingham: help needed for sorely stricken area', *Town Crier*, 28 May 1926.
68. 'South Wales Miners' Choir at the Central Hall', *Town Crier*, 4 June 1926.
69. Watchman, 'A well-deserved tribute', *Town Crier*, 11 June 1926.
70. 'South Wales choir raises £1000', *Town Crier*, 8 October 1926.
71. Especially when you consider that the £3 13s 1 1/2d raised by singing at the end of a ward Labour Party youth section dance and concert was considered 'a big success'. *Town Crier*, 20 August 1926.
72. 'South Wales choir raises £1000', *Town Crier*, 8 October 1926.
73. *Town Crier*, 10 September 1926.
74. *Bradford Pioneer*, 9 June 1926.

75. 'A Welsh Miners' Choir in Russia', *Town Crier*, 19 November 1926.
76. *Bradford Worker: Official Strike Bulletin*, 11 May 1926.
77. There are numerous examples. One was a 'Grand Dance in aid of the miners' fund' hosted by the West Birmingham Labour Party'. *Town Crier*, 28 May 1926.
78. Branson, *History of the Communist Party of Great Britain*, p. 118.
79. Francis, *Miners Against Fascism*, p. 107.
80. [IWM, SCW, SA] 12942/1.
81. Laurie Lee, *Red Sky at Sunrise* (London, 1993), p. 434.
82. Ibid., p. 476.
83. [IWM, SCW, SA] 12942/1.
84. Ibid.
85. Ibid.
86. Ibid.
87. Francis, *Miners Against Fascism*, p. 242.
88. Ibid., p. 293.
89. Watson, 'Alan Bush and left music', p. 83.
90. Ray Pegg, 'A song for the people: the story of Clarion', *WMA Bulletin*, July–August 1975, p. 1. The observation was a common one. Bob Doyle, who signed up to the International Brigade as an idealistic teenager, recalled his abiding memory of his experiences in Spain: 'they sang at every opportunity'. [IWM, SCW, SA] 12942/1. The idea was parodied by Tom Lehrer in 'Folk Song Army' from his 1965 album 'That Was the Year That Was'.

> Remember that war against Franco?
> That's the kind where each of us belongs.
> Though he may have won all the battles
> We had all the good songs.

http://members.aol.com/quentncree/lehrer/
91. Hannington, *Unemployed Struggle*, pp. 89–90.
92. *Town Crier*, 28 April 1939.
93. Over a quarter of the 2,000 British volunteers in Spain died in the conflict.
94. 'Jim Connell and the Red Flag', *Labour Magazine*, vol. VII, no. 11, March 1929.

Chapter 5 The Best Music Available

1. *Labour's Who's Who* (1927), p. 193.
2. J.S., 'Music notes', *Town Crier*, 17 October 1919.
3. H. G. Sear, 'The men behind the music', *Town Crier*, 3 April 1925.
4. In Sear's articles it is much to Mendelssohn's discredit that he 'never had the fierce struggle for existence which is the common lot of artists', whereas Schubert is praised for being 'a peasant's son'.
5. H. G. Sear, *Town Crier*, 3 April 1925.
6. H. G. Sear, 'On discrimination', *Town Crier*, 10 April 1925.

7. H. G. Sear, 'Chamber music', *Town Crier*, 8 October 1926. 'Almost every household has a piano'.
8. H. G. Sear, 'The men behind the music: Mozart', *Town Crier*, 29 May 1925.
9. H. G. Sear, 'The men behind the music: Schubert', *Town Crier*, 17 July 1925.
10. H. G. Sear, 'Chamber music', *Town Crier*, 8 October 1926.
11. H. G. Sear, 'The men behind the music: "Papa" Haydn', *Town Crier*, 1 May 1925.
12. H. G. Sear, 'The men behind the music: Mozart', *Town Crier*, 29 May 1925.
13. H. G. Sear, 'More about songs', *Town Crier*, 24 December 1925.
14. H. G. Sear, 'An open letter to plain people', *Bradford Pioneer*, 11 November 1932.
15. H. G. Sear, 'The orchestra', *Town Crier*, 19 June 1925.
16. H. G. Sear, 'The men behind the music: Rachmaninoff', *Town Crier*, 15 October 1926.
17. H. G. Sear, 'Towards real musical comedy', *Town Crier*, 11 September 1925.
18. H. G. Sear, 'The men behind the music: Rossini', *Town Crier*, 10 July 1925.
19. H. G. Sear, 'Songs and singers', *Town Crier*, 23 October 1925.
20. H. G. Sear, 'The men behind the music: Elgar', *Town Crier*, 30 July 1926.
21. H. G. Sear, 'The men behind the music: Tchaikovski', *Town Crier*, 11 June 1926.
22. Anon., 'Mr. H. G. Sear's lectures on music and musicians', *Town Crier*, 10 September 1926.
23. *Bradford Pioneer*, 4 January 1929.
24. *Bradford Pioneer*, 15 February 1929.
25. *Bradford Pioneer*, 1 March 1929.
26. *Bradford Pioneer*, 15 February 1929.
27. *Bradford Pioneer*, 1 March 1929.
28. *Town Crier*, 14 January 1927.
29. *Town Crier*, 2 October 1925.
30. H. G. Sear, 'Making music live: the secret of great playing', *Town Crier*, 6 November 1925.
31. *Town Crier*, 11 December 1925.
32. *Town Crier*, 25 June 1926.
33. The Strand Theatre became the National Centre of the Guild of Arts.
34. Arthur Bourchier, *Art and Culture in Relation to Socialism* (London, 1926), p. 6.
35. Ibid., p. 15.
36. H. G. Sear, 'A holiday concert party', *Town Crier*, 13 August 1926.
37. Bourchier was actually an admirer of Trotsky and if he was politically out of step with his ILP colleagues, it was probably that he was to the left of them.
38. *Town Crier*, 23 April 1926.

39. Art was, however, to seek the truth. In *The Glastonbury Festival Movement* (Glastonbury, 1922), Boughton refers to the importance of an artist's 'ideas of truth and beauty' (p. 8).
40. Boughton served an invaluable apprenticeship under Sir Granville Bantock at the Midland Institute School of Music in Birmingham.
41. Michael Hurd, *Rutland Boughton and the Glastonbury Festivals* (Oxford, 1993), p. 3.
42. Stanley Sadie (ed.), *The New Grove Dictionary of Music and Musicians*, Vol. 3 (London, 1980), p. 97.
43. Ibid., p. 98.
44. Ibid., p. 99.
45. Rutland Boughton, *The Reality of Music* (London, 1934), p. ix.
46. Boughton, *The Glastonbury Festival Movement*, p. 3.
47. Ibid.
48. Hurd, *Rutland Boughton*, pp. 356–64.
49. *Town Crier*, 26 March 1926.
50. Hurd's biography gives details of Boughton's very complicated love-life.
51. Hurd, *Rutland Boughton*, p. 188.
52. Ibid., p. 174.
53. *Worker's Weekly*, 12 February 1926.
54. Hurd, *Rutland Boughton*, pp. 175–7.
55. '. . . it is clear that Wagner's ideas were very near to those of Marx'. Boughton, *The Reality of Music*, p. 154.
56. Ibid., p. 152.
57. F.B., 'Opera fortnight', *Bradford Pioneer*, 6 February 1925.
58. 'Wagner himself may have been less aware than Shaw of the political implications of his masterpiece.' Boughton, *The Reality of Music*, p. 151.
59. Anon., 'Opera at the Repertory Theatre', *Town Crier*, 8 July 1921.
60. *Town Crier*, 16 July 1921.
61. Boughton, *The Glastonbury Festival Movement*, p. 8.
62. Anon., *Town Crier*, 8 July 1921.
63. H. G. Sear, 'Rutland Boughton's new opera: "The Queen of Cornwall"', *Town Crier*, 7 January 1927.
64. Hurd, *Rutland Boughton*, p. 164.
65. Boughton, *The Glastonbury Festival Movement*, p. 9.
66. Hurd, *Rutland Boughton*, p. 177.
67. Ibid., p. 184.
68. This is interesting because Fyfe was not broadly considered to be 'MacDonald's man'. When MacDonald complained about the contents of the paper in 1924, Fyfe replied: 'The "Herald" is the organ, not of your government, nor of a Party, but of the Labour Movement' (cited in Ross McKibbin, *The Evolution of the Labour Party 1910–1924*, Oxford, 1974, p. 230).
69. Hurd, *Rutland Boughton*, p. 171.
70. Ibid., p. 185.
71. Boughton, *The Reality of Music*, pp. 146–9.

72. '[Schoenberg's] is the art of the exquisite but sincere *poseur*' (ibid., p. 161). '[Stravinsky] may peddle rotten music but at least it is typical of the final decadence of a people' (ibid., p. 164).
73. Richard Hanlon and Mike Waite, 'Notes from the left: communism and British classical music', in Andy Croft (ed.), *A Weapon in the Struggle: The Cultural History of the Communist Party in Britain* (London, 1998), p. 75.
74. Donald Brook, *Composer's Gallery* (London, 1946), p. 32.
75. Hurd, *Rutland Boughton*, p. 176.
76. Randall Swingler and Alan Bush, *Left Song Book* (London, 1938).
77. [NMLH] 372.1 WMA *Tribute to Alan Bush on his Fiftieth Birthday* (1950).
78. Anthony Payne, 'Alan Bush', *Musical Times*, April 1964, p. 263.
79. Ibid.
80. Scott Goddard, 'Alan Bush: propagandist and artist', *Listener*, 23 April 1964, p. 697.
81. Payne, 'Alan Bush', p. 264.
82. Goddard, 'Alan Bush', p. 697.
83. Ibid.
84. Payne, 'Alan Bush', p. 263.
85. Goddard, 'Alan Bush', p. 697.
86. Hanlon and Waite, 'Notes from the left', p. 76.
87. Swingler and Bush, *Left Song Book*.
88. Nancy Bush, *Alan Bush: Music, Politics and Life* (London, 2000), pp. 17–18.
89. [NMLH] 372.1 WMA, *Tribute to Alan Bush*.
90. [EM/PS] Ailie Munro, 'Folk music, politics and the Workers' Music Association' (WMA Occasional Paper, March 1988).
91. Sadie, *Grove Dictionary*, Vol. 3, p. 502.
92. Payne, 'Alan Bush', p. 264.
93. Ibid., p. 265.
94. Ian Watson, 'Alan Bush and left music in the thirties', *Gulliver*, no. 4, 1978, pp. 86–7.
95. Anti-Stalinist might be a more appropriate description for pieces such as his Symphony No. 3. He had been a consistent anti-Stalinist throughout the period, only changing his point of criticism from Trotskyism to humanism.
96. Ian Kemp, *Tippett: The Composer and His Music* (London, 1984), pp. 26–7.
97. Ibid., pp. 29–31.
98. Ibid., pp. 31–2.
99. J. J. Plant, 'Obituary of Michael Tippett', *Revolutionary History*, vol. 7, no. 1, 1998. Reprinted at http://www.michael-tippett.com.
100. *Town Crier*, 27 January 1922.
101. [NMLH] Socialist Sunday Schools Box 4(D) 'The Youth Called Ideal' script.
102. *Bradford Pioneer*, 2 January 1931.

103. Ibid.
104. [NMLH] Socialist Sunday Schools Box 4(D) 'The Youth Called Ideal' script
105. Joseph Kerman, *Musicology* (London, 1985), p. 11.
106. A number of 'avant-garde' composers were attracted to the political left and are referred to in Hanlon and Waite, 'Notes from the left'.

Chapter 6 A Music of Their Own

1. Chris Waters, *British Socialists and the Politics of Popular Culture 1884–1914* (Manchester, 1990), p. 98.
2. David Harker, *Fakesong: The Manufacture of British 'Folksong', 1700 to the Present Day* (Milton Keynes, 1985), p. 231.
3. The Folk Song Society and the Folk Dance Society merged in 1932.
4. It is unclear precisely which text this would have been. It was quite likely to have been one of many Cecil Sharp collections aimed at schoolchildren (such as *A Book of British Song for Home and School*, 1902) or a more recent collection based on similar research.
5. There is a wide literature on these issues, ranging from Harker, *Fakesong*, and Georgina Boyes, *The Imagined Village: Culture, Ideology and the English Folk Revival* (Manchester, 1993) to disputes in journals such as *History Workshop*, in articles and correspondence on Cecil Sharp and other folksong characters and controversies.
6. A. L. Lloyd described Sharp as 'a Socialist with a ready sympathy for working people and a keen recognition of their qualities; yet his was an ideology of primitive romanticism with a vengeance'. *Folk Song in England* (London, 1967), p. 13.
7. Whether this was to 'help to mystify the workers' culture in the interests of bourgeois ideology', as Harker would have it, is a separate question.
8. *Town Crier*, 2 July 1920.
9. Alec Hunter, 'Back to Merrie England', *Labour Magazine*, vol. II, no. 4, August 1923, p. 155.
10. Boyes, *The Imagined Village*, p. 51.
11. Ibid., p. 14.
12. Lloyd, *Folk Song in England*, p. 21.
13. Antonio Gramsci, 'Problems of history and culture: the intellectuals', *Selections from Prison Notebooks* (London, 1971), p. 4.
14. Boyes, *The Imagined Village*, p. 24.
15. Hunter, 'Back to Merrie England', p. 156.
16. Rutland Boughton, 'The Arts as a part of the worker's life', *Labour Magazine*, vol. II, no. 7 (November, 1923), p. 302.
17. Ibid.
18. He tended to divide 'British folk song' between Celtic, Northumbrian (by which he meant literally north of the Humber rather than the modern county) and English folk regions. Folk England was just the south and the Midlands. Actually this could have been part of a wider

and bizarre (very) Little Englandism, as he regularly referred to the north as 'the country that lies between England and the Celtic lands'. Rutland Boughton, *The Reality of Music* (London, 1934), p. 35.

19. 'There is little difference between the howl of a dog, the cry of the gibbon . . . and the song of the Australian aborigines . . . in that sound we have the beginnings of musical art.' Ibid., pp. 2–3.

20. H. G. Sear, 'Music for children', *Town Crier*, 11 March 1927.

21. Joseph Kerman, *Musicology* (London, 1985), p. 168.

22. Ian Watson, 'Alan Bush and left music in the thirties', *Gulliver*, no. 4, 1978, p. 88.

23. Roger Laidlaw, 'The Gresford disaster in popular memory', *Llafur*, vol. 6, no. 4, 1995, p. 123.

24. A. L. Lloyd, *Come All Ye Bold Miners* (London, 1978).

25. Laidlaw, 'The Gresford disaster', p. 140.

26. Even so there was often quite a lot of money in these music halls and in some of the 'stars' who were elevated from working-class communities, such as Tommy Armstrong. However, while the southern music hall evolved into large-scale variety clubs through the twentieth century, northern halls evolved into the working men's and social club circuit. Some of the big northern music-hall stars, like George Formby and Gracie Fields, made their money in southern halls and, of course, on the big screen.

27. Boyes, *The Imagined Village*, p. 15.

28. [WYA-Bfd] 59 D89 Souvenir programme. The dances included two untitled morris dances, 'I Loved a Maiden Fair' and 'All in a Garden Green'.

29. [WYA-Bfd] 59 D89 Such as the 'Pied Piper of Hamelin' (*sic*) and 'Love Is Out of Season, When the Gorse Is Out of Bloom'.

30. [WYA-Bfd] 59 D89 These were songs with actions – an important aspect of the infant music syllabus for Bradford children published some years later – such as 'Strawberry Fair' and 'A Lawyer He Went Out One Day'.

31. [WYA-Bfd] 59 D89.

32. Eric Hobsbawm, 'Birth of a holiday: the first of May', in *Uncommon People: Resistance, Rebellion and Jazz* (London, 1999), p. 151.

33. *Town Crier*, 3 June 1921.

34. *Town Crier*, 6 May 1927.

35. [WYA-Bfd.] 5D87/7/10. A photograph of one such pageant design shows a horse-drawn cart with children of all ages standing around a tall maypole. Sharing the cart is a particularly severe-looking middle-aged woman – the jollity of the spring festival seems conspicuously absent from the Great Horton Socialist Sunday School here.

36. Hobsbawm, 'Birth of a holiday', p. 152.

37. Ibid., p. 160.

38. *Town Crier*, 30 April 1926.

39. *Town Crier*, 19 March 1926.

40. *Town Crier*, 25 March 1927.

41. Stephen Jones, *The British Labour Movement and Film, 1918–1939* (London, 1987), p. 140.
42. Paddy Scannell and David Cardiff, *A Social History of British Broadcasting*, Vol. 1: *1922–1939 'Serving the Nation'* (Oxford, 1991), p. 181.
43. Ibid., p. 182.
44. Ibid., p. 207.
45. Ibid., p. 205.
46. Ibid., p. 206.
47. For exact figures see a variety of sources, including James J. Nott, 'Popular music and the popular music industry in Britain', D.Phil thesis, University of Oxford, 2000.
48. Stephen Jones, *Workers at Play: A Social and Economic History of Leisure, 1918–1939* (London, 1986), pp. 10–22.
49. Scannell and Cardiff, *British Broadcasting*, Vol. 1, p. 209.
50. Ibid., p. 210, paraphrasing *Melody Maker*, April 1932.
51. Eric Hobsbawm, 'The Duke', in *Uncommon People*, p. 351.
52. David Harker, *One for the Money: Politics and Popular Song* (London, 1980), p. 29.
53. Scannell and Cardiff, *British Broadcasting*, Vol. 1, p. 193.
54. Ibid.
55. Ibid., p. 189.
56. Ibid., p. 182.
57. Ibid., p. 184.
58. Ibid., p. 193.
59. Ibid.
60. Ibid., p. 195.
61. Ibid., p. 221.
62. Ibid., pp. 184–5.
63. Nott, 'Popular music'.
64. Jones, *Workers at Play*, pp. 38, 52.
65. Ibid., p. 53.
66. Ibid., p. 56.
67. Ibid., p. 57.
68. Nott, 'Popular music', p. 107.
69. Comparatively not a bad living either. Scottish pianist Arthur Allen was paid £5 a week in the summer and £7 a week in the winter when employed by 'Maximes' in Edinburgh – a popular 1920s dance hall. This wage was 'several times the average working wage'. Frank Bruce, '"There were bands, bands everywhere": working in the leisure industry, 1916–1950', *Scottish Labour History Society Journal*, no. 32, 1997, p. 44.
70. Stephen Jones, *The British Labour Movement and Film, 1918–1939* (London, 1987), p. 77
71. Bruce, 'Working in the leisure industry', p. 41.
72. Ibid., p. 47.
73. Ibid., p. 50.

74. Ibid., p. 45.
75. Ibid., pp. 40–60. This article studies an oral history project with one musician (Arthur Allen) who played piano in a variety of bands and venues or as accompanist for soloists. He also learned to play the Wurlitzer by copying a church organist, so that he could play at a cinema (organists were still employed after the advent of the talkies).
76. *Town Crier*, 21 January 1921.
77. Jones, *Workers at Play*, p. 150.
78. As well as Gareth Williams, *Valleys of Song* (Cardiff, 1998), Welsh working-class culture (particularly that promoted by the South Wales NUM, which began its own miners' eisteddfod after the Second World War) is considered in Hywel Francis and David Smith, *The Fed: A History of the South Wales' Miners in the Twentieth Century* (London, 1980).
79. Dan Griffiths (ed.), *What is Socialism? A Symposium* (London, 1924), p. 38.
80. 'It is sunlight opposed to darkness; concord resolving discord; peace and plenty in place of plunder and penury; fresh air and freedom instead of filibustering and filth.' Hampson was fond of alliteration!
81. *Bradford Pioneer*, 9 December 1921.
82. *Bradford Pioneer*, 23 April 1920.
83. Boyes, *The Imagined Village*, pp. 7–9.
84. Both Chris Waters and Dave Russell refer to the influential nature of Haweis' *Music and Morals* (London, 1871). The influence may have been less direct than is suggested here – merely that Haweis opened the way to a general discussion of the moral effects of music which eventually influenced socialists. Waters pointed to a direct influence on Edward Carpenter and also mentioned that some correspondents to the *Clarion* (pre-First World War) referred to Haweis' work. Like Boughton, Haweis refers to 'Mr Darwin's gibbon' when discussing the development of music.
85. Haweis, *Music and Morals*, p. 570.
86. Eric Hobsbawm, 'Jazz comes to Europe', in *Uncommon People*, p. 355.
87. Arthur Bourchier, *Art and Culture in Relation to Socialism* (London, 1926), p. 11.
88. *Bradford Pioneer*, 8 December 1922.
89. *Town Crier*, 7 January 1921.
90. Eric Hobsbawm, 'The people's swing', in *Uncommon People*, pp. 369–70.
91. Ibid., p. 371.
92. Eric Hobsbawm, 'Jazz comes to Europe', p. 363.
93. *Town Crier*, 30 April 1926.
94. *Town Crier*, 11 September 1925.
95. *Town Crier*, 16 and 30 April 1920.
96. *Town Crier*, 28 January 1921.
97. For example, 'The dance held at the Suffolk Gardens in the evening was very successful. Labour Party officials, SPGB-ers, Youth

members, ILP-ers and Fabians – all got together famously.' *Socialist*, October–November 1934. The article did not say whether they 'got together' on the dance floor or in the discussion!

98. One such band was the 'COLNA' Dance Band, which advertised in the *Town Crier*, 17 September 1926. 'The "COLNA" Dance Band (Labour) is now open for engagements. Moderate Charges.'
99. Ewan MacColl, *Journeyman: An Autobiography* (London, 1990), p. 156.
100. Ibid., p. 157.
101. *Bradford Pioneer*, 3 February 1922.
102. *Town Crier*, 27 May 1927.
103. *New Leader*, 2 July 1926.
104. *Railway Review*, 16 January 1919.
105. Anon., 'Oxford Bags at Aston!', *Town Crier*, 4 September 1925.
106. [EM/PS] Secretary of the Workers' Music Section, 'Music Section wakes up: a singing group in every troupe', *Workers' Theatre Movement Monthly Bulletin*, no. 3, February 1931.
107. Watson, 'Alan Bush and left music', pp. 80–90.
108. The Red Megaphones had been formed that year out of the split in the Clarion Players. Their programme included 'several parodies of popular songs'. MacColl, *Journeyman*, p. 169.
109. Lines like 'Comrades from sports' field and Salford's dark mills,/ Hikers who tramp over Derbyshire's hills' echo famous MacColl songs like 'Dirty Old Town' and 'I'm a Rambler'.
110. [EM/PS] *Workers' Theatre Movement Monthly Bulletin*, no. 3, February 1931.
111. [EM/PS] *Red Stage*, no. 1, November 1931.
112. [EM/PS] *Red Stage*, no. 4, March 1932.
113. Ibid.
114. Ibid.
115. Hobsbawm, 'Jazz comes to Europe', p. 363.
116. [EM/PS] *Red Stage*, no. 5, April–May 1932.
117. This was probably a reference to the Manchurian crisis at the same time. The crisis was certainly amongst the subjects – sometimes considered rather distant, obscure and sectarian – discussed at Young Communist League meetings, according to MacColl, *Journeyman*, p. 184.
118. [EM/PS] *Red Stage*, no. 6, June–July 1932.
119. Such as 'The Docile Workers' to the tune of 'There was a Lady Loved a Swine', which ran 'There was a Premier loved the Poor'. *Town Crier* 17 June 1921. This was taken from *The Bolo Book* (1921?), which was a Labour Publishing Company publication. Other songs from it included 'Here We Go Round the Vicious Circle' to the tune of 'Here we go round the Mulberry Bush'. *Town Crier*, 9 September 1921.
120. [EM/PS] *Red Stage*, no. 6, June–July 1932.
121. Roy Palmer, *The Sound of History* (London, 1988), p. 264.
122. Lloyd, *Folk Song in England*, p. 317.
123. Review of a new Labour 'Community Song Book', *Town Crier*, 22 July 1927.

124. Lloyd, *Come All Ye Bold Miners*, p. 64.
125. [EM/PS] *Red Stage*, no. 6, June–July 1932.
126. 'The Left Theatre', *Socialist*, July–August 1936.
127. Watson, 'Alan Bush and left music', p. 81.
128. Ibid., p. 88.

Conclusions

1. Malcolm Hardman, *Ruskin and Bradford* (Manchester, 1986), p. 221.
2. Topic began life in 1939 as the label of the WMA, bringing out recordings of 'The Red Flag' and 'The Internationale' as well as folk music.
3. Tom Steele, *Alfred Orage and the Leeds Arts Club, 1893–1923* (Aldershot, 1990).
4. Anne Janowitz, *Lyric and Labour in the Romantic Tradition* (Cambridge, 1998).

Bibliography

Primary sources

Manuscripts

Imperial War Museum
  Spanish Civil War sound archive (IWM-SCW-SA)
  12942 – 'In our hearts were songs of hope'
  A:8851/9 – oral history interviews

Modern Records Centre, Warwick (MRC)
  TUC archives, individual union archives
  MSS.135.7 – TUC unemployment relief activities
  MSS.292.135.2 – National Demonstration of Unemployment
    documents
  MSS.192.CA/4 – National Union of Clerks, the *Clerk*
  MSS.127/NU/4 – National Union of Railwaymen, *Railway Review*

National Museum of Labour History, Manchester (NMLH)
  Labour Party Archives
  Socialist Sunday School records
    4.D SSS music, scripts, miscellany
  Song books and pamphlets
    372.1 Workers' Music Association ephemera

Ruskin College Library
  The Ewan MacColl and Peggy Seeger Archives (EM/PS)
  Select issues of *Red Stage, Workers' Theatre Movement Monthly
    Bulletin*
  Workers' Music Association occasional papers

West Yorkshire Archives Service, Bradford (and Keighley) (WYA)
  Bradford ILP and Labour records, minutes, souvenirs, etc.
    5D87/1 Heaton ILP minutes
    5D77/5 Bradford ILP miscellany
    5D87/7 Bradford ILP photograph collection

59 D89 ILP International Fair, 1925, Souvenir Programme
Keighley ILP, Women's Labour League and Social Committee
minutes
2D80/A Keighley ILP minute books
2D80/B Keighley ILP Women's Committee minutes
2D80/C Keighley ILP Social Committee minutes
Socialist Sunday School song books and other sheet music
2D80/F SSS songbooks

Newspapers and periodicals

Bradford Pioneer
Bradford Worker: Official Strike Bulletin
Clarion
Daily Herald
Labour Magazine
Labour Monthly
New Clarion
New Leader
Railway Review
Railwayman
Red Stage
Socialist
Socialist Leaguer
Sunday Worker
Town Crier (Birmingham)
Worker (Glasgow)
Worker's Dreadnought
Workers' Theatre Movement Bulletin

Books

Anon., *Rego and Polikoff Strike Songs*, London, 1929.
Blatchford, Robert, *Merrie England*, London, 1908.
—— *My Eighty Years*, London, 1931.
Boughton, Rutland, *The Glastonbury Festival Movement*, Glastonbury, 1922.
—— *The Reality of Music*, London, 1934.
Bourchier, Arthur, *Art and Culture in Relation to Socialism*, London, 1926.

Bradford ILP, *Bradford Independent Labour Party International Fancy Fair: Souvenir Programme*, Bradford, 1925.

Carpenter, Edward, *Towards Industrial Freedom*, London, 1917.

—— *Chants of Labour* (6th edn), London, 1922.

Griffiths, Dan (ed.), *What is Socialism? A Symposium*, London, 1924.

Haweis, Hugh, *Music and Morals*, London, 1871.

ILP Publications Department, *Labour's Song Book*, London, 1931.

Labour Publishing Company, *Labour's Who's Who*, London, 1924.

—— *Labour's Who's Who*, London, 1927.

Lee, Jennie, *Tomorrow is a New Day*, London, 1939.

Morris, William, *News from Nowhere and Other Writings*, London, 1993 (*News from Nowhere* first published 1890).

National Council of British Socialist Sunday School Unions, *Socialist Sunday School Tune Book 12*, n.d.

—— *Socialist Sunday School Hymn Book*, 1910 [WYA].

—— *Socialist Sunday School Hymn Book*, 1925 [WYA].

Sharp, Cecil, *English Folk Song: Some Conclusions*, London, 1936.

Swingler, Randall and Bush, Alan, *The Left Song Book*, London, 1938.

Trevor, John, *The Labour Church Hymn Book*, 1891 (and updated version, 1906).

Tressell, Robert, *The Ragged Trousered Philanthropists*, London, 1993 (first published 1914).

Articles

Anon., 'The right to leisure', *Worker*, January 1919.

—— 'Opera at the Repertory Theatre – The Immortal Hour', *Town Crier*, 8 July 1921.

—— 'An "eistedfodd" for labour', *Town Crier*, 14 August 1925.

—— 'The ILP Arts Guild', *Bradford Pioneer*, 4 September 1925.

—— 'Oxford Bags at Aston', *Town Crier*, 4 September 1925.

—— 'A triumph for the other Pioneer', *Bradford Pioneer*, 20 November 1925.

—— 'The South Wales Miners' Choir: why they have come to Birmingham', *Town Crier*, 28 May 1926.

—— 'South Wales Miners' Choir at the Central Hall', *Town Crier*, 4 June 1926.

—— 'Mr H. G. Sear's lectures on music and musicians', *Town Crier*, 10 September 1926.

—— 'South Wales choir raises £1000', *Town Crier*, 8 October 1926.

—— 'A Welsh Miners' Choir in Russia', *Town Crier*, 19 November 1926.

—— 'Jim Connell and the Red Flag', *Labour Magazine*, vol. VII, no. 11, March 1929.

—— 'Class struggle and art – on the occasion of the tenth anniversary of Lenin's death', *International Theatre*, no.1, 1934.

—— 'The Left Theatre', *Socialist*, July–August 1936.

Bevan, Aneurin, 'Challenge of the Hunger March', *Socialist*, November 1936.

Boughton, Rutland, 'The Arts as part of the worker's life', *Labour Magazine*, vol. II, no. 7, November 1923.

—— 'Choral music and the socialist ideal', *Daily Herald*, 19 March 1924.

—— 'Boughton breaks with Morrison', *Sunday Worker*, 7 July 1929.

—— 'Lies for choral singing', *Railway Review*, 28 July 1933.

Court, Sydney A., 'Music and the people: a message to the labour movement', *Labour Magazine*, vol. II, no. 10, February 1924.

F.B., 'Opera fortnight', *Bradford Pioneer*, 6 February 1925.

Gramsci, Antonio, 'Problems of history and culture: the intellectuals', in *Selections from Prison Notebooks*, London, 1971.

—— 'Why we need a Cultural Association', in *Pre-Prison Writings*, Cambridge, 1994, pp. 35–8.

Graves, Charles, 'The £.s.d of bands', *Sphere*, 13 July 1935.

Hunter, Alec, 'Back to Merrie England', *Labour Magazine*, vol. II, no. 4, August 1923.

J.S., 'Music Notes', *Town Crier*, 17 October 1919.

Lenin, V. I., 'L. N. Tolstoy', in Maynard Solomon (ed.), *Marxism and Art*, Brighton, 1979, pp. 174–7.

Mus. Bac., 'The Pioneer Choir concert', *Bradford Pioneer*, 27 March 1925.

Ramsden, Jack, 'A national CVU contest at Sheffield', *Clarion*, May 1928.

Salway-Wallis, C., 'Socialism and song: a plea for music: make meetings merrier, *Town Crier*, 16 January 1925.

Sear, H. G., 'The men behind the music', *Town Crier*, 3 April 1925.

—— 'On discrimination', *Town Crier*, 10 April 1925.

—— 'The men behind the music: "Papa" Haydn', *Town Crier*, 1 May 1925.

—— 'The men behind the music: Mozart', *Town Crier*, 29 May 1925.

—— 'The orchestra', *Town Crier*, 19 June 1925.

—— 'The men behind the music: Rossini', *Town Crier*, 10 July 1925.

—— 'The men behind the music: Schubert', *Town Crier*, 17 July 1925.

—— 'Towards real musical comedy', *Town Crier*, 11 September 1925.

—— 'A plea for pure music', *Town Crier*, 2 October 1925.

—— 'Songs and singers', *Town Crier*, 23 October 1925.

—— 'Making music live: the secret of great playing', *Town Crier*, 6 November 1925.

—— 'More about songs', *Town Crier*, 24 December 1925.

—— 'The men behind the music: Tchaikowski' (*sic*), 11 June 1926.

—— 'The men behind the music: Elgar', *Town Crier*, 30 July 1926.

—— 'A holiday concert party', *Town Crier*, 13 August 1926.

—— 'Chamber music', *Town Crier*, 8 October 1926.

—— 'The men behind the music: Rachmaninoff' (*sic*), *Town Crier*, 15 October 1926.

—— 'Labour choirs and orchestras', *Town Crier*, 22 October 1926.

—— 'Rutland Boughton's new opera: "The Queen of Cornwall"', *Town Crier*, 7 January 1927.

—— 'Music for children', *Town Crier*, 11 March 1927.

—— 'An open letter to plain people', *Bradford Pioneer*, 11 November 1932.

Secretary of the Workers' Music Section, 'Music Section wakes up: a singing group in every troupe', *Workers' Theatre Movement Monthly Bulletin*, no. 3, February 1931.

Trotsky, Leon, 'Proletarian culture and proletarian art', in Berel Lang and Forrest Williams (eds), *Marxism and Art*, New York, 1972, pp. 62–9.

V.Eff., 'Casey and Dolly', *Bradford Pioneer*, 14 December 1928.

Watchman [William Chamberlain], 'A well-deserved tribute', *Town Crier*, 11 June 1926.

Secondary sources

Books

Adorno, Theodor, *Quasi una Fantasia: Essays on Modern Music*, London, 1992.

Ainsworth, Jim, *Accrington and District, 1927–1934: The Cotton Crisis and the Means Test*, Hyndburn and Rossendale TUC, 1997.

Bellamy, Joyce M. and Saville, John, *Dictionary of Labour Biography*, Vol. VI, 1982.

Boyes, Georgina, *The Imagined Village: Culture, Ideology and the English Folk Revival*, Manchester, 1993.

Branson, Noreen, *History of the Communist Party of Great Britain, 1927–1941*, London, 1985.

Briggs, Asa, *The History of Birmingham, Vol. II: Borough and City, 1865–1938*, London, 1952.

Briggs, Asa, *The History of Broadcasting in the United Kingdom, Volume One: The Birth of Broadcasting*, Oxford, 1961.

—— *William Morris: Selected Writings and Designs*, London, 1962.

Briggs, Asa and Saville, John (eds), *Essays in Labour History*, London, 1967.

—— *Essays in Labour History, 1918–1939*, Vol. 3, London, 1977.

Brook, Donald, *Composer's Gallery*, London, 1946.

Brown, Tony (ed.), *Edward Carpenter and Late Victorian Radicalism*, London, 1990.

Burnett, John, Vincent, David and Mayall, David (eds), *The Auto-biography of the Working Class: An Annotated Critical Bibliography*, Brighton, 1987.

Bush, Nancy, *Alan Bush: Music, Politics and Life*, London, 2000.

Clarke, John, Critcher, Chas and Johnson, Richard, *Working-Class Culture: Studies in History and Theory*, London, 1979.

Colls, Robert, *The Collier's Rant: Song and Culture in the Industrial Village*, London, 1977.

Croft, Andy (ed.), *A Weapon in the Struggle: The Cultural History of the Communist Party in Britain*, London, 1998.

Ehrlich, Cyril, *The Piano: A History*, London, 1976.

Foot, Michael, *Aneurin Bevan, Vol. I: 1897–1945*, London, 1962.

Francis, Hywel, *Miners Against Fascism: Wales and the Spanish Civil War*, London, 1984.

Francis, Hywel and Smith, David, *The Fed: A History of the South Wales Miners in the Twentieth Century*, London, 1980.

Goorney, Howard and MacColl, Ewan (eds), *Agit-prop to Theatre Workshop: Political Playscripts, 1930–1950*, Manchester, 1986.

Gramsci, Antonio, *Selections from Prison Notebooks*, London, 1971.

—— *Pre-prison Writings*, Cambridge, 1994.

Graves, Pamela M., *Labour Women: Women in British Working-class Politics 1918–1939*, Cambridge, 1994.

Hannington, Wal, *Unemployment Struggles 1919–1936: My Life and Struggles amongst the Unemployed*, Wakefield, 1973.

Hardman, Malcolm, *Ruskin and Bradford*, Manchester, 1986.

Harker, David, *Fakesong: The Manufacture of British Folksong, 1700 to the Present Day*, Milton Keynes, 1985.

—— *One for the Money: Politics and Popular Song*, London, 1980.

Herbert, Trevor (ed.), *Bands: The Brass Band Movement in the Nineteenth and Twentieth Centuries*, Milton Keynes, 1991.

Hurd, Michael, *Rutland Boughton and the Glastonbury Festivals*, Oxford, 1993.

Janowitz, Annie, *Lyric and Labour in the Romantic Tradition*, Cambridge, 1998.

Jones, Stephen G., *Workers at Play: A Social and Economic History of Leisure, 1918–1939*, London, 1986.

—— *The British Labour Movement and Film, 1918–1939*, London, 1987.

Kemp, Ian, *Tippett: The Composer and His Music*, London, 1984.

Kerman, Joseph, *Musicology*, London, 1985.

Lang, Berel and Williams, Forrest (eds), *Marxism and Art*, New York, 1992.

Laybourn, Keith, *The Rise of Socialism in Britiain, c.1881–1951*, Stroud, 1997.

—— *Britain on the Breadline: A Social and Political History of Britain, 1918–1939*, Stroud, 1998.

Lee, Laurie, *Red Sky at Sunrise*, London, 1993.

Lewis, Oscar, *Children of Sanchez*, London, 1962.

Lloyd, Albert L., *Folk Song in England*, London, 1967.

—— *Come All Ye Bold Miners*, London, 1978.

MacColl, Ewan, *The Shuttle and the Cage: Industrial Folk Ballads*, London, 1954.

—— *Journeyman: An Autobiography*, London, 1990.

Mackerness, E. D., *Social History of English Music*, London, 1964.

—— *Somewhere Further North*, London, 1974.

McKibbin, Ross, *The Evolution of the Labour Party, 1910–1924*, Oxford, 1974.

Marriott, John, *The Culture of Labourism*, Edinburgh, 1991.

Mason, Laura, *Singing the French Revolution*, New York, 1996.

Nettel, Reginald, *A Social History of Traditional Song*, New York, 1969.

Palmer, Roy, *The Sound of History: Songs and Social Comment*, London, 1988.

Poole, Robert, *Popular Leisure and the Music Hall in Nineteenth-century Bolton*, Lancaster, 1982.

Russell, Dave, *Popular Music in England, 1840–1914: A Social History*, Manchester, 1987.

Sadie, Stanley, *The New Grove Dictionary of Music and Musicians*, London, 1980.

Samuel, Raphael, *Theatres of the Left, 1880–1935: Workers' Theatre Movements in Britain*, London, 1985.

Scannell, Paddy and Cardiff, David, *A Social History of British Broadcasting, Vol. I: 1922–1939*, Oxford, 1991.

Schafer, M., *British Composers in Interview*, London, 1963.

Seaman, L. C. B., *Life in Britain Between the Wars*, London, 1970.

Solomon, Maynard, *Marxism and Art*, Brighton, 1979.

Steedman, Carolyn, *Childhood, Culture and Class in Britain: Margaret McMillan, 1860–1931*, London, 1990.

Steele, Tom, *Alfred Orage and the Leeds Arts Club, 1893–1923*, Aldershot, 1990.

Taylor, A. R., *Brass Bands*, London, 1979.

Tiratsoo, Nick (ed.), *From Blitz to Blair*, London, 1997.

Vincent, David, *Poor Citizens: The State and the Poor in Twentieth Century Britain*, London, 1991.

Waters, Chris, *British Socialists and the Politics of Popular Culture, 1884–1914*, Manchester, 1990.

Watkins, K. W., *Britain Divided: The Effect of the Spanish Civil War on British Political Opinion*, Edinburgh, 1963.

Watson, Ian, *Song and Democratic Culture in Britain*, London, 1983.

Williams, Gareth, *Valleys of Song: Music and Society in Wales, 1840–1914*, Cardiff, 1998.

Williams, Raymond, *Keywords: A Vocabulary of Culture and Society*, London, 1988.

Witkin, Robert, *Adorno on Music*, London, 1998.

Wright, Anthony and Shackleton, Richard, *Worlds of Labour: Essays in Birmingham Labour History*, Birmingham, 1983.

Articles

Bevan, Clifford, 'Brass band contests: art or sport?', in Trevor Herbert (ed.), *Bands: The Brass Band Movement in the Nineteenth and Twentieth Centuries*, Milton Keynes, 1991, pp. 102–19.

Bruce, Frank, '"There were bands, bands everywhere": working in the leisure industry, 1916–1950', *Scottish Labour History Society Journal*, no. 32, 1997.

Capaldi, Jim, 'Charles Seeger', *Folk Scene*, April 1979, reprinted on: http://ourworld.compuserve.com/homepages/jimcapaldi/charless.htm

Drake, Peter, 'The Town Crier: Birmingham's labour weekly, 1919–1951', in Anthony Wright and Richard Shackleton (eds), *Worlds of Labour: Essays in Birmingham Labour History*, Birmingham, 1983, pp. 103–22.

Goddard, Scott, 'Alan Bush: propagandist and artist', *Listener*, 23 April 1964.

Hall, Duncan, '"More than a pleasant way to pass the time"?: Alan Bush and socialist music between the wars', Alan Bush Trust webpages: http://www.alanbushtrust.org.uk (October 2000).

Hanlon, Richard and Waite, Mike, 'Notes from the left: communism and British classical music', in Andy Croft (ed.), *A Weapon in the Struggle: The Cultural History of the Communist Party in Britain*, London, 1998.

Hobsbawm, Eric, 'Birth of a holiday: the first of May', in *Uncommon People: Resistance, Rebellion and Jazz*, London, 1999.

—— 'The Duke', in *Uncommon People: Resistance, Rebellion and Jazz*, London, 1999.

—— 'Jazz comes to Europe', in *Uncommon People: Resistance, Rebellion and Jazz*, London, 1999.

—— 'The people's swing', in *Uncommon People: Resistance, Rebellion and Jazz*, London, 1999.

Howe, Margaret, 'A small corner of Lakeland: memories of the EFDS in the thirties', *English Dance and Song*, vol. XLVII, no. 3, autumn–winter 1985, pp. 18–20.

Laidlaw, Roger, 'The Gresford disaster in popular memory', *Llafur*, vol. 6, no. 4, 1995.

Lloyd, A. L., 'Workers' songs in England: a summary account' [typescript] [EM/PS].

Marshall, John, 'Folk song as a political weapon', *Folk Scene*, no. 10, August 1965, p. 11.

Mason, Tony, 'Hunger . . . is a very good thing', in Nick Tiratsoo (ed.), *From Blitz to Blair*, London, 1997.

Munro, Ailie, 'Folk music, politics and the Workers' Music Association', *WMA Occasional Paper*, March 1988.

Nairn, Tom, 'The nature of the Labour Party', in New Left Review (ed.), *Towards Socialism*, London, 1965.

Nield, Keith, 'Edward Carpenter: the uses of utopia', in Tony Brown (ed.), *Edward Carpenter and Late Victorian Radicalism*, London, 1990, pp. 17–32.

Payne, A., 'Alan Bush', *Musical Times*, April 1964.

Pegg, Ray, 'A song for the people: the story of Clarion', *WMA Bulletin*, July–August 1975.

Reid, F., 'Socialist Sunday Schools in Britain, 1892–1939', *International Review of Social History*, no. 11, 1966, pp. 18–47.

Russell, Dave, '"What's wrong with brass bands?" Cultural change and the band movement, 1918–1964', in Trevor Herbert (ed.), *Bands: The Brass Band Movement in the Nineteenth and Twentieth Centuries*, Milton Keynes, 1991, pp. 57–101.

Watson, Ian, 'Alan Bush and left music in the thirties', *Gulliver*, no. 4, 1978, pp. 80–90.

Wright, Martin, 'Robert Blatchford and the Clarion movement', in Tony Brown (ed.), *Edward Carpenter and Late Victorian Radicalism*, London, 1990, pp. 74–99.

Yeo, Stephen, 'A New Life: the religion of socialism', *History Workshop Journal*, no. 4, 1977, pp. 5–56.

Theses and dissertations

Boughton, John, 'Working-class politics in Birmingham and Sheffield, 1918–1931', Ph.D. thesis, University of Warwick, 1985.

Cloonan, Martin, 'Politics and pop music: the "top twenty" road to socialism?', diploma thesis, Ruskin College, Oxford, 1986.

Nott, James J., 'Popular music and the popular music industry in Britain', D.Phil thesis, University of Oxford, 2000.

Shelley, Christopher, 'Birmingham Co-operative Party in the 1930s: co-operation and the labour movement', Ph.D. thesis, University of Warwick, 1987.

Whithall, Keith, 'The Voluntary Organising Committee in the Musicians' Union, 1935–1939: a study in rank and file trade unionism', diploma thesis, Ruskin College, Oxford, 1976.

Internet resources

Alan Bush Trust
http://www.alanbushtrust.org.uk/

Chelmsford TUC – Songs and Poetry
http://wkweb.cableinet.co.uk/maljan/Newsongs.html

Information on Kurt Weill
http://www.hnh.com/composer/weill.htm

'Songs of Irish Labour' by Helen Sheehan
http://www.dcu.ie/wcomms/hsheehan/lsong.htm

Tom Lehrer Lyrics
http://members.aol.com/quentncree/lehrer

The Official Michael Tippett Website
http://www.michael-tippett.com/

Index